LOVESICK JAPAN

LOVESICK JAPAN

*Sex * Marriage * Romance * Law*

MARK D. WEST

CORNELL UNIVERSITY PRESS
ITHACA AND LONDON

First published 2011 by Cornell University Press

Printed in the United States of America

Library of Congress Cataloging-in-Publication Data

West, Mark D.
   Lovesick Japan : sex, marriage, romance, law / Mark D. West.
     p. cm.
   Includes bibliographical references and index.
   ISBN 978-0-8014-4947-5 (cloth : alk. paper)
  1. Sex customs—Japan. 2. Love—Japan. 3. Marriage—
Japan. 4. Divorce—Japan. 5. Japan—Social life and customs.
I. Title.
   HQ18.J3W47   2011
   306.810952—dc22   2010044494

Cloth printing   10 9 8 7 6 5 4 3 2 1

CONTENTS

ACKNOWLEDGMENTS

Many people who helped with this book would be mortified if their names appeared here. Thanks go to the large number of people who freely but anonymously shared their stories with me and helped shape this book.

I can thank other people more publicly. For helpful conversations and comments on the manuscript, I thank Yuri Fukazawa, John Haley, Don Herzog, Atsushi Kinami, David Leheny (my spectacular referee), Y. A. Lin, Alison MacKeen, Kevin McVeigh, Curtis Milhaupt, Bill Miller, Mark Nornes, Yoshihiro Ōhara, Mark Ramseyer, Carl Schneider, Scott Shapiro, Marc Spindelman, Yukiko Tsunoda, and Sarah Zearfoss.

I also received helpful comments at presentations hosted by the University of Chicago, Columbia University, Harvard University, the Japan Society, the University of Michigan, the Museum of Sex, and Washington University in St. Louis.

My work is supported by the endowments of the Nippon Life Insurance Company and the Sumitomo Bank, Ltd., at the University of Michigan Law School, as well as by contributions to the school from Nagashima Ohno & Tsunematsu and Oh-Ebashi LPC & Partners. I also received generous funding from the University of Michigan's Center for Japanese Studies.

Explanatory Notes

Names are given in American order: John Smith, not Smith John.

All yen amounts are converted to dollars at the rate of $1 = 100 yen. The actual rates were 144.79 in 1990, 107.77 in 2000, and 93.68 in 2009. The differences won't matter.

To protect the privacy of the litigants, courts often use pseudonyms or generic labels like "plaintiff" and "defendant" instead of party names. Unless otherwise stated, if the court or case reporter uses the real name of a party, I use it. If not, to keep the players straight and to preserve some humanity in the opinions, I named the parties.

Court cases in Japan generally begin in one of three places: summary court (438 courts, for civil cases with damages claimed of less than $14,000 and petty criminal cases), family court (50 courts, with 203 branches and 77 local offices, for domestic relations and personal status cases), or district court (50 courts and 203 branches, for everything else). District courts hear appeals from summary courts. Eight high courts hear appeals from district courts and family courts. The Supreme Court is the highest court.

LOVESICK JAPAN

INTRODUCTION

In 1999, a man was prosecuted for committing "obscene acts" with two girls, eight and eleven years old.[1] The Shizuoka District Court judge in the case based his written description of the facts in part on the statement of Haruko, the eleven-year-old:

> The defendant delivered newspapers in the neighborhood where Haruko lived. He would give snacks to Haruko and her elementary school friends and talk about games with them. He would get close to the girls and touch their backs, or he would touch their breasts and claim that his hand had slipped. These things caused him to be known as a pervert. After he kissed one of the girls, Haruko's mother warned her not to get too close to him.

The particular words the judge uses to describe the action are important. The judge employs an omniscient voice but uses words that are more befitting an eleven-year-old than a jurist. Instead of calling the defendant a "strange person" or something similar, the court called him a pervert, an *ecchi ojisan*—literally, perverted uncle. *Ecchi* is the Japanese pronunciation of the English letter *H,* a slang term that is said to have first appeared in the mid-1960s as shorthand for the Roman alphabet spelling of *hentai,* a word that means perverted.[2] *Ecchi* can mean perverted, but it can also be used as a noun to refer to sex acts. A court normally uses *ecchi* only when it is quoting someone. *Ojisan* (literally, uncle) is a term applied to middle-aged men. The combination of *ecchi* and *ojisan* appears only twice in all of Japanese case law, once in 1988 and once in 2006, both times as quotes of sexually abused seven-year-old girls.[3] The court's use of the language here in its own voice places the impending crime squarely within a stereotypical predatory story line by highlighting the childlike innocence of the victims. The court continues:

> About two weeks before the crime, Haruko saw the defendant [playing] with a Game Boy. When she said, "I wish I had a Game Boy," the defendant said, "I'll buy you one." They agreed to meet at 12:30 on the last Sunday in April at the parking lot in front of the Citizens' Hall. The defendant wrote his cell phone number on the back of his business card and gave it to her.
>
> Because Haruko knew that the defendant was a pervert and worried a bit that he might take her away in his car, she decided to change their meeting spot to Hamamatsu Station, which was near stores, so she would not have to get into a car. She called his cell phone from a public phone and said, "Let's meet at Hamamatsu Station." She lied, saying, "My mother works near the station, so I'll have her drop me off, and I'll go home with her at 4." The defendant complained, "Just let your mother go off by herself," but in the end, she was able to get him to agree. Because Haruko did not know what might happen to her if she met him alone, a week before the meeting, she invited her friend Natsuko.

Again the court takes the child's perspective. It attributes to Haruko the words "I wish I had a Game Boy" (*ge-mu bo-i iina*). A more literal translation might be a singsong "I suuuuuuuure do like that Game Boy you've got there," a childish and indirect way of asking for a treat. And again the court used the word pervert (*ecchi*) instead of a more proper label.

On the day of the planned meeting, Haruko and Natsuko took the bus to Hamamatsu Station, where they met the defendant:

> When the defendant met Haruko and Natsuko, he quickly said, "Let's go," but just as they were about to go buy the Game Boy, he said, "I left my

wallet in the car," and he tried to get them to go to the car with him. Haruko and Natsuko sat on a bench and said, "We'll wait here." The defendant got on the escalator and beckoned for the girls to come. Haruko and Natsuko watched him for a bit, then said, "OK, let's go." Because the defendant had said that he had left his wallet in the car, the girls thought that if they didn't go get it, they wouldn't receive Game Boys.

As the three of them walked toward Hamamatsu Station, they came upon a store that was selling Pokémon rings. The defendant said, "Oh, they're really cute. It's OK, pick one out for yourself." Haruko and Natsuko each picked one, and the defendant paid three dollars each out of his wallet. [In a separate portion of the opinion, the court said that Haruko noticed then that the defendant had his wallet despite the fact that he had said it was in his car.]

At the crossing signal at the Ito-Yokado [store], Natsuko saw a friend; they had a few words, and then they reached the parking garage. The parking garage was scary, and Haruko and Natsuko said, "It looks like ghosts will come out, and I hate being here." The defendant said, "I'm going to buy it for you, so come on," and the girls, thinking they had no choice, boarded the elevator and headed toward the fifth floor, where the defendant's car was parked. Haruko said, "Hurry up and get what you left." The defendant opened the passenger side door and said, "It's OK, so get in" and "If people see us, they'll think something is strange, so get in," and the girls had no choice but to get in.

The narrative from the girls' perspective continues to set the stage. The girls know that something is wrong with the parking garage—it's scary. But it is scary not in the language of an educated judge; it is spooky because "it looks like ghosts will come out" (*obake ga deshō*). The court attributes that line to both of the girls. Surely they did not say it simultaneously, but it is the mood that matters, not the identity of the speaker. When the defendant opened his car door and convinced the girls to get in because the scene would appear "strange" to passersby, the court conveyed the defendant's increasing creepiness.

When the three got in the car, the defendant took an unequivocally devious step, which the court's buildup has made inevitable:

"If you want [the Game Boy], do *it*." Because Haruko didn't know what he meant, she said, "What's *it*?" to which the defendant replied, "*It* is *it*." Haruko asked again, "So what is *it*?" to which the defendant replied, "*Ecchi*."

The meaning of *ecchi* here is imprecise; it might mean intercourse or it might mean some other sexual act short of that. Upon hearing it:

> Haruko said, "Why do we have to do such a thing? That's not what we said." She became angry and turned toward the window, facing away from the defendant. The defendant turned to Natsuko, and in such a way that Haruko would hear it, said, "I wonder why she's so angry? It's not such a big deal."
>
> Haruko and Natsuko said they wanted to get out of the car to talk about it, and the defendant opened the door to let them out. They talked for ten to fifteen minutes, saying, "I really want that Game Boy. I wonder how much he'll give us" and so forth. Finally, Haruko turned to the defendant and asked, "How much will you pay us"? The defendant said, "If you let me touch you, I'll give you $300," to which Haruko and Natsuko said, "We won't let you touch us." The defendant then said, "OK, just photographs. Please." The girls talked to each other, saying, "What should we do? A photo lasts forever." They could not decide, and they asked the defendant again, "How much will you give us?"

The defendant and the girls eventually settled on $150. The defendant readied his car for the photography session, taping newspaper to the windows so that no one could see inside. The girls took off their clothes, and the defendant took five instant photos of the girls together and ten of each girl separately. The defendant then asked the girls to sit in the *taiikusuwari* pose, a position frequently used in elementary school assemblies but also a favorite of pornographers, in which a seated girl places her knees together and tucked toward her chest, with her feet remaining on the floor.

> The girls were embarrassed and would not open their knees. The defendant begged, "Please, spread your legs. If you spread them I'll give you $200." The girls did so, and the defendant took pictures of them in a pose in which the place where you pee could be seen. The defendant took pictures of the girls in several poses, and Haruko began to feel embarrassed over their nakedness and the pictures. She didn't talk much while the pictures were being taken, and at the end, she thought, "This is dangerous. I shouldn't be doing this."

There are no quotes in that passage other than those that are marked. The court called the genital area "the place where you pee" (*oshikko wo suru tokoro*). By speaking as a child here, the court seems to be pushing us, and not very gently, to view the situation through the victims' innocent eyes. But using the child's voice as heard by the defendant also encourages us to see the world through the lecherous eyes of a pedophile.[4] It is not clear which perspective the court is suggesting (consciously or otherwise) that we take, but either view frames the impending acts as frightening, unconscionable, and sick.

The court finalized its narrative by saying that the girls dressed, got out of the car, received their $200 each, and bought their Game Boys.

The events thus molded into a story, the court turned to analyze the defendant (whose testimony it dismissed as unbelievable). The court changed its tone entirely. After noting that dozens of pornographic magazines, videotapes, CD-ROMs, and photographs of underage girls were found wrapped in cardboard in the defendant's attic (and given to authorities by the defendant's wife), the court began to dissect the defendant's psyche:

> These pornographic tapes and books had titles such as "White Paper on Lolitas" and "Dangerous Old Guy and Lolita Part 2" and contained many Lolita Complex images such as girls who appeared to be junior high school students in school uniforms performing sex acts with men, elementary school–age girls urinating outside, and three junior high age girls posing naked indoors.

The court went on to describe the contents of the seized illegal CD-ROMs, which included "pictures of young girls' genitals," "pictures of junior high school girls performing fellatio," and "naked girls whose vaginas were penetrated by sex toys." The court now has abandoned the language of a child; it is explicitly reporting on things that a child would not, and speaking in clinical, definitively adult language.

The court, which apparently had no psychiatric testimony before it, then diagnosed the defendant's illness as if it had expertise in doing so:

> The existence of these perverted videotapes and so on shows that the defendant has a Lolita Complex, an unusual sexual perversion. Unsatisfied with virtual reality, the defendant expanded his sexual desires into the real world. He began by taking lurid pictures of girls in their underwear, and then his desires became stronger, to the point at which he took lurid pictures of nude girls.

The court then shifted tone yet again, turning from its pseudoscientific diagnosis to a moralistic sermon that situated the defendant in the decline of society:

> The collapse of sexual taboos, the destruction of various attachments of social meaning to the mystery of sex, the removal of the male chauvinism that surrounds sex, and the recognition of the reality of sex for what it actually is can in some sense be said to be a sign of social advancement. However, the pleasure that accompanies sex has led recently to sexual hedonism, the collapse of the family system, and adultery. The lack of moral principles regarding sex is enough to make one cover one's eyes. People have forgotten to think deeply about the fact that every person's actions have meaning in a person's life.
>
> Sex for all living creatures performs the essential function of ensuring survival and prosperity; for humans, it serves the additional function of supporting the foundational group unit of society, the family (the epitome of *Gemeinschaft,* on which humans necessarily depend). In other words, as opposed to one-sided civil society (*Gesellschaft*), in the family, which is typically comprised of a husband, a wife, and young children, people relate to each other with their whole selves in multifaceted ways, and in so doing they hope to maintain a lasting lifestyle based on deep love [*fukai aijō*] and trust. Sex in particular performs the role of cultivating the bond between husband and wife that creates and supports love [*aijō*]; it serves the purpose of providing children with emotionally stable development so that the next generations of mature adults may be sent into the social world. Accordingly, "sex" is a valuable thing that should not be treated lightly [*yasuuri...mono de wa nai*].
>
> A climate in which sex is treated negligently creates a generation that does not consider the overwhelming significance of the family, the basic foundational unit of society, and there is at the very least a risk that this generation will pass on the trait to the next.[5]

The defendant's act, for which he was sentenced to two and a half years in prison, thus was contrasted with a model of sex as a bond that "supports love" in marriage and promotes "emotionally stable development." The defendant's act hurt not only his victims but the whole of society for generations to come. That social collapse was apparently already in process before the defendant acted, as "the pleasure that accompanies sex has led recently to sexual hedonism, the collapse of the family system, and adultery." The judge hinted at his dismay with another social problem when he spoke of sex as "valuable"; although he was not chastising these girls in particular, he seems to be referring obliquely to the phenomenon of compensated dating (prostitution or paid dates by underage girls) as another sign of social decline.

The summary case note in the *Hanrei Times* law journal that introduced the opinion—almost certainly written by the judge himself[6]—further argued that the defendant's behavior was symptomatic of broader trends:

> Lately it has been estimated that one million young people lock themselves into their rooms. These young people are unable to interact with others; they simply sit in front of their computers and enter their own world. These avoidant personality and social withdrawal disorders have recently become a focus [for society]. It is a part of the "aging society with a declining birthrate" [*shōshi kōrei shakai*].[7]

With that flourish, the framing of the defendant's simple, time-limited acts as symptoms of a full-blown social epidemic is complete. To make the necessary links, the court appropriated at least four distinct voices, each for a specific purpose, into its powerful monologue. Its use of a girl's voice (at times as heard by the defendant) to tell the facts sets up the chilling tale and emphasizes the defendant's depravity. After the facts comes the analysis, first in a cold, investigator's voice to describe the pornographic evidence, then in the voice of a medical expert to diagnose a psychological complex. Finally, we hear the voice of a social critic lamenting the ills of society, measured against the idealistic yardstick of marital love and sex: cornerstones, apparently, of Japanese society.

The court has accomplished some essential goals of a judicial opinion: it has shown that the defendant's conduct was illegal (and despicable) and that he deserved a particular punishment. But the interesting aspect of this particular court opinion is not its seemingly predetermined outcome; rather, it is the way the judge tells the story, the way his words tell us something not just about the defendant but about the judge's worldview, his morality, and ultimately about Japanese law and society.

In this book, I use a comprehensive body of evidence—2,700 publicly available court opinions—to explore a particular vision of love, sex, and marriage in Japan. The opinions are from diverse areas such as family law, criminal law, torts, contracts, immigration, and trusts and estates.

They reveal an important, official perspective on how real individuals in Japan confront the painfully human issues that surround love, sex, and marriage.

Court opinions usually contain facts, analysis, decisions, and commentary. Sometimes judges' views of love, sex, and marriage emerge from the presentation of the facts. Among the recurring factual elements in the case law are work-induced commuter marriages, abortions forced or at least prompted by men, compensated dating, late-life divorces, termination fees to end affairs, sexless couples, Valentine's Day heartbreak, "soapland" bath-brothels, and home-wrecking hostesses. In many cases, these elements are irrelevant to the judgment, and yet judges choose to include them in the narrative anyway.

Sometimes it is the *non*factual elements of the opinions that are most revealing. Especially when combined with the facts, these portions—analysis, decisions, commentary—often suggest broad problems in love, sex, and marriage. Love, for instance, is highly valued in Japan, but in judges' opinions, it usually appears as a tragic, overwhelming emotion associated with jealousy, suffering, heartache, and death. Other less debilitating emotions and conditions, including "feelings," "earnestness," and "mutual affection," appear in unexpected areas of the law such as cases of underage sex and adultery. Sex in the opinions presents a choice among (a) private "normal" sex, which is male-dominated, conservative, dispassionate, or nonexistent; (b) commercial sex, which caters to every fetish but is said to lead to rape, murder, and general social depravity; and (c) a hybrid of the two in which courts commodify private sexual relationships. Marriage usually has neither love nor sex; judges raise the ideal of love in marriage and proclaim its importance, but virtually no one in the cases achieves it. Instead, married life is best conceptualized as the fulfillment of a contract.

Taken as a whole, the judges' opinions describe a Lovesick Japan. By "lovesick," I do not mean languishing with love as a teenager might pine for a sweetheart. Nor do I use lovesick as a substitute for loveless (lacking love) or lovelorn (the pain of unrequited love), though aspects of each apply. In this book, I use the word "lovesick" to describe a society in which a complex set of chronic and evolving problems is revealed in the ways people conceptualize and discuss love and the related components of sex and marriage. In the court opinions, lovesickness most often appears as a presupposed absence of physical and emotional intimacy, affection, and interconnectedness in personal relationships, an absence that stands in stark contrast with courts' clear recognition of the value and significance of other emotions.

Many scholars have thoughtfully analyzed love, sex, and marriage in Japan.[8] Potentially related social problems, including the low birthrate and social shut-ins as seen in the Child Predator case, as well as a low number of male-female relationships, a rising divorce rate, and high rates of abortion, sexual dissatisfaction, and suicide, also have been explored in depth.[9] What I offer is a distinct new perspective: a state-endorsed institutional view of love, sex, and marriage and their related problems.

As I analyze Lovesick Japan, I also explore the role that law plays there. In a previous book, *Law in Everyday Japan,* I showed the extensive role of law in everyday scenarios such as employee working hours, lost and found, and karaoke noise complaints.[10] Those findings contrasted sharply with the traditional view of Japan as a place where law takes a backseat to harmony, hierarchy, and relationships.

In this book, I show that the influence of law in Japan is more pervasive still, and in a very important arena: Japanese judges, who have significant discretion, play a surprisingly direct role as arbiters of emotions in intimate relationships. Take love. We tend to think of love as a warm, spontaneous emotion that lies on the opposite end of the spectrum from cold, calculating law (and lawyers?). Law is about rules; love (and for that matter betrayal, forgiveness, tragedy, endurance, and the rest of the spectrum) is natural and free.

But the cases show that love is inextricably linked with law. In case after case, Japanese judges opine on, and in one type of case actually are required by statute to determine, whether a person is in love, what other emotions a person is feeling, and whether those emotions are appropriate for the situation. In some cases, judges even determine whether a person's love is "natural," as opposed to some other kind of love. When judges eschew formalistic legal analysis and conduct a more visceral examination of emotions, they highlight the illusory nature of the line between what we think of as "law" and what we think of as "nonlaw" in an area that is central to being human.

These findings emerged from the cases to my surprise. I began this project after a discussion in my Japanese law class as to whether the Japanese Supreme Court in an important divorce case should have considered the love (or lack thereof) of the spouses. To follow up, I searched Lexis's online database of approximately 200,000 Japanese cases for cases involving love. I assumed I would find that by-the-book Japanese judges do not concern themselves with legally trivial matters of the heart.

I was wrong: I found love in the cases. But I found that love mattered mostly in criminal cases, *not* in cases about marriage and divorce, in which love is trotted out for the sake of showing its unattainability. I then expanded my search beyond love to marriage and divorce cases to see what, if not love, informed and motivated judges' decisions in those areas. That examination, and in particular an exploration of a long line of adultery-related marriage and divorce cases, led me to broaden my search to cases involving sex, as I found that the three concepts—love, sex, and marriage—were so intertwined in the cases that they needed to be examined together for each to make sense.

I found many of these cases on love, sex, and marriage using hundreds, or perhaps thousands, of keyword searches in the database, with little regard to legal categories. But law is not organized by keywords, so I also relied heavily on Japanese treatises and other scholarly works on particular legal topics to find additional cases. I focused on clearly relevant areas of the law such as breach of engagement, underage consensual sex, and illness as grounds for divorce. My case selection process in these specific areas of law was simple and decidedly inelegant: I read them all. Of course, I did not read all rape cases or all murder cases, though I found many to be relevant. In those areas, I focused on cases I found through searches, in secondary legal sources, and in citations from other opinions.

I then organized the cases for this book, sometimes by legal topic, sometimes by concept. I am able to present only a small fraction of the cases. I chose cases that are representative either of the legal topic or the concept, and sometimes both. If a case is an exception or comes from a small body of case law, I say so. Given the choice between an interesting case and an uninteresting one on the same point, I chose the interesting (and often footnote the uninteresting), but my primary concern was to choose cases that best exemplify a concept. Most of the cases are from the 1990s and 2000s, but I include a few earlier cases, sometimes to show the continuity (or lack thereof) of an idea over time.

I want to state four limitations up front. First, just as I pay particular attention to the particular words that judges choose and ignore to tell their stories, I understand that you might do the same to examine mine. I hope you won't. But the fact that you might suggests there is some danger of information distortion from the multiple levels of interpretation and translation.

Second, I do not claim *Lovesick Japan* to be unique. Every society has its own particular strain of lovesickness. But aside from a few comparisons to U.S. law to place Japanese law in context, I do not examine other lovesick societies. My simple focus is Japan's lovesickness as seen through the eyes of its judges.

Third, there are virtually no gays and lesbians in Japanese law, and accordingly homosexuality is virtually absent from this book. Sodomy, which makes prominent appearances in U.S. Supreme Court jurisprudence, is not a legal concept in Japan.[11] Same-sex marriage is unconstitutional (article 24 states that marriage is based on "the mutual consent of *both* sexes") and a subject of neither lawsuits nor debate. The online database contains only sixty-three opinions in which the word homosexuality (*dōseiai,* literally, same-sex love) appears. That smattering of cases offers no clear vision: the most well-known case, a discrimination case from 1994, states that "the majority of citizens have not thought very deeply about homosexuality."[12] The *Lovesick Japan* that appears in this book, then, is almost entirely straight.

Finally, my dataset is full of outliers: court cases do not reflect the normal life of an average person in Japan. A dispute (or crime) becomes a court case only when it cannot be settled otherwise. Lawsuits in any country are a parade of oddities, and Japan is no exception.

But it is precisely because the cases do not perfectly represent everyday life that themes and patterns in both the facts and the rulings become visible. Unlike real life, which is full of meaningless, irrelevant, and random events, court opinions compress life experiences into a few ordered paragraphs of "facts." As we saw in the Child Predator case, a court opinion presents an overorganized reality: a neatly chiseled story with a beginning, a middle, and an end from which any bits of information the court deems irrelevant have been trimmed away. Consciously or otherwise, subtly or otherwise, judges choose, eliminate, emphasize, and downplay facts to justify their decisions or perhaps to tell a dramatic, convincing, or familiar story filled with socially salient elements. They decide when to start and stop the clock on the narrative, whom to include as actors, and whether those actors are unique or everyman. After the events have been reduced to a legal folk tale, the judge then may turn the story into a homily on socially acceptable behavior.[13] The reality-skewing purposiveness of these court opinions, well stocked with dramatic and literary devices like Chekhovian guns that emerge early and fire later, reveals a rich, complex, and ultimately discomforting picture of love, sex, and marriage in contemporary Japan.

Now, who are the storytellers, and how do they tell the stories?

1

JUDGING

Japanese judges and U.S. judges have little in common. Judges in the United States function in an unorganized hodgepodge of federal, state, and local systems; New York State alone has judges in more than 1,250 town and village courts. Some judges are elected, some are appointed, and most are former lawyers or practitioners. U.S. judges receive wildly disparate educations depending on which of the approximately two hundred U.S. law schools they attended. Some went to elite schools; some went to night school—and some judges in local courts never even finished high school.[1]

The Japanese judiciary is much more homogeneous. Consider Judge Tanaka. Tanaka is my invention, a fictional character based on a combination of facts from the literature (much of it written by judges) and countless interactions over the last two decades with Japanese judges, lawyers, and prosecutors. Obviously judges are individuals, but the amalgamated Judge Tanaka represents what it means to be a member of the Japanese judiciary.

Tanaka's first major career break comes in his senior year of high school, when he passes an examination that awards him admission to one of Japan's elite universities. He majors in law but he rarely attends classes; instead, he studies for the bar examination at a cram school. Soon, perhaps even as early as his junior year of college, he takes the bar exam, an exam which until very recently had a two percent pass rate. He passes on his third attempt, two years after he graduates from college, and is then admitted to the government-run Legal Research and Training Institute, where he is paid a stipend to study law.

Until 2004, the institute was Japan's *only* law school. Then, in response to cries from business and citizens that legal services were too scarce, the government revised the system to increase the number of legal professionals. Almost all lawyers, judges, and prosecutors (with a few exceptions) now must earn a degree from one of Japan's seventy-four graduate law schools.[2] Those graduates are required to study for at least one year at the institute before entering the profession. Institute graduates—and almost everyone graduates—can apply to be judges or prosecutors or can simply become lawyers. In this case, one of Tanaka's instructors at the institute happens to be a judge. He encourages Tanaka to interview for the judiciary and writes a glowing recommendation for him.

What was it about Tanaka that so impressed his instructor? What traits and abilities made him seem like a good candidate for the judiciary? A 2003 Osaka High Court case provides an insider's view of how young judges are chosen. That case begins in 1994, when the Supreme Court rejected institute student Naoki Kamisaka's application to enter the judiciary. Kamisaka sued the government over the decision, arguing that he had been discriminated against for having once participated in a controversial citizens' suit against the government. After losing in the Osaka District Court, Kamisaka appealed.

The Osaka High Court recounted several discussions between Kamisaka and his instructors, detailing how the instructors repeatedly discouraged him from applying to the judiciary and refused to write recommendations on his behalf. In one conversation, an instructor told Kamisaka that a judge was not the kind of person who is politically active or brings lawsuits. In another conversation, the instructors voiced a more central concern. According to the court:

> Instructor A...telephoned Kamisaka and told him, "Instructor B and I have both told you that you're more suited to being a lawyer than a judge,

and I just wanted to see what happened after that." "If you become a judge, you'll have a really rough time; you don't have what it takes, and you won't get along well with your colleagues. I don't think you can stick it out. It's a job that operates on the basic premise of deliberation." "A lawyer can be verbose [*jōzetsu*], but judges are different. They have to listen carefully to the claims of the litigants and [guide them]. I really think you're a lawyer type." "I know you're thinking about a lot of things, but I want to be very clear with you. In all likelihood you won't become a judge. But I can't say for sure because it's not really my decision."

The same instructor then said, "Your grades aren't a problem. You're in the top of the civil class. The problem is circumstances. Some students can't find law firm jobs, and this year there will probably be more than one hundred applicants for the judiciary. So people with bad grades or bad personalities are being told that they can't make it or that it will be difficult." In response, Kamisaka said, "Are you saying that I have a bad personality?" to which the instructor replied, "Yes, I guess that's right." Kamisaka said, "What's wrong with my personality?" and the instructor replied, "For starters, the Christian era system [is a problem]. Writing opinions like that will confuse litigants." "And that's just a typical example. The Christian era thing isn't about expressing some background thought. It's a matter of form, not content."

The court's opinion contains a lengthy discussion of whether Kamisaka's failure to use the Christian era system was indeed sufficient grounds for rejecting his application. The Japanese court system catalogs cases by a year, a letter, and a docket number. The year is recorded in the imperial system, not the Christian era system. For instance, Kamisaka's appeal was filed in the year 2000, which is known as Heisei 12 in the imperial system because it is the twelfth year of the Heisei emperor's reign. Civil appeals are designated by the letter "ne," and the docket number of Kamisaka's case was 2366. The official case citation, then, is Heisei 12 (*ne*) 2366. The court discussed the fact that Kamisaka had consistently ignored this convention while he was a student, choosing to write the year in the Christian era system instead—and, even more oddly, writing both the Christian era year and the docket number in Japanese characters rather than Arabic numerals.

Kamisaka argued that he chose the Christian era system because of "globalization" and the increasing number of foreign litigants in Japanese courts. The court dismissed those reasons and noted that the imperial system is widely used. It found that Kamisaka's incorrect method showed that he was "persistent in following his own thoughts and had an inflexible personality and character." The court denied his claim.[3]

From the U.S. perspective, two factors in the opinion stand out. First, the qualities that matter to becoming a judge in Japan are institute grades and personality. In the United States, law school grades are less directly relevant, as people usually become judges later in life after they have gained work experience. Personality might matter in the United States, but not necessarily, and certainly not as early in life. Second, the type of personality that the Japanese judiciary expects (or for which applicants self-select) is clear: straitlaced, thoughtful, works well with others, and conformist— traits that apparently are not expected of lawyers. The Christian era issue might seem trifling, but in the Japanese judiciary it was a clear reflection of a seriously incompatible personality.

Our hypothetical Judge Tanaka has both the grades and the personality necessary to obtain the job. After a year of formal study at the institute and practical training, he enters the judiciary as an assistant judge at a district court. On average, judges begin practice at age twenty-seven, compared to age twenty-nine for the overall pool of bar examination passers, but twenty-three- and twenty-four-year-old judges are not unusual.[4] Judges are more likely to have passed the bar on the first try, a feat that is interpreted as a sign of intelligence.[5]

Tanaka has become one of 3,416 judges and assistant judges, of which 499, or 14.6 percent, are women.[6] He is twenty-eight years old. It is his first job.

Tanaka earns about $27,000 per year.[7] Despite his education and elite status, that salary is about 20 percent lower than the average for all Japanese workers and about one-fourth of what Tanaka would have earned as a lawyer in an elite Japanese firm. It is also far less than the $169,300 salary of U.S. federal judges and is roughly half the salary of the recent law school graduates who serve as those U.S. judges' clerks. Still, Tanaka's job has nice benefits; he rents his government-owned apartment at about half of the market price.

As a young assistant judge, Tanaka sits exclusively on three-judge panels. In those panels, the presiding judge is a senior judge, in his fifties or early sixties. The "right-chair judge" (*migibaiseki*) is a mid-career judge, often in his forties. Judge Tanaka is the "left-chair judge" (*hidaribaiseki*), a judge who has less than five years' experience and is usually in his late twenties or early thirties.

These chair designations are literal. In a Japanese district courtroom, the three judges sit on three chairs on a raised stage that resembles that of a U.S. courtroom. The judges wear black robes and, as a result of their elevated seating arrangements, literally overlook the proceedings. The clerk and the stenographer sit below them. The witness box is in the center of the courtroom; witnesses face the judges. The parties and their attorneys sit on the left and the right of the courtroom on either side of the witness box, perpendicular to the bench, facing each other (and not the judges). Gallery space is designated for spectators, but the absence of a jury system makes most Japanese courtrooms relatively small.[8] There are no insignia, flags, or symbols of state authority in the courtroom.

The panel usually assigns cases initially to the left-chair judge—in this case, young Judge Tanaka. Tanaka conducts the initial three-judge conference that precedes the hearing of the case. After hearing the case, the judges meet for a decision-making conference, which typically lasts thirty to forty minutes. The conference usually begins with the oldest judge asking Tanaka's opinion. The dynamics of these conferences vary. One Tokyo District Court judge writes that some presiding judges believe that "I'm the presiding judge, so I need to show these regular-seat judges how powerful I am," while others enjoy a give-and-take that resembles a university seminar.[9] In each case, maverick behavior is discouraged.

After the conference, Judge Tanaka writes the first draft of the opinion. Unlike the United States, the required format for a judicial opinion in Japan is stated precisely by law and the details are spelled out in officially issued sample opinions and institute textbooks.[10] In a civil case, an opinion must contain a statement of the judgment, the facts of the case, and the reasons for the judgment, including a clear statement of the parties' claims.[11] In a criminal case, an opinion must contain a statement of the judgment, the facts that constitute the crime, an examination of evidence, the application of law, and the reasons for the sentence imposed, if any.[12] Virtually every opinion issued in Japan follows this strict pattern.

Run-on sentences and difficult vocabulary once made Japanese judicial opinions "the champion of terrible writing."[13] But since 1990, under the motto "judicial opinions that parties can read" (*tōjisha ga yonde wakaru hanketsubun*), judges have been instructed to write opinions more simply.[14]

Many judges of the older generation bemoan this change, claiming that it leads to less careful and less precise legal analysis. Many younger judges are happy to leave the turgid prose in the past.

If facts are undisputed by the parties, Judge Tanaka has considerable discretion as to whether or how much of those facts to include in the opinion.[15] If they are disputed but are merely background facts, the evidentiary standard for determining them is unclear, but it is lower than the standard for proving the material elements of a case.[16] Tanaka, then, has freedom to determine and use the facts to tell a comprehensive narrative "that parties can read." When he drafts his opinions, he includes as background some facts that are relevant to the *story* even if they have no direct, clear relevance to the *ruling*. Sometimes the result is a jarring juxtaposition of the banal with the sensational, but Tanaka believes the details give readers a more complete picture of the case.

When Tanaka has finished drafting the opinion, he gives it to the right-chair judge, who revises it if necessary and identifies questions that need further research. The presiding judge makes final revisions.[17] The presiding judge also must read the main text of the judgment aloud in court and, in a criminal case, a summary of the reasons as well.[18] Each opinion lists the name of each judge. With the exception of the Supreme Court, there are no concurring or dissenting opinions.

Japanese judges often tell me that they write their opinions "for the public." But the public rarely reads opinions. Excerpts from important opinions, such as those involving corporate takeovers or issues of religious freedom, occasionally appear in the newspapers. Otherwise the average citizen rarely encounters them, and, in most cases, even the legislature seems relatively uninterested.

Judges also write their opinions for the parties to the suit. Citing a Legal Training and Research Institute manual, one Japanese judge explains that "the highest function of an opinion is to inform the parties as to the content of the judgment and to give them an opportunity to consider whether to appeal." "But," he writes, "in reality, an opinion also is expected to play the role of persuading the losing party in the case [as to the correctness of the judgment]."[19] The opinions, then, often reveal judges' efforts to assure losing parties (including criminal defendants) that the court has carefully considered their claims. In so doing, they often portray the argument of both sides in more depth than the opinions of U.S. courts.

Judge Tanaka has another audience for his opinions that need not be mentioned in institute manuals: senior judges. Like almost all judges and assistant judges, Tanaka is transferred every three years. The quality of the post and the quality of the location to which is he transferred depend in part on his ability to impress senior judges and ultimately the Secretariat, the administrative arm of the Supreme Court. If his performance is sub-par, he can be terminated. Senior judges assess performance on the basis of factors such as hours worked and quality of written opinions. Judges are expected to work very long hours; in the Yokohama District Court, an announcement is made every night at 11 p.m.: "for the sake of your health, please go home."[20] Defining "quality" is difficult, but studies suggest that it includes political correctness.[21] As a standout, Tanaka gets the best posts in the big cities, Tokyo and Osaka.

The transfer system leads to courtroom circumstances that would be odd in the U.S. system. As Dan Foote notes, the combination of transfers and noncontinuous trials "means judges sometimes shift during the trial. Presumably because the identity of the judge is not supposed to matter, this change in judges is an accepted feature of the Japanese judicial system."[22]

Transfers affect virtually every judge. The entering class of 2000 had eighty-eight new judges, most of whom were between the ages of twenty-seven and thirty-one. By 2003, only nine had not been transferred (one of the nine died). The class of 1980 had sixty-eight judges, fifty-four of whom were transferred at least twice by 1986 (three of the remaining fourteen quit to become lawyers.[23]

At age thirty-one, after three years on the bench, Tanaka marries. As a member of Japan's bureaucratic elite, his spouse is of the appropriate social class and has the appropriate level of education. It is not uncommon for young judges to marry the daughters of their judge-instructors from the institute. Of course, it would be interesting for purposes of this book to know whether Tanaka actually loves his wife, or how often he has sex, but there is little information on those points from which to extrapolate a guess, and I suspect there is significant variance anyway.

Tanaka and his new wife continue to live in judiciary housing. Roughly sixty percent of judges live in one of the two thousand units set aside for the judiciary. Some complexes include bureaucrats from several different agencies and branches of government, and some are reserved solely for judges.

Judges generally praise the housing as inexpensive, safe places where "judges can develop relationships with each other." As two Osaka judges write, "it is not unusual for judges to meet in a housing complex and continue their relationships even after a transfer; there are more than a few cases in which judges end up living posttransfer in a housing complex with judges with whom they lived before the transfer."[24] Tanaka's wife spends time getting to know other judges' wives and, according to a book chapter written by two judges in 2004, "trading information on housework and childrearing."[25]

The combination of uniform education, transfers, and judiciary housing creates a strong social network for Tanaka. Unlike judges in the United States, he comes to know every judge who graduated from the institute with him and many, many others as well. If he does not know a particular judge, he usually knows another judge who does.

After five years on the bench, Tanaka is promoted to "special assistant judge." As a result of his new status, he is able to rule on cases on his own and serve as the right-chair judge.[26] The promotion is not automatic. But Tanaka is viewed as competent, and, like many young judges, his promotion was assumed.

Tanaka and his wife have two children, the first of whom was born in his sixth year as a judge, the second in his eighth year. Each time Tanaka is transferred, his family moves with him, his young children enter new schools, and his wife joins new social networks. Tanaka could refuse the transfers, but his career would suffer.

After ten years, three transfers, and thousands of hours reading records and writing opinions, Tanaka is promoted from assistant judge to judge. Again the promotion was not automatic, but it was expected. His annual salary becomes approximately $64,000, still far below both his market value as a top-notch lawyer and the salary of his U.S. federal counterparts. He must clear approximately three hundred civil cases per year for his caseload to stay "in the black" or he will not advance in the system.[27] To keep up with this case-a-day pace, Tanaka learns to write opinions quickly and to avoid some of the more difficult cases by persuading the parties to settle. He is rewarded with good posts, and each new one brings him a new docket of cases.

When it is time for Tanaka's children to attend junior high school, he and his wife decide that the children are too involved with activities at school and cram school (the goal of the latter is to place his children in elite high schools) to move when Tanaka is transferred. As a result of this decision, Judge Tanaka will live separately from his family for several years, returning home on weekends when possible.

For the remainder of his career, Tanaka is promoted through increasingly prestigious judgeships and administrative posts. He becomes a right-chair judge, a presiding judge, and finally a judge on one of eight high courts, which hear appeals from district courts. At the high court, his job changes little: appeals in the high court are considered continuations of lower court proceedings, and judges make rulings on fact and law just as in district court. Judge Tanaka retires from his senior position at the mandatory retirement age of sixty-five.[28]

I offer these stylized facts in part to show the difference between the U.S. and Japanese models and in part to explore how a judge's training and career path might affect both the way he writes opinions and the way in which he views the world. Before examining that relationship, I want to be clear: Japanese judges are among the smartest, most careful, and most dedicated workers I know. I find them as honest, trustworthy, and hardworking as members of any other profession in Japan or the United States; in most cases, more so. They agonize over difficult decisions, which they are aware can have dramatic consequences not only for the parties involved but for society as a whole. Most aim diligently to fulfill the societal expectations set forth in 2000 by the Justice System Reform Council which call for "judges who are full of humanity, kind, and warmhearted" and "who do their best to listen intensely to litigants, to understand their feelings, and never to look down on them from the bench."[29] And in the specific context of love, sex, and marriage, Japanese judges struggle admirably with a complex reality that falls short of the ideal.

However diligently they may strive, judges are subject to a variety of institutional influences and pressures. Four institutions seem particularly relevant to the ways judges might view cases involving love, sex, and marriage. First, the seniority system fosters top-down conformity. Young judges rise and fall with the evaluations of the older judges with whom they work. Although exceptions exist, senior judges are far more likely to impress their vision of love, sex, and marriage on young judges than the other way around. The opinions, then, are largely the product of a group of senior entrenched bureaucratic elites, a relatively homogeneous group that includes few women, either as authors of opinions or as workplace colleagues. It would be no surprise if the opinions expressed conservative, paternalistic, or outdated views.

Second, no matter how much a judge wants to please his elders, in some cases he simply cannot overcome his youth and inexperience. As Judge Etsuo Shimozawa reflects:

> Thirty years or so ago, I was twenty-seven and still single. At that young age, I was assigned to cases with two veteran [lay person] mediators, and as a family court judge I was in charge of mediating family cases of marital discord, such as divorce and so on. At that time, the only things I knew about marriage or male-female relations were from books. Actually I was very immature; I had never even held a girl's hand and I knew nothing about the subtleties of relationships between men and women. When I look back on those days now, I see that I was pretty daring, or maybe I should say that I had a lot of nerve.
>
> But as I mediated cases of marital distress day after day, I found opportunities for new discoveries daily, and I learned a lot. Little by little, I began to understand things such as what might cause a couple to fall into mutual distrust, conflict, disharmony, and ultimately to a complete breakdown of the marriage.[30]

Of course, many judges eventually fall in love, have sex, and marry; there is even a published divorce case in which a suing spouse happens to be a judge (the court allowed him to divorce his schizophrenic wife).[31] But Judge Shimozawa, at least, was deciding cases in which knowledge of the complexities of relationships would seem essential, and he seems to have been sorely lacking in that department.

Third, the transfer system and judiciary housing create a homogeneous and insular world in which judges often are separated from their families in commuter marriages and live life with few acquaintances outside the judiciary. As some Japanese commentators argue, judges "do not know the world."[32] Judges can go for days without speaking to anyone other than other judges. Of course, this situation does not necessarily make any judge "lovesick." But it is no small leap to speculate that this lifestyle might cause judicial views on love, sex, and marriage to deviate from or lag behind public norms.

Finally, the Japanese judge's career path limits important professional interactions. Few members of the bench have significant experience outside the courtroom. Unlike U.S. judges, with a handful of exceptions, Japanese judges have never practiced law. Most Japanese judges have never represented a client, which means that, among other things, they have never played the role of lawyer-as-psychologist. Of course, some distance from the actual parties to a case is desirable for a judge, but the lack of one-on-one interaction with the kinds of people who appear in the cases before them might lead some judges to view litigants as relatively impersonal legal actors.

One might expect Japanese judges, then, to write straightforward, dry opinions that don't rock the boat; as Mark Ramseyer and Eric Rasmusen have argued, the Japanese bureaucratic judiciary "is not an institutional structure likely to foster judicial independence."[33] True, especially in the politically charged contexts on which Ramseyer and Rasmusen focused. But in cases of love, sex, and marriage, Japanese judges often seem completely unreserved about using the language of love, raising intimate and emotional issues that seem unrelated to the legal question at hand, or editorializing at length on matters of the heart.

In some cases, judges go further than editorializing: they create precedents that dramatically change the rules of love, sex, and marriage, with little or no legislative authority. In those areas, at least, if U.S. judges wrote the opinions that Japanese judges do, they would be criticized by some for "judicial activism" and "creating law." But in Japan as in the United States, the reality of judiciary-led legal change is complex. Japan is a civil law country; its legal system is based on five main codes, a constitution, and various limited statutes. Many provisions are quite broad and require extensive interpretation. For instance, article 709 of the Civil Code, the basic tort provision, provides that "a person who has intentionally or negligently infringed any right of others, or legally protected interest of others, shall be liable to compensate any damages resulting in consequence." From this statute, judges must assess liability in a broad range of situations, from medical malpractice to automobile accidents to sexual harassment: all are governed by article 709, which remains constant over time despite changes in the applicable situations. When judges interpret and apply the provision, they have significant discretion to create—or not—standards, tests, and doctrines to justify their rulings and to ensure uniformity of the law. Some of those standards, tests, and doctrines are highly formalistic (as we will see in the divorce context), but a significant number focus on less "legal" factors such as emotion (in murder cases) or normality (in sex cases).

The precedents created through this process influence future decisions. As the Tokyo District Court has noted, lower court decisions may differ from Supreme Court precedent "only when the latter are based on clearly irrational reasoning, or when the basic situation on which the latter is based has changed dramatically, or when remarkably unreasonable results would follow because of special circumstances in the case before the court.[34] Former Supreme Court Justice Masami Itō expresses a similar view but notes the (small) possibility that lower court opinions can spark change as well:

> When a lower court reveals a judgment that is contrary to a Supreme Court judgment, and especially if many lower courts share that attitude, the Supreme Court will hear the appeal and can take the opportunity to reconsider and re-examine the rationality of its precedent. There are examples of lower court decisions that trigger change in Supreme Court precedent in this way. But examples of this practice are very rare, and most lower court judgments that are opposed to Supreme Court judgments are exceptions that will be overruled.[35]

As Itō's comment demonstrates, legal change is a conversation among many different players that often lacks clear rules, processes, and results. Higher courts set the course of statutory interpretation and may overrule lower courts if they find their interpretation or application of law to be incorrect. Lower courts examine prior rulings in an attempt to ensure uniformity, but they use their discretion to distinguish precedents and push the law in different directions. Legislatures creates statutes for courts to interpret, and courts interpret them in ways that may or may not have been intended. Scholars interpret both statutes and opinions, and their views, often formed independently from actual cases, are sometimes followed and cited by judges.

One of the particularly complicated players in this legal conversation is society. Sometimes judges must interpret laws that they know were deeply contested at their passage or are the subject of shifting contemporary debate. That knowledge might not necessarily change a judge's ultimate ruling, but it might change the language the judge uses.

Sometimes judges in Japan are *required* to look to society. Judicial answers to some of the most difficult questions, such as whether a marriage is "irretrievably broken," whether a relationship is "earnest," whether certain sexual practices are "normal," and even whether a sex organ is "remarkably malformed" such that it could "embarrass" a person[36]—are examined by Japanese judges according to the "sense of society" (*shakai kannen, shakai gainen,* or *shakai tsūnen*) or by standards of "public morality" (*kōshū dōtoku* or *kōjo ryōzoku*). Courts apply the standard—which was invented by courts[37]—in many areas of Japanese law, including religious freedom,[38] property rights,[39] and employee dismissal.[40] It is, as one scholar explains, "among the most frequently used phrases in Japanese judicial opinions. In judgment after judgment, Japanese judges invoke the 'sense of society' as a controlling source of value and standard for their decisions."[41]

Of course, there is no monolithic "sense of society" in Japan, and in a few cases, courts unwittingly reveal as much. In a 2007 Supreme Court case, for instance, a woman applied for spousal benefits under the Welfare Pension Act following the death of the man with whom she had lived in a spousal relationship for forty-two years. Because the couple was never officially married, the applicant argued that she was eligible for benefits as a "person who has not filed a notification of marriage but actually has a relationship similar to a marital relationship," a provision intended to cover common-law (*naien,* or de facto) spouses.[42] The problem for the Court was that her putative husband was also her uncle, and as such the marriage would have been illegal under the Civil Code (art. 734). The Supreme Court began its analysis by invoking the "sense of society" (*shakai tsūnen*) regarding marriages between relatives:

> Under the rules and law of marriage and generally socially accepted ideas, common-law marriage between blood relatives within the second degree of kinship is extremely unethical and against the public interest. Therefore, even if persons in such a common-law marriage live together as husband and wife in a socially accepted (*shakai tsūnen*) way, they are not eligible for [bene-fits]... because the marriage is unethical and against the public interest.

But the Court then implied that the sense of society in some communities might differ:

> Nevertheless, it is well known that marriage between relatives frequently occurred in Japan in order to secure successors for farmlands or other reasons. In [the wife's] community, due to regional characteristics, marriage between relatives occurred with some frequency, and common-law marriages between uncle and niece also occurred. It seems that in her particular community and among her relatives, there are examples of such common-law marriage that were accepted without opposition.

The wife won. The Court adopted her local community's view, finding that "from the beginning, the marriage could hardly be regarded as unethical or antisocial." But it did not directly address the fact that the local view also was a sense of some segment of society, that multiple senses of society existed, or that it was flouting the dominant sense of society.[43]

The "sense of society," then, is a term of art, or perhaps a placeholder for some other concept. Japanese judges have told me they have three primary strategies for determining it. First, in many cases they simply guess. These guesses might incorporate clues from outside the courtroom, or they might result from an entirely internal thought process.

In other cases, judges invoke the "sense of society" as a rhetorical crutch to justify decisions in difficult cases. Cases of love, marriage, and sex often involve messy he-said/she-said questions of fact, and the emotional stakes are often particularly high. Japanese judges must resolve the factual issues, decide the legal issues, and in almost every case write an opinion (if they cannot persuade the parties to settle). In these cases, the Japanese judge deserves pity, for there is little room for fudging or ducking issues, even in emotionally fraught cases (like adultery) in which, as one judge told me, "most of the time, everyone is lying to some extent." A judge might invoke the "sense of society" in such cases as a means of insulating himself from the kind of criticism he might receive if he were to express an opinion as his own.

Finally, a judge will sometimes approach the sense of society in a prescriptive manner, stating not what he thinks the sense of society *is* but what he thinks it *should be*. As we will see, the Japanese judiciary tends to be conservative, and it sometimes deliberately expresses normative views that run counter to the sense of society but reflect the judiciary's elite perspective.[44] Still, as John Haley has noted, Japanese judges believe that "the judiciary itself would suffer were the public ever to perceive that judges were freely deciding cases out of…any extreme personal ideological bias at odds with what they would themselves consider the 'sense of society.'"[45] If judges push on countervailing social mores, they do so carefully, with attention to how their decisions will be received both by the public and by senior judges.

But I have found that Japanese judges sometimes can be oblivious to the assumptions that underlie their prose. I discussed this book project at length with several Japanese judges. They showed great interest, and a few asked if I had examples of their own writing; in one instance, I did. I showed the judge the opinion under which his name was signed as presiding judge and pointed to descriptions in the facts that seemed to me to reflect some interesting views on relationships. After reading the case, he expressed embarrassment, told me that he agreed with my interpretation, and then requested that I not tell his colleagues what his words revealed (I didn't, but the case is in this book).

This combination of purposefully and accidentally revealing language paints a rich picture of the views of Japanese judicial elites—very smart, highly educated people in prestigious government offices—on love, sex, and marriage. Occasionally that vision is charming, kind, and encouraging. But it is often highly disturbing.

2

LOVE

Love abounds in Japan. Japan's popular prime-time soap operas are often about love and obstacles to obtaining it. The music and film industries thrive on love songs and romantic comedies. Stores sell out of cakes and candy on Christmas Eve, Valentine's Day, and White Day, days said to be the most romantic of the year. Bookstores are full of modern romance novels, classic Japanese love stories, and shelves of books that teach how to find true love. Cell-phone novels with titles like *Eternal Dream* and *Deep Love,* written by and for young women, are one of the latest manifestations of pop-culture love.[1]

Some of these entertainment genres celebrate the power of love as a beautiful, many-splendored thing. But the most striking feature of Japanese love narratives is their strong emphasis on suffering and pain. In Japan, love is often portrayed as a problem—an irresistible, destructive, and life-threatening condition. Of course, Japan is not the only nation to describe love in that way. Unavoidable tragedy is at the center of much of Western romance literature—not to mention American murder ballads and lonesome country standards.[2]

But love in Japanese court opinions is often darker and even more difficult to overcome. In this chapter, I explore the dark side of love in three kinds of Japanese court cases: suicide, murder, and stalking. Characters in these ominous-sounding tales should not be expected to live happily ever after, and they don't. But the depiction in the opinions of love as suffering extends beyond tragic endings to places in the narrative that need not be bleak: the judges' applications of laws and nuanced recitations of the facts that occurred *before* the tragedy. Judges' depictions of love even extend beyond the particular facts of the cases, as they discuss the facts against the backdrop of what they view as widely shared assumptions about love. The resulting narratives usually describe love as if it naturally could not be anything other than an overwhelming, disorienting force to which people unwittingly cede self-control.

Before turning to the cases, let us examine the context for this dark side of love in Japan.

Love in Context

Several words in Japanese translate to "love." Shinmeikai's standard Japanese dictionary, *Kokugojiten,* defines one translation of love, *ren'ai,* as "a condition in which one has special feelings of affection for a particular member of the opposite sex, wants to be alone together, and with feelings of wanting to join together if possible, experiences extreme sadness when it is not possible." Compare that definition to the *Oxford English Dictionary:* "that state or feeling with regard to a person which manifests itself in concern for the person's welfare, and also often desire for his or her approval; deep affection, strong emotional content." The focus in English is the other person, the loved; the focus in Japanese is wanting and sadness.

Surveys suggest the pervasiveness of the heartbroken definition in Japan. Before turning to them, I want to acknowledge that I am somewhat skeptical of the results of some of the surveys in this book, in part because people are not always truthful, even with themselves, about love, sex, and marriage. Nevertheless, even the studies that have questionable results are helpful tools for understanding the context for judicial opinions on love, sex, and marriage, as they show the questions and issues that researchers from universities, corporations, and most interestingly the government find important enough to ask. And when the results correlate with the cases, we should at least examine possible connections.

One study compared attitudes toward love and romance among students from the United States, Germany, and Japan. It found that German and U.S. students valued romantic love more highly than Japanese and that, among the three, the Germans were the most "passionate" insofar as they were most likely to forgo economic security for love. It also found the Japanese response to be "the most complex." Some Japanese responses reflected traditional romantic ideals: for example, Japanese respondents were more likely to agree that "a woman should expect her sweetheart to be chivalrous on all occasions" and that "to be truly in love is to be in love forever." Yet Japanese respondents were also significantly more likely than German and U.S. respondents to agree with the statements "When you are in love, you are usually in a daze" and "Jealousy usually varies directly with love; that is, the more in love you are, the greater the tendency for you to become jealous."[3]

In a second study, three researchers from Osaka University asked 178 Japanese university students "What is love to you?" (*anata ni totte ren'ai (ai) to ha nan desuka*). The researchers coded the 247 responses they received into fifteen categories, as listed in table 2.1.

As the table shows, respondents volunteered a broad range of descriptions of love. The two most common responses were "love gives energy and power to life" and "love is complex and sometimes leads to pain." But the gender split is significant: "love gives energy and power to life" was the response of more than a quarter of women but less than twelve percent of men—and it was also the only statistically significant difference in the survey. One in five women found that "love is important and vital" but fewer than one in nine men agreed. Crucially, the two male responses tied for first place were "love is complex and sometimes leads to pain" and "love is smug and full of assumptions and misunderstanding."

The gap in male and female perceptions of love correlates with both a separation of the sexes and strictly defined gender roles in Japan. From an early age, the degree of separation between boys and girls at Japanese schools is usually far greater than in U.S. ones. The workplace too is often sexually segregated, as women continue to have difficulty in obtaining management positions and often work part-time. So separated, many men form friendships exclusively with other men and women with other women.

Men and women in Japan seem to interact in meaningful ways infrequently. A 2006 government survey—and note here that the government cares—found that 52.2 percent of single men and 44.7 percent of single

TABLE 2.1. What Is Love to You?

Response	Male response % (Rank)	Female response % (Rank)	Overall response %
Love brings energy and power to life	11.7 (4)	25.5 (1)	16.5*
Love is complex and sometimes leads to pain	15.5 (1)	14.6 (6)	15.2
Love is about trust and kindness	11.7 (4)	21.8 (2)	15.2
Love is important and vital	11.7 (4)	18.2 (3)	13.9
Love advances a person and leads to growth	11.7 (4)	18.2 (3)	13.9
Love is smug and full of assumptions and misunderstanding	15.5 (1)	5.5 (13)	12.0
Love is vague, puzzling, unclear, and cannot be understood	12.6 (3)	9.1 (10)	11.4
Love gives comfort and causes feelings of happiness	9.7 (8)	10.9 (7)	10.1
Love is fun	9.7 (8)	7.3 (12)	8.9
Love is about earnest caring and fondness	3.9 (13)	16.4 (5)	8.2
Love is instinctive and causes excitement	5.8 (11)	10.9 (7)	7.6
Love is realistic: a compromise, requires money, is about sex, etc.	8.7 (10)	5.5 (13)	7.6
Love is a wonderful thing that I would like to try	4.9 (12)	9.1 (10)	6.3
Love is inessential and merely adds value to life	1.9 (15)	10.9 (7)	4.1*
Love is about being with or wanting to be with a companion	3.8 (14)	3.6 (15)	3.8

* Denotes statistically significant difference between sexes at the 95% confidence interval.

Source: Yūji Kanemasa, Jun'ichi Taniguchi, and Masanori Ishimori, Ren'ai no Ime-ji to Kōi Riyū ni Oyobosu Isei Kankei to Seibetsu no Eikyō [Effects of Opposite Sex Relationships and Sex on Images of Romantic Love and Reasons for Attraction], 1 *Tainin Shakai Shinrigaku Kenkyū* 147 (2001). Table revised from original.

women between the ages of eighteen and thirty-four had no relationship *of any sort* with any member of the opposite sex, not even friendship. In the 30–34 age group (the oldest surveyed), 24.3 percent of the men and 26.7 percent of the women said they were virgins—and 11 percent of the men and 18 percent of the women declined to answer the question, suggesting that the actual numbers might be higher.[4] Another study found that 30 percent of Japanese men have never been in love, a percentage far higher than in Russia (12 percent) and the United States (13 percent).[5]

Part of the reason for the phenomena these data represent might be strictly defined gender roles. It is cliché but true to note that gender stereotypes permeate Japanese culture. Female themes of *enka* ballads are beauty, passivity, and longing; the male theme is dogged commitment to a path and following it until the end.[6] In manga comic books, male characters are said to be direct, cool, eager, and brazen; female characters are said to be kind, cute, cooperative, and shy.[7]

Judges adopt similar gender stereotypes. The adjective "feminine" (*onna rashii*) is used sparingly in court opinions, but when it is, it usually refers to physical attributes: makeup, shoes, and certain poses and styles of sitting.[8] Feminine is used in the cases to refer to a woman who is fashionable or to a woman who is "large-breasted and has a nice body."[9] A young girl who plays with other girls is considered to be engaged in a feminine activity.[10]

By contrast, the cases usually apply the adjective "masculine" (*otoko rashii*) to character and actions. Whether in the course of quoting or summarizing testimony or on their own, courts have labeled as masculine the following actions: doing one's job,[11] paying a debt,[12] providing a urine sample as ordered,[13] taking responsibility for criminal actions,[14] admitting the truth about a sexual relationship,[15] playing "muscle-to-muscle" American football,[16] making decisions,[17] and speaking one's true intentions to a superior.[18] Some actions are said to be masculine in context: for a *yakuza* gang member, killing as instructed or as expected is masculine[19]; for at least one firefighter, masculinity could be found in the settlement of a dispute by duel-like punching.[20] Many actions are labeled as *not* masculine, including being too comical, concerning oneself with trifling matters, attempting to evade punishment, and of course appearing feminine.[21]

This gender split is prominently on display in the "love theory" (*ren'ai ron*) section that exists in virtually every large Japanese bookstore. The books in this section share three defining qualities. First, few of them resemble the marriage improvement, self-improvement, or even relationship books found in U.S. bookstores. Instead of offering practical advice about how to manage or cope with existing relationships, love theory books are devoted to the pursuit of true love. They teach self-discovery, goal-setting, self-promotion, how to dress appropriately, and how to converse with the opposite sex.

Second, few love theory books are written by psychologists or other professionals. Some are written by celebrities, but many are unclassifiable one-shots, such as *The Underground Theory of Love,* a book based on interviews with women in the sex trade. It begins by instructing the reader that "normal love enters the heart and connects to the body. Sex-shop love enters the body and connects to the heart."[22]

Finally, as with the large number of translated Harlequin romance novels sold in Japan, most love theory books are written for women.[23] In many bookstores, the "love theory" books are merged with feminist books into one overarching section: Theory of Woman/Theory of Love. The spines of the books are often pink, the titles are written in cutesy fonts, and the cover art—full of wide-eyed girls, hearts, and flowers—is pitched to female readers. These books belong to a larger catalog of works that purport to teach femininity, including cookbooks, which often are more about preparing meals correctly for children, husbands, and boyfriends than cooking. The idea behind women's books seems to be that although there are very few good men are out there, the right man can be found—and caught—with the right set of techniques.

For men, however, the fundamental premise differs. For men, the idea seems to be that there are many, many good women out there, but they are unavailable to most men, or at least to most *Japanese* men. As a best-selling 2008 book about Japan's growing "crisis" of people who do not or cannot marry explains, "No matter where one goes in the world—Morocco, Indonesia, Mexico—one finds Japanese women married to local men. Japanese women can use love to go anywhere in the world.... But, and please excuse me for saying it, Japanese men are the least sought-after men in the world."[24] Japanese women need to target selectively, but Japanese men, the idea seems to be, should simply take what comes along.

Japanese love theory books for men are usually shelved in the miscellaneous section, not the love theory section, and their subjects include personal hygiene, sex, social skills, and the cultivation of masculinity—not exactly love theory. A typical example is *Health and Physical Education for Thirty-Year-Olds.*[25] The 2008 book was initially marketed at stores in Tokyo's electronics market, Akihabara, an area said to be teeming with tech-savvy but socially challenged men who have never dated, or perhaps even spoken to, a woman. It quickly became the best-selling book on Amazon. com's Japanese site, amazon.co.jp. The book teaches readers how to talk to a woman ("it is like playing catch"), what to do and not to do on a date ("do not go to a computer shop"), when sex will happen ("most couples do it after approximately one to three months of dating, which means three to eight dates"), how to prepare for sex ("trim your fingernails"), and how to remove clothing (a woman will be "less embarrassed" if the man removes her t-shirt from behind). Roughly two-thirds of the book is about sexual techniques and positions, all illustrated by a seemingly happy cartoon couple. One of the book's stated goals is to help thirty-year-old virgins whose sexual experience has been limited to watching adult videos and playing sexual role-playing computer games. Accordingly, it instructs that there are differences between those media and real sex: real sex does not occur outdoors, requires a condom, happens with the lights off, and does not involve ejaculation in the woman's face ("most women dislike it").

Despite all the interest, the Japanese vocabulary of love is relatively new. Japanese translators of Western literature in the late nineteenth century had no word to convey the dominant understanding of love as a combination of devotion, affection, longing, friendship, and equality. Translators could have used *ai,* which translates to "love" in English, but according to some accounts, *ai* was at that point more closely associated with passion and could only be used by a superior to an inferior[26]; according to others, *ai* simply denoted beauty and had religious overtones[27]; and according to still others, it was linked too closely to parental and sibling love.[28] Translators could have used *koi,* but it was considered to be too sexual.[29] According to the most cited historical account, a new term for love, *ren'ai,* was coined in the 1870s by combining the characters *koi* and *ai.*[30] By the 1890s, translators had begun to use *ren'ai* regularly to convey the Western concept of love.[31]

Contemporary Japanese has several words for love. As a high court noted in a 2009 trademark infringement suit over the use of the word *rabu,* a Japanized version of the English word *love, rabu* is "well known in Japan" and synonymous with the nouns *ai, aijō,* and *koi,* and with the verbs *hito wo aisuru* (to love a person), *koi wo suru* (to be in love), and *suki ni naru* (to fall in love, or to come to like).[32] Still, courts almost always use one of three words to express feelings roughly comparable to the English concept of love: *ai, aijō,* or *ren'ai. Ai* translates to love in English, while *aijō* translates a bit awkwardly to "feelings of love." Lovers have *ai* and *aijō* for one another, but so do friends, parents, children, and pets.[33] *Ren'ai* is used mostly for lovers, including young couples, persons in extramarital affairs, and perhaps newlyweds; it implies a dating or romantic relationship.[34] The only time *ren'ai* applies to married couples is when it is used to distinguish "love" marriages from marriages that were arranged (a distinction I will discuss later).

"I love you" translates most smoothly and directly into Japanese as *aishiteru.* But *aishiteru* rarely appears in the law. In the published case law, it appears only as reported speech—for instance, later in this chapter by a woman being strangled by her husband and by another woman after she has been beaten, and in chapter 3 in an emotional distress case in which a man denies having said it.[35]

The phrase "I love you" is rare in Japanese society as well. Expression of fondness and attraction often take the form of *sukida,* which is sometimes translated as "I love you" but perhaps more accurately as a bit closer to the less committed "I like you."[36] This aspect of love is a subject of serious academic discourse in Japan. Studies indicate that although young Japanese people favor direct expressions of love, those expressions rarely take place between spouses.[37] The scarcity of such expression during marriage has been attributed not to lack of love but to embarrassment[38] and to a feeling that love in marriage is superficial and "I love you" a "fatuous form of flattery."[39]

A Japanese bank campaign provides an intriguing glimpse into the lack of straightforward declarations of love among married couples. In 2000, the Sumitomo Trust and Banking Company began "Love Letters at Sixty" (*60sai no Rabu Reta-*), a promotion in which it asked sixty-something married couples to submit romantic missives they had written to their spouses. The only requirement was that the words fit on the back of a postcard. The campaign became an annual one, and by 2008, NHK press had published roughly one thousand love letters over the course of eight annual volumes and was receiving more than ten thousand entries per year.

The sponsor, Sumitomo Trust, awards prizes to the writers of the best letters. The 2008 grand prize winner was Noriyuki Miyakawa, a sixty-seven-year-old husband. Forty years ago, Noriyuki reminisced in his letter, he promised to come home early from work one day. But he forgot. When he finally did arrive home in the middle of the night, his wife was not waiting up for him as usual but already in bed. She told him, "I waited for you at the station." His response was "What's the matter with you, stupid? Lots of things happen at work!" The last line of his letter was "I'm sorry, Chieko."[40]

The love letter as apology or as an expression of gratitude is a common motif. Very few letters explicitly mention love, and fewer still say "I love you." Of the fifteen letters the sponsors chose in 2008 for the runner-up "gold prize," only one said "I love you"—and it was an apology from a wife for her inability to say those words to her husband in person. The theme of regrettable silence runs throughout the collected letters. One husband writes, "It took me forty years to learn to tell you properly 'it's delicious' about the food you prepare. So it will take me five more years to learn to say 'thank you.' And then to tell you 'I love you'... well, I'll do my best."[41] A braver husband writes: "Next Sunday I'll tell you 'I love you' [*aishiteruyo*], so please don't laugh."[42]

Wives also write of their inability to express romantic feelings. One fifty-one-year-old woman wrote the following to her husband, whose transfer to an overseas job had forced them into years of long-distance marriage (*tanshin funin*): "On the day I go to meet you, I romp around on purpose and act a little weird. I do that to cover up my joy and my loneliness, but someday I'd like to actually express those feelings in words. I'll probably cry if I do."[43]

At the same time, neither husbands nor wives seem to have any *expectation* of verbal expressions of intimacy. As one sixty-two-year-old wife wrote in her love letter to her husband:

> I've never heard you say "I like you" or "I love you" [*sukida toka aishiteru toka*]. But I still hold dear other words that you've told me. Before we were married, when you gave me my Christmas present, you said, "I've just learned for the first time how great it is to give a present." I wonder if you remember those words from forty years ago.[44]

A fifty-seven-year-old wife echoes:

> I'm not very bright. I've made lots of mistakes. And yet you've never strongly scolded me. You're a reserved person. But I really like that you're a reserved person. Even though my memory is not so good, I remember every time you've said, "Thank you." If I weren't with you, I would surely be a sad person.[45]

The unspoken nature of the feelings in these letters is seen in Japan as a romantic ideal: true love does not need to be spoken, it simply *is*. Part of the reason for the idealization might be that the comfortable affection of mature, mellowed couples stands in such stark contrast to a view of love that we will now see in the cases: emotional upheaval.

Love in the Law

When Japanese judges write about love, it is rarely about the sugary sentiments seen in love letters, and it usually is unrelated to the idealized love sought by readers of love theory books. Instead, judges write of the dark, disruptive side of love. It appears frequently in court opinions in three particularly lurid kinds of cases: love suicides, murder, and stalking. It rarely appears elsewhere.

Love Suicides

The publication of Jun'ichi Watanabe's 1997 novel *Lost Paradise* (*Shitsura-kuen*), in which a fifty-four-year-old married man falls in love with a thirty-seven-year-old married woman, struck a national nerve. The love-struck pair commits suicide. Watanabe explains the male protagonist's feelings about the suicide: "Kuki came to think that people regard a love suicide as something tragic or crazy because they see only the outer shell, when the souls of the man and woman involved have moved elsewhere."[46]

On one hand, as we see here, love suicide is described as "tragic" or "crazy." On the other hand, love suicide is romanticized in Japan, as evidenced by the success of this very novel (and its accompanying film and television miniseries). Japanese fiction is filled with tragically romantic themes of geisha/client suicide, adulterous wife/lover suicide, failed suicide, and half-failed double suicide, in which one party is left to carry on after a lover's death and his or her own failed suicide attempt.[47]

In real life, it is difficult to determine how frequently love suicide occurs. The word for love suicide, *shinjū,* refers not only to suicides of lovers but also to joint suicides involving family members. Those suicides are often covered by the media but are not necessarily common. One study (and the fact that this study exists suggests the importance of the topic) finds that of 194 joint suicide cases reported in the *Asahi Shinbun* newspaper over a six-year period, 64 were mother-child, 30 were husband-wife, 29 were the entire household, 22 were father-child, and 20 were unwed love suicides—but the vocabulary of *shinjū* makes it difficult to tell precisely what those figures mean.[48]

Love suicides appear in the case law most frequently when one lover's suicide is successful and the other survives. The following Love Hotel Suicide case is exemplary. Kimiko and Tetsuo met in the Self-Defense Forces, Japan's military. Kimiko was 21 and had recently enlisted; Tetsuo was 40, married, a father, and Kimiko's superior officer. Kimiko, the court explained, "was raised by her mother after her parents' divorce, which occurred when she was in elementary school.... She had a kind, easily sweet-talked personality."

Kimiko and Tetsuo began in November 2004 an "adulterous relationship" (*furin kankei*) which was discovered in January 2005. At that point, their superiors instructed them to end the relationship immediately. When Tetsuo's wife learned of the relationship, Tetsuo attempted suicide. He failed. He was transferred to a base in Yokosuka. Kimiko's superiors advised her not to see him again, but she continued to meet him secretly on weekends and holidays. She made plans to resign from her post when her term was completed in March 2006 so that she could move closer to Tetsuo.

But in September 2005, one of Kimiko's female friends introduced her to a single man, Masa, who was only two years older than she and stationed at the same base. They began to "e-mail each other and go on drives together."

Despite explicit orders from her mother, Kimiko also continued to e-mail and phone Tetsuo. When she met him in December, however, she told him of her new relationship, announcing that "I can't go with you to Yokosuka" and "I have a new boyfriend, so we have to break up." At the same time, Kimiko assured her mother that she and Tetsuo were just friends.

Still Tetsuo continued to contact her. He called and begged her to stay in the relationship, saying, "I just want to be with you no matter what kind of relationship you want." They finally made plans to meet for one last date in Kyoto on February 17, 2006. Meanwhile, Tetsuo's e-mail continued, and Kimiko told her mother that "Tetsuo keeps e-mailing me, saying that he wants to die, that he can't eat, he can't work, he can't sleep and so on. I really feel sorry for him. I want to break up with him but I just can't."

In January, four months after they met, "Kimiko kissed Masa for the first time, and around February 4, they had sex (this was the only time they had sex)." The next day, according to Kimiko's diary, she fought with her mother about Tetsuo and his frequent hang-up calls while they were shopping at a local Jusco department store. "Mom's not rational," Kimiko wrote. She went on to write that she bought Tetsuo a "cute" Valentine's Day necktie. She also bought chocolate for Masa, which she gave him on Valentine's Day. When one of her girlfriends e-mailed, asking who her "main" guy was, she replied: "My main guy is Masa, and I'm struggling to break it off with Tetsuo."

Yet Tetsuo remained in the picture. On Valentine's Day, he e-mailed her: "I can't sleep. Will you pretend to be my girlfriend until Sunday?"

And again on February 17, just before they met: "I want to see you in that denim miniskirt one last time."

Kimiko and Tetsuo met as planned on the seventeenth at Kyoto Station. They checked into a nearby love hotel. Love hotels are designed specifically for sex: they can usually be identified by large neon signs and are located in red-light districts and at highway exits, areas to which they are confined by national law and local zoning regulations. Kimiko and Tetsuo might have chosen a love hotel over a regular one for several reasons. Love hotels offer anonymity; there is no front desk, and no credit card or identification is required. They are also relatively inexpensive: although love hotels usually lack the amenities of a luxury hotel (such as a concierge), they offer other amusements, such as a karaoke system, a massage chair, a large bath, or perhaps a heart-shaped rotating bed underneath a mirrored ceiling, at less than half the price of a regular room. Because love hotel management and patrons are accustomed to any noises that might emerge from behind closed doors, love hotels are also known as refuges where couples can have uninhibited sex that will not be heard or interrupted by children or parents, who might be sleeping in the next room of a crowded, thin-walled Japanese house. For the same reasons, love hotels are sometimes sites for crime, including prostitution, underage sex, and occasionally rape and murder. Still, while many people might be embarrassed to be spotted at a love hotel, a love hotel visit would not be considered particularly abnormal either for a clandestine affair or for a married couple.[49]

When Kimiko and Tetsuo arrived at the love hotel, she gave him his present, the necktie she had bought for him. While Kimiko was in the bath that night, Tetsuo used Kimiko's cell phone to call his rival, Masa. Tetsuo told Masa that he was dating Kimiko and that Masa should stay away from her. The couple spent the night together. On the eighteenth, they rented a car in Himeji, and Kimiko practiced driving (she planned to graduate from driving school the following month). They spent the night of the eighteenth in another love hotel.

Around noon on the nineteenth, Kimiko phoned her mother to let her know that all was well. At 6:30 that evening, Kimiko and Tetsuo went to two drug stores, where Kimiko bought twelve sleeping pills and seventy-two sedatives. Fifteen minutes later, they checked into an Osaka love hotel, where they took the pills and slit their wrists with a fruit knife and a razor.

They tried to hang themselves but were unsuccessful. They decided to sleep until the drugs and the bleeding caused their deaths.

The pair awoke around midnight when the love hotel manager called to tell them that they had stayed too long to receive the three-hour "rest" rate and would be required to pay for a full night. The drug doses had been too small and the cuts too shallow to induce death. They tried again to hang themselves in the bathroom but again were unsuccessful. Tetsuo then strangled Kimiko—with the necktie she had given him. He reported the incident to the police at 7:55 a.m. Police found no evidence of struggle.

Tetsuo testified that he had told Kimiko repeatedly that he wanted to die. Kimiko responded, he said, by assuring him that "if we were together, I'd die for you" and "let's take sleeping pills, cut our wrists, and bleed to death." Tetsuo also said that Kimiko instructed him to strangle her with the necktie after their attempts proved unsuccessful. He asked if she were sure, and when she said yes, he used the necktie to strangle her. He then tried to hang himself and cut his wrists, but when he did not die, he decided to call the police.

At trial, prosecutors attempted to prove that Tetsuo had committed murder as specified in article 199 of the Penal Code: "A person who kills another shall be punished." Tetsuo argued that he had merely participated in a suicide, a crime governed by article 202: "A person who instigates or assists another to comment suicide or kills another at the request or with the consent of the latter shall be punished." The penalty for murder is higher than the penalty for assisted suicide.

The statutes gave no further guidance, leaving the court to conduct its own investigation on its own terms. The court briefly examined the physical evidence. It found that the couple had indeed tried to hang themselves. It did not accept the prosecution's theory that Kimiko bought the drugs to help her sleep; if she had sleep issues, the court reasoned, she would have purchased them on their first night together, not the third. The court found no evidence that Kimiko resisted.

The court's analysis turned not on the physical evidence but on the question of whether Kimiko was in love (*aijō*—feelings of love) with Tetsuo. If Kimiko had been in love with him, the court reasoned, she consented to a love suicide and Tetsuo should receive the shorter sentence accorded in cases of homicide to which the victim consented. Conversely, if Kimiko was *not* in love, she did not consent, and Tetsuo was a murderer who deserved a longer sentence.

From a U.S. legal perspective, this is a fascinating way of framing the case. Although laws differ from state to state, an inquiry by a U.S. court probably would focus on Tetsuo's state of mind. Tetsuo seems to have intended Kimiko's death (though his lawyer might argue otherwise), but was he insane? Did he suffer from an "extreme emotional disturbance"? Was there some sort of "heat of passion?" And what of Kimiko's state of mind? Did she manifest consent? Was Tetsuo reckless or negligent in believing that she consented? U.S. law, focusing on intent, categorizes mental states and then attempts to determine if a particular defendant's thought process falls into those categories.

The Japanese court in this case does away with those intent-based complications and heads straight to the emotional core of the matter by asking whether the parties were in love. Doing so might avoid some legal fictions, but it also causes a couple of problems. First, by focusing on love in this way, the court tacitly recognized that love is a legitimate, or at least not unimaginable, motive for suicide. Surely that is not the message the state wants to send: in fact, the government has set an official goal of a 20 percent reduction in the suicide rate from 2007 to 2016.[50]

Second, and more centrally, the court has required itself to answer questions that seem unanswerable. How can anyone determine whether two people, one of whom died at the hands of the other, were in love?

Prosecutors in the case sought to help the court make that determination by using Kimiko's statements. They argued that Kimiko's e-mail message in which she agreed to meet "one last time" confirmed that she had been trying to end her relationship with Tetsuo. "It is clear," they argued, "that Kimiko's love for Masa had cooled to a great degree."

The court disagreed, citing the "facts" of love as follows:

1. Kimiko spent two complete days with Tetsuo through February 17, and they stayed together in a love hotel.
2. On the fifth of the same month, Kimiko bought a necktie for Tetsuo. On the same day, she expressed some unease with Masa in her diary, when she wrote, "Despite all of that, I found a necktie for him and bought it." While [the "despite all of that" language] suggests some feelings of irritation or dissatisfaction, it also may raise suspicions that she was unable to throw away her love for Tetsuo.

3. According to [Kimiko's friend's] testimony, she could not confirm directly that Masa and Kimiko had begun dating in earnest. Moreover, during the two days she was with Tetsuo, Kimiko did not contact Masa, which raises some suspicions as to the depths of her feelings for him.

In consideration of these facts, it cannot be denied that Kimiko still was in love to some degree with Tetsuo. (The prosecution argues that the necktie was purchased only to assuage Tetsuo, who had been making hang-up phone calls to her mother. But as the previously mentioned diary shows, Kimiko's feelings were complicated, and she could not throw away her love....)

Moreover, above and beyond the fact that it cannot be said that Tetsuo and Kimiko were not in love, Tetsuo, who had previously attempted suicide, elicited sympathy from Kimiko when he said, "I want to die. I want to die." Furthermore, with the feeling that this was to be their last meeting, they spent two days together, and as the time for them to part drew near, Kimiko, who had a tenderhearted tendency to agree with anything a person said or thought, sympathized with Tetsuo, who hinted that he would commit suicide after they parted. It is not unthinkable that she would have consented to joint suicide by saying something indirect, such as "I'll die if it's with you."

Each of the court's three points reflects assumptions about love and death. First, the court interpreted the fact of Kimiko's and Tetsuo's visit to a love hotel as a sign of love or romance, and not as a purely sexual arrangement—notwithstanding the widely held view of love hotels as destinations for sex. Second, the court placed a great deal of emphasis on Kimiko's emotional conflict—her confusion, not joy. The court did not require her to speak explicitly of love, or even of fondness, in her diary. The evidence that mattered to the court was her ambivalence, as manifested by her inability to resist the urge to buy Tetsuo a necktie. Third, the court noted that Kimiko was a gullible personality "type," implying that some people are simply more likely than others to consent to death. By describing Kimiko at the beginning of the opinion as having a "kind, easily sweet-talked personality" (*yasashiku hito no iinari ni nariyasui*), a phrase that seems superfluous in this context, the court was able to bolster its claim later in the opinion that her kindness and gullibility may have induced her to consent to a joint suicide just to spare Tetsuo from having to die alone.

Evidence of the court's views on love also lies in what the court chose to omit. For example, the court did not require that Kimiko's relationship with Tetsuo be exclusive; it found love even though Kimiko had another suitor—a suitor whom she told her friend she preferred to Tetsuo. Nor was Kimiko required to profess her love; even Tetsuo, who had a strong interest in claiming that Kimiko had declared her love to him, apparently never made any such claim. Focusing instead on the love hotel, the necktie, and Kimiko's personality, the court found love, accordingly found Tetsuo guilty only of aiding suicide, and sentenced him to only six and one-half years in prison for Kimiko's homicide.[51]

If the case had been tried in a U.S. courtroom, because of the importance of intent, lawyers for both sides likely would have presented expert psychiatric testimony. In a New York case, for example, lawyers presented testimony from a psychiatrist to show that a defendant had a "passive-dependent personality disorder" and that she had a "dependent, child-like character structure,"[52] much like Kimiko seems to have had. Japanese courts are required in criminal cases to give "due consideration" to opinions of psychiatric experts regarding mental disorders, so it would not have been unusual for attorneys in Kimiko's case to present such evidence.[53] But they didn't, or at least it did not appear in the opinion—and the court seems to have had no difficulty making its own diagnosis.

It seems likely that both Tetsuo and the easily sweet-talked Kimiko suffered from depression. The medical literature shows that depression is closely associated with suicide,[54] and Japan has one of the highest suicide rates in the world—including nearly three people per day who are determined by police to have killed themselves because of "male-female problems" not unlike Kimiko's (another three victims per day do so because of "marital discord").[55] The actual incidence of depression in Japan is unknown, but there is consensus that it is underreported, underdiagnosed, and undertreated. Underreporting is due at least in part to the significant stigma of depression in Japan.[56] Until very recently, mental health care was available only on an inpatient basis in psychiatric hospitals, and admittance to such a facility implied incapacitating long-term mental illness not only for the patient but for the family as well.[57]

The stigma associated with depression is related to popular understandings of the illness and its causes. When surveyed, Japanese people were far more likely than Australians to attribute depression and other mental illnesses to "nervousness" and "weakness of character," rather than genetics, the factor most frequently cited by the Australians.[58] Even the word for depression (*utsubyō*) in Japanese carries stigma; when asked to label stories of mental health issues, Japanese people were far less likely than Australians to use psychiatric labels such as "depression."[59] When pharmaceutical companies sought to introduce next-generation antidepressants (selective serotonin reuptake inhibitors, or SSRIs) to Japan in 1999 (Luvox) and 2000 (Paxil), one of their first tasks was thus to change the image of depression by relabeling it a "cold of the heart" (*kokoro no kaze*).[60]

In the absence of easy access to mental health professionals, or even a familiar language for talking about mental illness, diagnosis and assessment of the meaning or context of mental illness often occurs not on the psychiatrist's couch but in the courtroom. The results are frequently difficult to reconcile. In a divorce case filed in 2006, for instance, the husband-plaintiff claimed that his lengthy separation from his wife was grounds for divorce. The wife countered that she had been depressed during the separation and that she now intended to work on the marriage. The Nagoya Family Court found that "although the defendant's actions at the time of the separation were influenced by depression and as such are not her fault, it is an unavoidable fact that the plaintiff lost all desire to reconcile during that period." Saying nothing more about depression, the court ordered a divorce. But when the wife appealed to the Nagoya High Court, that court held that "because it is possible that the wife's behavior that led to the husband's thoughts of divorce were influenced by her depression, the husband should wait for her to recover, and he should wait for the opportunity to look forward to…married life when the influence of her illness has disappeared." The court denied the divorce and offered no explanation for its reversal of the Family Court. It kept the couple together against one spouse's will, a phenomenon we will see in more detail in chapter 6.[61]

In love suicide cases, the focus is not depression but love. In a 2001 case, the Sapporo High Court described the facts as follows:

> In February 1998, the [thirty-three-year-old] defendant met the victim, who came as a customer to the pub at which the defendant worked. They soon began dating. The victim had a husband and children, and as such their relationship was an extramarital affair. After that, the woman became pregnant with the defendant's child and had an abortion. In October 1998, the defendant left the nightlife business [*mizu shōbai*] and began working as a long-haul trucker. In January 1999, he was hospitalized after an epileptic seizure, and from the time the victim cared for him for about one month as he recovered, he fell madly in love with [*tsuyoi ren'ai kanjō*] her.

At about the same time, she began to work as a hostess in a snack bar. The defendant was jealous of her interactions with male customers and asked her to leave the business. The victim began to dislike the defendant because of these things that he said, and she began to avoid him. Despite this change, the defendant continued to follow her around and wait near her house for her to come home.

After a heated encounter in which the victim pleaded with the defendant to leave her alone, he stabbed her twice in the chest. She begged him to take her to the hospital, pledging to quit her job if he did so. He put her in his car, where she begged him more: "I really will quit my job. I won't tell anybody that you stabbed me. Just take me to a hospital." The defendant had other ideas:

> The defendant planned to stop by his house so he could die together with her, but he trembled as he heard these words. After a short amount of time passed because of his inability to start the car, he was faced with the decision of whether to go to his house to commit love suicide or to take her to the hospital. He started the car before he could decide, and he reached a crossing at which he could either go straight to the hospital or turn right and go to his house. He decided to forget his plans for going home and to believe her words. Deciding that her death now would be unacceptable, he turned right and they arrived at the hospital.

The victim lived. Curiously, at no point in its opinion did the court question the underlying logic of love suicide. It simply explained that the defendant had abandoned his intent to kill and was for that reason entitled to a reduced sentence of four and one-half years imprisonment.[62] The use of the language of unrequited love—*madly* in love—suggests the court felt the defendant's emotional state was relevant to the abandonment question, and the relevant emotion was not jealousy but love.

Japanese courts have ruled in many similarly scripted love suicide and family suicide cases. In one 2002 case, for instance, a wife strangled her sixty-eight-year-old husband in a hotel with a bathrobe belt in a planned double suicide designed to prevent them from becoming a burden to their children in their old age. Her suicide attempt failed, and she received a three-year sentence, suspended for four years (meaning that she will not serve her three-year sentence if she commits no other offense in the next four years).[63] In another case in which a man strangled his married girl-friend in a failed suicide pact, the court sentenced him to three years.[64] The trend is relatively constant over time: in a well-publicized case from the 1950s, a woman and her lover attempted to poison and gas themselves because their parents would not consent to their marriage. They decided that they would kill the woman's nine-year-old daughter from a previous marriage as well, on the ground that it would be sad for her to grow up without parents. In the end, the child died and the adults lived. The court denounced the evils of both love suicide ("a social problem that must be coldly condemned") and parent-child suicide ("completely inapposite to a mother's love"). But it also gave each of the defendants a three-year sentence, suspended for three years, again resulting in no jail time.[65]

Given the apparent begrudging acceptance of love suicide in the courts, it might seem that a claim of failed love suicide would be a convenient way to escape liability for murdering one's lover. It happens. A 2007 case concerned a (married) fifty-five-year-old businessman and his lover of eighteen years, a bar hostess. Suspicious that her lover was cheating, the bar hostess strangled him in his sleep with the electrical cord of a curling iron. After killing him, she attempted suicide by cutting her neck and chest and taking sleeping pills but to no avail.

In court, the hostess claimed that her lover had consented to a joint suicide. Unlike the Love Hotel Suicide case, the court assumed these two were lovers and did not investigate whether they were truly in love (and did not discuss marital infidelity, either). Instead, it found that the lover killed out of anger over her lover's affair and that she contradicted herself in her testimony when she said, "I didn't think that he would agree if I said 'die with me' or 'let's commit love suicide together.'" The court found her guilty and sentenced her to eleven years' imprisonment—but it did so only after seriously considering the possibility that the victim had consented to death in his sleep by curling-iron-cord strangulation.[66]

Finally, consider the painful love that arose from jealousy in the Kimono Belt Murder case. Yasuo and Kumiko had been married for nearly twenty years in 2006; he was a pediatrician and she managed his clinic. In 2004, Yasuo began e-mailing a "particular woman." Kumiko discovered the e-mail on January 28, 2006, while Yasuo was away on a business trip. She felt "shock over the betrayal." She wrote a suicide note to Yasuo and to her mother. When Yasuo returned the next day, she pledged to divorce him, became emotional, and cut the back of his head with scissors.

The court stopped the narrative there, resuming with the night of February 14, Valentine's Day, some two weeks later. While Yasuo was brushing his teeth, Kumiko grabbed the belt of a kimono, wrapped it around her own neck, and said, "Now I'm going to die on you [*shinde yaru*]. I'm going to do to you the thing that you hate the most." She climbed over the handrail on the second floor of their home and stood on the edge, about fifteen feet above the first floor. When Yasuo did not stop her, she said, "You're thinking it would be good if I die, aren't you," "I see the real you," "You're the devil," and "You betrayer." Kumiko slapped him in the face. He slapped her back. She said, "Oh, now you want to kill me?" and "A person who kills another person has no right to live." She tried to return to the other side of the handrail. Yasuo did not allow her to come back; instead, he pulled on the ends of the belt, strangling her. Kumiko said, "But I love you! Why?" [*aishiteru noni, dōshite*], and then lost consciousness. Kumiko's statement stands out in the court's narrative not only for its pathos but also because it could have come only from Tetsuo's testimony.

Kumiko fell to the first floor. Yasuo went downstairs and found her body crumpled with the belt still around her neck. He stepped on the belt with his foot and pulled the other end with his hand, strangling her to death.

Despite the "I'm going to die on you" language to a spouse, the court saw the case as murder, not assisted (love) suicide. It sentenced Yasuo to nine years' imprisonment, explaining that the sentence took into account Yasuo's remorse, the various payments he had made to Kumiko's mother, his lack of criminal history, and a letter signed by 2,129 of his nursing students, fellow doctors, friends, patients, and acquaintances. The court was nevertheless notably harsh with Yasuo, noting that he had killed "a perfectionist, a person who would not treat lightly mistakes or wrongdoing.... To think that a woman like Kumiko, as a wife, could be asked to view a relationship with another woman as just a way for a man to relax is simply asking too much."[67] She loved him—according to his testimony as recounted in the court's narrative, those were her last words—and with that love came her dramatic death.

Murder

The 1936 Sada Abé murder case, in which the defendant strangled her lover and carried his penis around for three days, is one of the most notorious crimes of twentieth-century Japan. In William Johnston's insightful study of the crime and its place in Japanese sexual and social history, he quotes Abé:

> When I suggested that we commit a double suicide or run off together, [lover Kichizō] Ishida said that he wanted to go on meeting me at teahouses. When we met, Ishida had already made a success of himself and his business. There was no reason for him to think of committing suicide or of running off. I knew all too well that he would refuse my suggestions and didn't even think of double suicide or of running off as serious options. So in the end, I decided that there was nothing I could do but kill him and make him mine forever.[68]

Johnston then comments on Abé's statement:

> These were words of love—more accurately, of desire—not of anger and hatred. Abe's desire to make Ishida hers forever had the ring of a marriage proposal or pledge of commitment. Her decision to murder came from her positive feelings about their relationship combined with her recognition of the impossibility that it could continue on terms she could accept.[69]

Johnston seems to have it right: the murder was not about anger, hatred, or sex, as many had thought. It also seems correct to say that the murder came from positive feelings, not negative ones. But was it really above *love,* framed as desire or otherwise? Might it have been better characterized as obsession, domination, fear, jealousy, helplessness, or despair (some of which Johnston mentions elsewhere)? Are those things aspects of love? Of desire? Of passion?

These are the kinds of questions that are often asked—by scholars, media, the public—when trying to explore the reasons behind some kinds of murder. They are not usually *legal* questions, as it is usually impossible to determine when a person is in love. But as in the suicide cases, Japanese judges have a way of determining when a person is in love in murder cases: it is accompanied by suffering, pain, and tragedy.

In one murder case from 2002, Michael, a Philippine citizen, sneaked into Japan in the cargo hold of a ship in 1997. Marie, also a Philippine citizen, was a bar hostess who arrived in Japan on an entertainment visa in 1996. She married Akihiro, a Japanese man, in April 1997. The court then made a statement of causation: "because" Akihiro frequently played mahjong outside of the house, Marie became "lonely," and she began having sex with Michael.

Michael knew of Akihiro and was possessive of Marie. On one occasion, Marie's cell phone rang when she was with Michael. Noticing that the call was from Akihiro, Michael answered and said, "We just finished having sex. Fuck you." Akihiro became enraged. He summoned Marie to his office, where he stripped her, handcuffed her to the toilet, and beat her, extinguishing cigarettes on her body.

After this attack, Marie left Akihiro and "seriously considered divorce." But when she heard a few weeks later that Akihiro was to marry another woman, she became jealous. She phoned Akihiro. They told each other that they "loved each other" (*aishiteru*), and Marie went to see him. They had sex that night.

The following morning, according to Marie, Michael entered the home she shared with Akihiro, showed Akihiro pictures of Michael having sex with her, and stabbed Akihiro to death in the heart. Michael's story differed. According to his version, Marie called him to the home, and when he arrived, she had already stabbed Akihiro. Michael and Marie were in agreement on their post-mortem actions: they took Akihiro's body to the bathtub, chopped it into pieces, put the pieces in trash bags, and threw the bags into the river. Prosecutors charged Michael with murder (and Marie with improper disposal of a corpse).

To evaluate these conflicting stories, the court first examined the forensic evidence (such as the amount of urine in Akihiro's bladder, to determine the time of death). But the primary factor in the court's decision was the nature of Marie's two relationships. If Marie's feelings for Michael were strong and her feelings for Akihiro were weak, perhaps she was the killer, and Michael was not. If Michael's feelings for Marie were strong, perhaps Michael had killed in a jealous rage.

Marie told the police, "My feelings were complicated. Of course, I was sad that my husband had been killed, but I was also amazed that [Michael] would love someone like me so much that he would kill my husband. I was happy that he loved me that much, that he loved me so much that he would commit murder. These feelings were mingled and complicated." In contrast, Michael claimed that Marie was his "sex friend" (*sekkusu furendo*), that they simply met for sex two or three times a week, and that he "did not love her."

If the court had thought Michael's admitted sexual relationship sufficient to cause a murderous jealous rage, the inquiry might have ended there. But it seems to have assumed that a mere sexual relationship could not provoke such extreme action. Only the far more powerful emotion of love could compel a person to commit such an irrational and heinous act.

The court launched an independent investigation into Michael's love. It noted that Marie had sex with a third man besides Akihiro at the same time that she was sleeping with Michael. Michael phoned the third man three times, once to ask why Marie was crying, once to announce that he had had sex with her, and once to state that he had a videotape of himself having sex with her. The court took these actions to be evidence of Michael's jealousy—and thus also of his love.

At the same time, the court uncovered what it regarded as even more reliable evidence of Michael's love. According to testimony, one of Michael's friends who dropped by Michael's house remarked that he looked as if he had not slept. When the friend asked why, Michael responded by pulling from his wallet a photograph of himself with Marie, on the back of which was written, "We will work together to get over this." In view of the friend, Michael cut the photo into pieces with scissors while sobbing, "I'm sorry." The court explicitly noted that this act as evidence that Michael had "deep feelings of love" (*fukai aijō*) for Marie—not merely love, but *deep feelings of love*. Deep love, the court found, was the motive to kill. The court found Michael guilty and sentenced him to fifteen years' imprisonment.[70]

The court, then, found evidence of Michael and Marie's love in suffering. Marie's love did not manifest itself as giddy daydreams or butterflies in her stomach; rather, she continued to profess love for her husband even after he handcuffed her to a toilet and beat her. Michael's love appeared not as romantic wistfulness over lost love but as a tragic, destructive emotional train wreck. He might jealously have destroyed the couple's photographs even if he had not been the murderer—but the court saw that act as evidence of guilt.

We have seen survey evidence suggesting that many Japanese people, especially men, believe that "Jealousy usually varies directly with love; that is, the more in love you are, the greater the tendency for you to become jealous."[71] The court's opinion expresses a similar sentiment. Although Michael's jealousy might have been fueled by feelings of possession, sexual attraction, or other complex emotions or disorders, the court declared it to be firmly rooted in love, ignoring the other possibilities.

The court based its telling of the story almost entirely on the testimony of non-Japanese witnesses, a fact that makes the court's narrative all the more interesting. Of course, it is not clear how the actual testimonies of the witnesses differed, if at all, from the story eventually penned by the court. But no matter what the courtroom drama was, the court presented the case through the lens of love as suffering.

This link between love and suffering in murder cases frequently emerges in the sentencing context. Japanese law has only one basic homicide statute (Penal Code art. 199): "A person who kills another shall be punished." Unlike the law of most U.S. states, Japan does not distinguish among first-degree aggravated murder, ordinary murder, and homicide that occurs in the heat of passion, due to provocation, or because of "extreme mental or emotional disturbance." Instead, Japanese judges make informal distinctions for sentencing purposes. One factor that is especially important is the defendant's emotions—including love.

One such case from 2003 involved twenty-three-year-old Hitomi Harada, the host of a satellite television program about professional wrestling, and twenty-six-year-old Hiroshi Tanahashi, a professional wrestler. According to the court, the two met after Hitomi sent Hiroshi a "fan letter," thus initiating a sexual relationship that lasted six months. Hiroshi then told Hitomi that he had another girlfriend, his "first love" (*hatsukoi*) from high school. Stunned by the news, "she hid her true feelings and had sex with him." He then told Hitomi that he wanted to continue his relationship with her anyway. She felt betrayed and decided that she would "kill him and then kill herself." She took a six-inch knife to bed with her and planned to kill Hiroshi in his sleep, but she was psychologically unable to do so.

The next morning, as Hiroshi headed off to practice, Hiromi begged him to stay for "just one more minute" while she lay in bed. "Well, just one minute, then," he said, as he turned his back to her and stared at the second hand on the clock, waiting contemptuously for exactly sixty seconds to pass. She suddenly felt that "if he left, he would never return, and she felt loneliness and desperation well up inside her, and she decided to kill him and herself. Then, she sat up in bed with her legs folded, pulled the knife out from under the covers where she had hidden it, grasped it with her right hand, and swung it up near her head." She stabbed Hiroshi twice in the back. He fled, and she chased him, naked, outside the house, but she was unable to inflict further injury to him (or to herself).

After finding Hitomi guilty of attempted murder, the court needed to determine her sentence. It described the act in context, noting that it occurred "when the defendant heard from her beloved's [*saiai no hito*] mouth that he wanted to date the woman who was his first love." The court's superfluous description of the victim as the defendant's "beloved" is intriguing. Perhaps it was trying to communicate to the defendant that it at least had listened carefully to her testimony. But the word is also frequently used in the case law to present the victim in a sympathetic light, as when the Tokyo District Court found in a different case that a wife had been murdered by "the husband who was supposed to be her beloved."[72]

In Hitomi's case too, the court seems to have been employing "beloved" to portray the defendant as a lovestruck, suffering creature—a victim of love. It found that Hitomi had taken responsibility for her actions, had reached an appropriate financial settlement with Hiroshi, and had been "forgiven" (*yūjo*) by him. It sentenced her to three years in prison (prosecutors had sought five years' imprisonment) but suspended the sentence for four years so that she served no jail time.[73]

Consider a second sentencing case from the Wakayama District Court. Masako was engaged to Teraya; they had known each other seven or eight months. He began to behave oddly. They met at a coffee shop to talk. There he told her that he suspected her of seeing another man and that he no longer wanted to marry her. She begged him to change his mind. That night, Masako revealed to Teraya that she was pregnant with his child and pleaded for him to stay with her. His attitude did not change. When he kissed her, she bit his tongue as hard as possible and then strangled him with an electric cord. He suffocated from the blood and the pressure on his windpipe. Prosecutors charged her with murder.

In sentencing Masako, the court noted that she was shocked, betrayed, young, and remorseful and that she acted on impulse. But equally telling was the setup of the story, in which the court found abundant love: the couple "fell in love with one another" (*aishiau*), Masako was afraid that their love (*aijō*) would end, and this was a "tragic case of the collapse of engagement and of the love [*ren'ai*] of a young man and woman." For the brutal murder, the court sentenced Masako to only two and one-half years in prison.[74] The case is from 1960, and I suspect that a contemporary court would place less emphasis on the engagement. But otherwise, the court's language is similar to that of modern courts, suggesting that the characterization of love as pain runs deep, even in the judiciary, and even back to a time in which love was not as socially prevalent as it is today.

The court's strategies with the husband-murdering Michael, the wrestler-stabbing Hitomi, and the tongue-biting Masako were remarkably similar. In each case, the court chose love as the appropriate means of framing the issues. In Michael's case, the court cited his spiteful love as evidence that he killed his lover's husband; in Hitomi's and Masako's cases, love was a reason to mitigate punishment for the fragile lover. In each case, spite, jealousy, or anger would have sufficed, but the language the court chose was love.

The language of passion and emotion as devices for judicial decision making is even more visible in the sentencing of death-penalty murder cases, in which judges have a starkly binary choice of life or death. Roughly two percent of Japan's murderers receive the death penalty.[75] The Japanese Supreme Court has held that imposition of the death penalty requires an examination of the nature of the crime, the defendant's motivations, the heinous nature of the crime, the number of victims, the pain felt by the victims' families, the influence on society, and the defendant's age, criminal history, and actions after the crime.[76]

As in the love suicide cases, the rhetoric of love often seeps into the death penalty standards, turning the judiciary into adjudicators of love. In cases in which love is an issue, the defendant tends to live if he is in love and die if he is not. The victims in the following three exemplary cases were, in order, the defendant's (a) girlfriend and four family members (the 1997 Hostess Family Stabbing case), (b) wife and two children (ages 10 and 17) (the 1991 Valentine's Day Murder case), and (c) wife and foster father (the 2007 Life Insurance Murder case). The perpetrators were all men, the facts have some similarities, and in each case the statute merely states that "a person who kills another shall be punished." Yet only the defendant in the third case was sentenced to death.

First, in the Hostess Family Stabbing case, the defendant, Hideo, was a forty-one-year-old bar owner. He hired Toshiko, age thirty-nine, to work at the bar as a hostess. They began a sexual relationship and he soon proposed marriage. When her family opposed the marriage and she refused Hideo's proposal, he became furious. He went to her house, where she lived with her family. Using a sashimi knife, he stabbed Toshiko, her seventy-one-year-old mother, and her three children, ages six, thirteen, and fourteen. Two died from blood loss.

The Tokyo District Court sentenced Hideo to death. It reasoned that he began his relationship with Toshiko and sought to marry her because he wanted to live in her newly constructed house and knew that she would receive an apartment as an inheritance. When she refused, he became angry, and he killed her and her family.

Hideo raised four arguments on appeal to the Tokyo High Court, two of which are relevant here. First, he argued that the district court failed to recognize his unstable mental state at the time of the crime. He argued that he was emotionally distressed and drunk. The high court disagreed; the lower court had considered the results of a psychiatric evaluation and had properly determined that Hideo was not drunk at the time of the killing. "At the time," the court declared, "the defendant was fully able to appreciate the wrongfulness of his actions."

Second, Hideo argued that he had been improperly sentenced. The high court first reviewed the district court's reasoning as follows:

> The defendant became attached [*shūchaku*] to Toshiko, pursuant to his feelings that he wanted to live with her or marry her. The lower court decision found, as a factor in sentencing, that "The direct cause of the crime was that the defendant, who lacked the ability to make a living on his own, would be able to live in a new house with Toshiko, with whom he had developed a sexual relationship, and he paired with her knowing that in the future he would be able to inherit her apartment as well." With no reference to the fact that the defendant had feelings of longing [*renbo*] and the passionate relationship [*aiyoku kankei*] of a middle-aged man and woman, the main reason behind the defendant's attachment to Toshiko would seem to be the pursuit of money.

The high court found a different motivation. It noted that Toshiko "showed the defendant kindness that he had never before seen in his relationships with women." There was evidence that Hideo became jealous when Toshiko flirted with customers and developed a "lingering attachment" (*miren*) to her. Finally, the court found:

> An examination of the defendant's history with women shows that he easily developed relationships and spoke of marriage and so on with female employees of restaurants and bars that he managed. Viewed from this perspective, it can be seen as natural that the main reason the defendant was attached to Toshiko was his strong feelings of longing [*renbo*] for her.

The court, then, found that Hideo's attachment to Toshiko was based on longing, lingering attachment, and jealousy, not monetary gain. That, along with additional evidence of suffering—namely, that shortly after the murders Hideo doused himself with lighter fluid in an attempt to kill himself—led the court to reduce his sentence. In the court's words, "we must hesitate to impose on the defendant the most extreme sentence and instead find it appropriate to impose a sentence of lifetime imprisonment, during which time the defendant can reflect deeply on his actions, spend all of his life praying for the repose of the victim's souls, and, with a grave attitude, can atone."[77]

The court did not invoke the evidence of Hideo's feelings for Toshiko in its discussion of Hideo's mental state; the important issues in that context were the psychiatric report and the evidence of intoxication. Nor did emotional longing excuse Hideo's actions. Instead, the court used Hideo's feelings in the sentencing stage, finding simply that "longing" and "lingering attachment" were less blameworthy motivations than money.

The court's logic is no more explicit than that, but it seems to be saying two things about the role of emotions. First, painful emotions like jealousy and longing are legitimate bases for a relationship. When the court discusses longing and monetary gain, it discusses them as motivations not for murder but for *attachment*. The court spared Hideo's life because his attachment to Toshiko was based on emotion and not a strategic calculation.

Second, the court implies that a person who is experiencing the pain of love deserves sympathy. It painted Hideo as a hapless suitor: he was smitten by Toshiko's simple acts of kindness because women in his prior relationships had never been so attentive, he was jealous of Toshiko's flirting with customers despite the fact that she was a hostess, and he frequently fell for his female employees quickly. In view of this history, it seems quite possible that Hideo, like the fifteen percent of Japanese men in the survey data, might have believed that love is "complex and sometimes leads to pain."[78] It also seems quite likely that the court gave Hideo a break not only because he had proper intentions when he entered into the relationship but also because his pain fit a familiar and sympathy-worthy pattern.

The Hostess Family Stabbing case focused on the defendant's emotional state and did not implicate Toshiko, the lover in the center of the turmoil, directly. In the following Valentine's Day Murder case, the court described a similar set of lovelorn emotions but turned the focus slightly toward the lover. The court began the troubled narrative of the defendant, Hisao, with the developmental problems of his younger daughter, who was born prematurely and was unable to speak. Hisao blamed his wife for the daughter's problems, as his wife had ridden a bicycle during her pregnancy despite his orders not to do so (a Japanese folk belief holds that riding on a bicycle or sitting on a cold surface during pregnancy can cause problems at birth).[79] As the daughter grew older, the topic became "taboo" conversation between Hisao and his wife.

The tensions produced by this taboo topic, the court said, made Hisao's house a terrible place to live. His older daughter started middle school and consistently had problems of absence, tardiness, and violations of school rules. Yelling in the home and parental trips to meet with middle school teachers became frequent.

Hisao began visiting a bar, where he met a hostess the court referred to as "[hereinafter,] the lover [*aijin*]," a word used exclusively for adulterous relationships.[80] "The lover" is not a frequently used term in Japanese court opinions: usually such a woman would be referred to as the "adultery partner" (*furin aite*). But this court used "the lover" fifty-seven times in its nine-page opinion. According to the opinion, "the couple began a sexual relationship, and the joy he felt was such that it could not even be compared to his ordinary married lifestyle. He became unable to forget the lover, he called her every day, arranged dates, and saw her secretly."

The relationship escalated. Hisao bought the lover gifts of clothing and furniture. He paid her rent at a new apartment that he arranged for her. Every day he would meet her at her apartment, they would have sex, and he would drive her to the bar where she worked. He had a vasectomy for her. They took trips together.

But eventually the relationship began to sour. Hisao began to discover "aspects of his lover's personality that he did not like." He ended their relationship. And yet two weeks later, his "lingering affection" (*miren*) for her brought the two together again.

At home, Hisao's relationship with his wife, who knew of the lover, worsened. They talked of divorce. Hisao began to think that things might be better if the entire family were "killed in an auto accident."

The last straw came on the night before Valentine's Day. It is worth noting here that Valentine's Day has played a fateful and conspicuous role in this chapter; Hisao's case is the third in which Valentine's Day emerges as the backdrop for a love-fueled death (and I did not choose those cases for that purpose). As in the United States, Valentine's Day in Japan is usually celebrated with dinner dates and gifts of chocolate. In Japan, women give chocolate to men, with a careful distinction made between *girichoco,* chocolate given out of obligation, and *honkichoko,* chocolate given out of true feelings. Men reciprocate with chocolate on White Day, a 1978 invention of the National Confectionary Industry Association, a month later.

In the Love Suicide case, Kimiko bought Tetsuo a necktie on Valentine's Day and he strangled her with it five days later. In the Kimono Belt Murder case, Yasuo strangled Kumiko to death after he pushed her over the railing on Valentine's Day. The day arises in other problematic legal contexts as well. In an action brought by a jilted wife against her husband's mistress (more on this kind of lawsuit in chapter 5), the Tokyo District Court noted specifically that until divorce was imminent, the couple "spent Valentine's Day together as usual" (on White Day the following month, the husband brought the wife a present and a divorce notice, the reasons for which she did not understand until she learned of the other woman).[81] The reference to Valentine's Day served as emotional evidence of the health of the couple's relationship.

On the eve of this particular Valentine's Day, Hisao visited his lover at her bar and asked if he could call on her the next day. She "flatly refused" him, and he was struck with "how completely different her attitude was from the previous year's Valentine's Day." Dejected, he returned home. He was greeted by the "neighborhood wives" in front of his home who said, "You're really home early, aren't you? That's rare." These comments, the court said, made him "hateful and angry," words that suggest impending doom.

The mood and the story now turn palpably darker. Hisao's house was empty and there was no food on the table. Irritated, he fixed his own dinner and began to drink. When his family returned home, he went out to play pachinko. When he ran out of money, he returned home, carrying an aluminum baseball bat that he apparently had prepared before he left. He found his forty-three-year-old wife and his ten-year-old daughter asleep upstairs. He beat his wife once in the head with the bat; she turned, expressed pain, and he beat her twice more. He went to his ten-year-old's room and struck her twice in the head as she slept. She died.

Hisao's older daughter, seventeen years old, tried to escape. He caught her. They struggled over the bat, but Hisao won. His daughter held her hands in front of her face and pleaded for her life repeatedly: "I'm sorry, I'm sorry, Dad. I'll quit school and get a job! I'll leave home!" "It's too late for that," Hisao responded. He hit her in the face with the baseball bat. When she fell to the ground, he beat her head twice more. She died.

Hisao went to the front door and retrieved a kerosene tank that he had prepared. He went upstairs to the master bedroom, soaked a bedsheet in kerosene and lit it on fire next to his wife's body. When she appeared to stir, he pressed her face into the bed with his hand until she died. He went to his ten-year-old daughter's room, poured kerosene on her body and around the room, and set fire to a cushion that lay on top of her. She died. He burned the house to the ground.

When the Fukuoka District Court characterized Hisao's mental process prior to the grisly killings, it discussed Hisao's daughter's developmental problems but focused on Hisao's lover: "The sexual relationship he began with the lover was better than anything he had experienced before.... When his relationship with the lover soured, he became mentally distressed and unable to think logically.... He began to think that if he killed his family members he would become free and able to improve his relationship with the lover.... The sinking relationship with the lover was a primary cause." Moreover, the court explained, "until [Hisao] began seeing the lover, he was an upstanding citizen who lived a normal social and home life."

Prosecutors sought the death penalty, but the court, after citing a psychiatric report that maintained that Hisao was aware of the wrongfulness of his actions, sentenced him to life imprisonment. Hisao's emotions saved him. His cold lover crushed him on Valentine's Day; his pain was therefore legitimate, and the rules of normal behavior were suspended for him.[82]

Prosecutors appealed the sentence to the Fukuoka High Court. (Japan's constitution prohibits double jeopardy, but prosecutors may appeal acquittals and sentences because the trial and its appeals are considered to be a single jeopardy.[83]) That court found that Hisao's crimes were not premeditated and that he did not have an antisocial or criminal nature. Instead, the crimes occurred as a results of Hisao's "worsening relationships with his lover and his wife" (the high court used the term "lover" forty-eight times in eight pages). Then, after the court stated that it "cannot help but feel sympathy for the victims' families," it affirmed the lower court's ruling, holding simply that Hisao's crimes did not merit death.[84]

In both the Hostess Family Stabbing case and the Valentine's Day Murder case, suffering love saved the defendants from the gallows. But sometimes the logic works in reverse. In the Life Insurance Murder case, company executive Kiyotaka Ōyama was charged with murdering his foster father in 1998 and his wife in 2000 in order to receive $730,000 in life insurance proceeds. Ōyama hit his sixty-six-year-old father on the head with an iron dumbbell, propped him up in a car, and slammed the car into a wall to make the death appear accidental. He killed his wife, thirty-eight-year-old Hiromi, by drowning her in the bathtub after giving her sedatives and having sex with her. He then dumped her body in the sea from a pier at Hiroshima Port and claimed that she had fallen into the water during a fishing trip.

Prosecutors argued that because Ōyama's motivations were coldly monetary (and thus devoid of emotion), he deserved the death penalty. Ōyama argued that he deserved life in prison because his motivations were more complex. In his father's case, he claimed, he killed in part because the two disagreed about how to liquidate his bankrupt firm and in part because he suspected that his father had killed his mother, whose death had been ruled a suicide. The Hiroshima High Court sided with prosecutors and found that Ōyama killed his father to receive insurance money, which he used to pay off massive debts.

Ōyama then argued that he killed Hiromi because she "kept badgering him about how the insurance proceeds were to be divided," and he feared she would discover his crime. As the court explained, "The defendant thought that if [Hiromi] discovered his lies, she would be disgusted with him, divorce him, and marry another man. As he had these thoughts, he decided that if he killed her, he would prevent her from the distress she would otherwise feel upon learning the truth, and at the same time he would save himself from the sight of Hiromi marrying another man." His claim rested on love:

> Through his counsel…, the defendant argues that his motivation to kill cannot easily be explained. It is impossible to understand, he argues, how he could form an "extremely strong intent" to kill his wife, whom he loved deeply [*fukai aijō*]. There is a huge disconnect, he claims, between brooding

over the fact that his beloved wife [*saiai no tsuma*] would not forgive him for his actions and killing her, and therefore no adequate explanation has been offered for why he killed his wife or of the events that preceded her death. It is clear, he argues, that there is no way to reconcile his deep love for Hiromi with the charge that her murder evidenced his lack of love for her.

The court responded in turn to the defendant's argument by using his own language of love:

> The defendant decided to kill [Hiromi] to prevent her from learning the truth and divorcing him. It can therefore be said that the defendant's "love" [punctuation in original] ultimately meant simply that he did not want to lose her, wanted to keep her for himself and away from other men, and wanted to prevent her from being stolen away. Motivated by these factors, he decided to kill his wife. His argument that his motivation to kill Hiromi was not adequately explained has no merit.

In another section of the opinion, the court examined the appropriateness of the death penalty. It described the heinous nature of the crime: Hiromi was killed while she was completely naked. She cried out "Why? Why?" as she struggled against the defendant in the tub. She called for their twelve-year-old son to help her as she drowned. She was only thirty-eight years old. She had two school-age children. Finally, "most significantly...there are no words to describe the pitifulness of the sadness [Hiromi] must have felt as she was betrayed by her husband, whom she had loved [*aishitsuzuketekita*] and trusted." The court ordered that Ōyama hang for his "cold-blooded" crimes.[85]

Love played three important roles in the Life Insurance Murder case. First, the court used Hiromi's love to highlight the depths of Ōyama's crimes. The most significant aspect of Hiromi's murder was not the children she left behind, the physical pain she experienced, or the dehumanizing way in which her body was unceremoniously dumped into the ocean—it was the suffering, painful betrayal by the husband whom she *loved deeply* (a finding for which the court offered no evidence).[86]

Second, that the couple had intercourse immediately before the murder reflected a further betrayal of Hiromi's feelings. The court stated that the couple "entered the warm bath together immediately after having sex, an act in which the love of a husband and wife are confirmed." The court, then, found love—and marriage—in the act of sex. The linking of the three, as we will see, is an atypical romantic statement for a court, an expression of an unachievable ideal. Here, the court seems to be using the expression for the specific purpose of turning Ōyama's love-confirming act into one of betrayal, increasing his blameworthiness in the murder of his loving wife.

Finally, the defendant's *absence* of love led to his death sentence. The defendant claimed that he loved his wife, but the court, defining love as separate from jealousy or possessiveness, found that he did not. If love was not behind the murder, if the killings could not be framed in the identifiable rhetoric of the defendant's suffering love, he should receive the maximum penalty.

In these death-penalty cases, then, as in cases of love suicide, love is a form of pain. In the Hostess Family Stabbing and the Valentine's Day Murder cases, the pain of love saved the defendants from the gallows, as courts seem to have found their emotions appropriate. Conversely, in the Life Insurance Murder case, the absence of pain, and the comparatively painful love of the victim, doomed the defendant, whose emotions were entirely inappropriate.

Consider a final type of love-as-suffering homicide case that has similarities both to the love suicide cases and the murder cases: euthanasia. In a 1985 case, a fifty-four-year-old woman learned she had terminal cancer. After enduring several hospital stays and chronic pain, she decided in 1990 that she wanted to die. Her husband of twenty-seven years attempted three times to help her do so. The first time, he placed his wife in their car and attempted to poison her with carbon monoxide fumes. He failed. The second time, he decided to die with his wife in a love suicide by driving their car off a cliff but they were unable to find a cliff.

The third time, the husband placed his wife in the bathtub and guided her hand with his as she cut her carotid artery with a razor. The cut was not deep enough. At her request, he sliced the artery again. She bled to death.

Pursuant to precedent, Japanese courts do not punish euthanasia if (a) the victim has a disease that cannot be cured with modern medical knowledge and technology and will lead to death in the near future, (b) the victim is in pain, (c) the killing is intended to ease the victim's pain, (d) the victim consents to the killing if he has the ability to make decisions, (e) the death is ("should be") effected by a doctor, and (f) the method used is appropriate according to the sense of society (*shakai tsūnenjō*).[87] The court found that in this case, the woman's husband failed the last two steps: a doctor was not involved, and other less painful methods of suicide were available. The court sentenced the defendant to three years' imprisonment, mercifully suspended for one year.[88]

The test and its application seem straightforward. But the court's decision contained one additional element, and by now it can easily be guessed. Before the court applied the test, it stated "for all of the victim's life, the defendant devoted all his energy into caring for and watching her, and accordingly we can confirm [*mitomerareru*] that their love as husband and wife [*fūfuai*] was wide and deep." The court's intent surely was to soften the blow of the guilty verdict, to clarify that although the defendant failed the legal test, he did not kill out of anger or hatred. The court could have done so with many different turns of phrase, but it chose to do so—as other courts have repeatedly done in similar situations[89]—with the rhetoric of love. The court gave no explicit basis for its determination of love, perhaps because the suffering of husband and wife was sufficiently clear evidence of its existence.

Stalking

In 1999, twenty-one-year-old university student Shiori Ino was stalked by an ex-boyfriend and his accomplices. She appealed to the police, who were unresponsive. She filed a complaint against the police for their inaction. Soon thereafter, she was stabbed to death near Okegawa station. The national outrage over the police's mishandling of the "Okegawa Incident" led to the passage of an antistalking law in 2000 by unanimous vote.[90]

The Antistalking Law criminalizes a list of broadly described activities, including "following, waiting near, or visiting the victim's home, office, school, or other places the victim frequents," "demanding to meet or interact with the victim when she has no obligation to do so," "making silent phone calls," and "acting or behaving extremely rudely to the victim." The law also provides that a person who commits these acts violates the law only if he "repeatedly" commits the acts against a victim (or the victim's spouse, relatives, or other persons with whom the victim is close) "for the purpose of satisfying feelings of love [*ren'ai kanjō*, alternatively, 'romantic' or 'amorous' feelings] or other feelings of affection for a specific person, or for the purpose of satisfying feelings of revenge [*enkon*, alternatively, 'grudge'] when one's love is unrequited."

This statutory language is striking: harassment is illegal under the statute *only* when it is based on "feelings of love or other feelings of affection...[or] feelings of revenge." If the court is persuaded that a harasser is not acting on feelings of love or love-fueled revenge, he is not stalking. Legislators pointed out problems of interpretation of love both when the bill was being revised and after its passage, but the language remained in the statute.[91] It is the only statute in all of Japanese law that contains the word *ren'ai* (love, or romantic relationship),[92] and the only one that requires a court to make a decision based on the existence of love between adults.

Most U.S. states define stalking as harassment that causes or is likely to cause fear, emotional distress, or harm. The victim is the focus: how was she or he affected by the behavior at issue? In Japan, the lens is reversed. Because harassment is illegal under the statute only when it is based on "feelings of love or other feelings of affection," it is the painful feelings of the *stalker,* not the victim, that are at issue.

Still, the Japanese statute has a U.S. parallel. In the domestic violence context in the United States, six states allow a person to request a civil protection order against a partner in an "intimate" or "romantic" relationship.[93] In one such state, Arkansas, a court found a "romantic relationship" where a couple "spent time outside of work together, they had sexual relations together 'multiple times'; they spent the night together; they went to eat and to the movies together, and they spent time together in the presence of the victim's children."[94] Other states require a "dating" relationship. In New Jersey, for instance, courts ask six questions (such as "How long did the alleged dating activities continue prior to the alleged acts of domestic violence?") that are so formulaic that courts literally fit the questions and their answers into a grid.[95]

The Japanese law for both domestic violence and stalking is different. In the domestic violence context, orders of protection can be filed only against a spouse, relieving Japanese courts of the task of determining whether a couple is "dating," "romantic," or "intimate" as required in those U.S. states.[96] In the stalking context, instead of focusing on objective evidence of a relationship as in New Jersey, the Japanese law focuses directly on the feelings of the stalker. The law's drafters could have specified those feelings in many different ways, perhaps as jealousy or possessiveness, just as they included a requirement of "feelings of revenge." But they didn't. To define stalking, they chose *love*.

Why did the legislature choose this formulation, which *requires* a court to determine the existence of love? As we have seen, courts make that judgment often, but why did the legislature unanimously mandate it? When the bill's sponsor, Representative Ryūji Matsumura, faced that question during committee deliberations, he said the legislation was intended to respond to the "common situations" of stalking ex-spouses and ex-lovers, as described by the National Police Agency. He then said that the "love" formulation was intended "to minimize the scope of regulation over citizens as much as possible."[97] Scholarly commentary on the law offers a similar explanation: the narrow language was intended to avoid problems of regulating harassment in the business context, in labor movements, and in religious activities, each of which would have been more controversial.[98]

The language is as ambiguous as it is broad. In the same committee deliberations, Representative Kantoku Teruya asked, "I have a pretty good understanding of what you mean by 'feelings of love' or 'feelings of revenge,' but what is your thinking on the phrase 'other feelings of affection'?" Matsumura responded:

> I am not a lawyer, so please bear that in mind, but "other feelings of affection" in the law [means] general feelings of liking someone [*sukina kimochi*] or feelings of affection [*shin'aikan*]...and not just pleasant [*konomashii*] feelings.... To take just one example, and this is only one example, if someone has feelings of longing for an actress or a newscaster whom they see on television, those are not "feelings of love," but they are "other feelings of affection."[99]

Matsumura's lack of a detailed explanation for "other feelings of affection" suggests that the language might present courts with difficulty. But consider the preface to Representative Teruya's question: he stated that he already had a good idea of what "feelings of love" meant. Teruya might simply have been posturing, but perhaps he *did* understand the meaning, or he at least understood that it is distinguishable from feelings that one has for an actress or a newscaster. Perhaps there is a consensus in Japan as to whether a person's feelings fit the Japanese conception of love.

The tone of court opinions on stalking suggests that the cases indeed are decided easily.[100] Some cases are particularly simple, as when an accused stalker specifically states in her deposition that she holds feelings of love for the lover.[101] Courts' all-knowing tone persists, though, even when stalkers claim they are *not* in love. In a 2004 Tokyo High Court case, the suspected stalker had distributed four letters and sixty-six naked pictures of his ex-girlfriend to mailboxes at her apartment complex. He claimed that his purpose was not to "satisfy his feelings of love" but "to make sure he had a way of communicating in order to end [*seisan shori*, alternatively, 'gain closure on'] the relationship."

The court noted that the two had dated, lived together, and planned to marry. The victim gradually grew to dislike the defendant, and she tried to end the relationship. She was initially unsuccessful; he continued to send her presents and proposed to her. She finally stopped having sex with him and then ignored his phone calls and e-mails. After his arrest, the court said, "the defendant's statement clearly shows mixed feelings of love and hate [*aizō*], and his letters were threatening and critical. Even if the defendant is correct that his purpose was to ensure a method of communication in order to end the relationship, it still can be said that he was acting to satisfy his feelings of love." The court found him guilty.[102]

In a similar case from 2007, the defendant, Tetsuya, was charged with stalking his thirty-year-old ex-wife, who had custody of their children. The evidence showed that at various times he had waited for her at her apartment, pressured her to talk to him, jumped over a fence onto her veranda, pushed her, and spied on her at work from his car. Tetsuya argued that he committed these acts not "to satisfy his feelings of love" but because he was curious about how his children were being raised.

As in the previous case, the court reviewed the evidence of love. The victim testified that Tetsuya had said, "You're coming home in the morning after spending the night with a man? Have you got a boyfriend? Get together with me one more time." The victim's father testified that Tetsuya told him that he still had feelings (*suki*) for his ex-wife. The court found the statements credible.

The more important factor to the court seems to have been Tetsuya's own statements. Tetsuya claimed that he could not be in love with his ex-wife because he already had a girlfriend at the time of the incidents. The court found that he indeed had a girlfriend but that the relationship began after he stalked his ex-wife. With no girlfriend at the time, he must have remained in love, the court reasoned, with his ex and be therefore guilty.

The court sentenced Tetsuya to two years' imprisonment, suspended for four years—in other words, no jail time.[103]

Return now to the Okegawa stalking case, the case that led to the Antistalking Law's passage. The presiding judge in the 2001 murder trial at the district court, Yoshiharu Shimoyama, was forced to recuse himself after he was caught dozing during the trial. Seven years later, he was arrested—for stalking a female court employee thirty years his junior. The Kofu District Court found the e-mail that he sent to her cell phone "cunning and vicious," characteristics the court deemed compatible with the requisite feelings of love.[104]

The courtroom might seem to be a particularly awkward place for determinations of love to occur. But as we have seen, Japanese judges frequently extrapolate love from the facts of the cases while interpreting the rules of the state. That process reveals a complex and fascinating relationship between the "law" of the state and the "nonlaw" of everyday life, a tangled knot in which the statutory categories of aiding suicide, murder, and stalking are defined not by a purportedly precise analysis of mental states as in the United States but by a more intuitive examination of emotions.

In conducting these examinations, with no legislative guidance, judges could have defined or described love any way they wished. Perhaps something like this:

> Love is patient, love is kind. It does not envy, it does not boast, it is not proud. It is not rude, it is not self-seeking, it is not easily angered, it keeps no record of wrongs. Love does not delight in evil but rejoices with the truth. It always protects, always trusts, always hopes, always perseveres. Love never fails.[105]

Comparing Japanese courts' conception of love differs to this prescriptive Biblical ideal is unfair, but the extent of the difference between the two is staggering. Although I cannot be sure if love in Japanese opinions delights in evil, it seems to miss every other point in the checklist. With Japan's ostensibly strict rules of interpersonal behavior, we might have expected courts to define love either dispassionately or in ways not too dissimilar from the Biblical version to stifle disorderly, out-of-control emotions. And yet the picture of Japanese love that emerges from the opinions is that of an uncontrollable force that allows for the weakening of rules of ordinary behavior, a love full of danger, heartache, excitement, excess, and tragedy.

Some of those aspects of love surely are desirable: although patience and kindness are nice, who has a quarrel with excitement? But what seems to be missing from most of the cases is a caring, interpersonal connection. Qualities like nurturing and sustainability might be difficult for judges to determine, but they seem no more so than lovesick pain and suffering, factors on which they routinely rely.

3

Coupling

How do people in Japan reach the tragic state of love? How do they meet, and how do they enter into marriage or other long-term relationships? And what happens to the seemingly unsustainable love as presented by the courts as the years go by?

In this chapter, I first examine how matches are made Japan. The methods for choosing companions are often awkward and dangerous, and, at least in the vision set forth by courts, many people making those choices seem to disregard love, intimacy, and emotional compatibility in favor of more calculated matching criteria.

I then turn to marriage. Loveless marriages happen everywhere. But in Japanese court opinions, loveless marriage often is an expectation—not sad, and certainly not a tragedy. Japanese judges sometimes hold up love as an ideal in some mythical perfect state of marital bliss, but they do not view it as a necessary component of actual marriages. Given the conception of love as an uncontrollable, disturbing, and confusing emotion as we saw in the previous chapter, the separation of love and marriage seems perversely necessary and imminently practical, for marriage seems unlikely to survive long-term turmoil.

Matching

At Japanese matchmaking agencies, the factors that matter to people who are choosing a partner include weight, height, age, schooling, hobbies, and economic status[1]—factors that matter in the United States as well. The United States has its own matching quirks; religion, for instance, surely is much more significant as a sorting device than it is in Japan. Japan has at least two other factors that play a lesser role in the United States.

First, some people seeking mates use blood-type matching to attempt to decrease the odds of personality clash.[2] Type As are considered cautious, meticulous, and like structure; type Bs are unrestrained, cheerful, and quickly lose interest in things; Os are generous and expressive; and ABs are a moody and conflicted combination of A and B. The stereotypes are well known. When surveyed college students were given a list of personality traits and asked to match them with one of the four blood types, agreement was nearly unanimous; for instance, the word "precise" (*kichōmen*) was attributed to type As by 86 percent.[3] (Again, the survey's very existence is intriguing.)

Second, at least for marriage, genetics and family background matter, sometimes to the extent that prospective spouses hire private investigators to examine each other surreptitiously. These records need to be inspected to ensure that, as one ethnography found, "the prospective partner has not been raised in a defective environment, indicated by incidences of suicide, divorce, crime, and the like."[4]

But make no mistake: looks matter. On this point we have data from the academy, corporations, and the government. First, consider a survey of 156 college students (78 men, 78 women). The students were asked to what factors they would attribute success or failure in love. The three most popular responses were personality (32.9 percent), looks (15.0 percent), and luck (10.9 percent). When asked what factors led to success in love for a friend, the importance of personality remained the same, but the importance of looks (22.1 percent) increased significantly (luck fell to 5.9 percent). When asked what led to love for an enemy, luck suddenly became very important

(24.1 percent), personality became less important (14.5 percent), and looks became much more important (23.7 percent).[5]

Second, a corporate survey from 2007 found that 39.4 percent of men fell in love at first sight, while only 22.3 percent of women (and only 12.8 percent of women in their thirties) did.[6] Looks matter, then, but mostly for men.

Finally, the Ministry of Health, Labor, and Welfare—and again, note that the government finds this issue sufficiently important to devote resources to it—found similar results in a 2004 survey of single men and women ages twenty to thirty-two regarding their "conditions" for marriage. Respondents were asked to choose up to three conditions. The top seven reported conditions are in table 3.1.

The interesting gaps between the sexes are in economic power and looks. For economic power, only 1.3 percent of men cared about that characteristic in a potential wife, presumably because women are unlikely to be economically powerful. The "looks" category was third place for men, just edging out a wife's ability to take care of the household: almost as many men say they value a wife's homemaking abilities as her looks. The least important condition for women, with only 7.3 percent, was a potential husband's physical appearance.

These data, reliable or otherwise, are merely one window into the importance of female beauty, which arises in courts as well. While riding her bicycle in 1992, Hanako was hit by a car. She injured her face, teeth, and legs. She sued the driver in Kobe District Court. The calculation of damages for aftereffects of an automobile accident is easy in Japan: Japanese law

TABLE 3.1. Conditions for Marriage (Percentages)

	Men	Women
Personality	82.0	78.7
Values/Compatibility	65.3	61.3
Salary/Economic power	1.3	57.3
Looks	27.3	7.3
Understanding and cooperation regarding my career	15.3	14.0
Similar hobbies	16.0	8.0
Ability and willingness to take care of house and children	25.3	30.0

Source: Ministry of Health, Labor, and Welfare, Shōshika ni Kansuru Ishiki Chōsa Kenkyū [Survey Research on Consciousness of the Declining Birth Rate], Aug. 13, 2004, available at http://www.mhlw. go.jp/topics/bukyoku/seisaku/syousika/040908/dl/0010.pdf.

rates injuries from Class 1 to 14,[7] and the Federation of Bar Associations specifies a range of damages for each class.[8] The damage charts at the time of Hanako's accident specified a maximum of $27,000 in aftereffect damages for "facial disfigurement." Hanako aimed high and claimed $35,000.

Hanako argued that "as a young, single woman," her scarring would cause her to "feel a significant amount of unease about love [*ren'ai*] and marriage in her future." The sentiment is often repeated in Japan; a woman who is disfigured or otherwise seen as defective might sadly be described as one who "cannot become a wife" (*oyome ni ikenai*), an expression that has no male equivalent.

The court disagreed. It held that "love and marriage are about charm as a human being, not just outward appearances, but the essence of a person.... We confirm that despite her injuries, she has not lost her inner charm." It awarded her $30,000 in aftereffect damages—more than the chart specified, but less than she had sought.[9]

Hanako's judges seem to have taken a holistic approach to beauty and relationships, but not all courts do. When assessing damages of $70,000 in a 1993 botched breast surgery case, the Fukuoka District Court specifically noted that "as an unmarried twenty-five-year-old woman" the plaintiff would have fears not only about breastfeeding but also about "her future marriage."[10] In a 2008 case over a similar surgery that left the defendant without her right breast, the court awarded damages based in part on the "passive" attitude toward love and marriage that the surgery had caused.[11] (The causal relation is unclear.)

By contrast, Hanako's judges focused on her inner charm. But the very law on which their judgment was based tells a different story. Under the relevant statute, had Hanako been male, her "facial disfigurement" would have been worth about half the amount that she could receive as a woman. Male facial disfigurement is the lowest form of the lowest class on the damages chart. The difference in value between male and female beauty is so significant that the Tokyo District Court held (in 1999) that a man who lives and works as a woman (in the night entertainment industry) may claim higher "female" disfigurement damages precisely for that reason.[12] Had Hanako, with or without her inner charm, been a man, her damage award would have been lower.

The situation may be changing. In a 2010 case, a man who suffered severe facial burns at work brought a workers' compensation claim against the state, claiming that his award was inadequate. The state, properly using the same chart used by the court to determine Hanako's damages, had awarded the man an amount less than that which he would have received if he were a woman. The Kyoto District Court held that at least in this workers' compensation context, the difference in damages based on sex was unconstitutional.[13] In so ruling, the court rejected the state's argument that facial disfigurement causes higher levels of "emotional pain and feelings of disgust from third parties in daily life" in men than women, an argument the state based in part on sales of cosmetics and advertising expenses for women's fashion. The impact of the decision on future cases in other contexts remains unclear, but the state's articulation of its position suggests that the issue is far from settled.

Until the late nineteenth century, beauty is said to have mattered little in marriage in Japan, as marriages were arranged and served largely as a method to combine households.[14] But as late nineteenth-century intellectuals in Japan studied the West, where romantic love was viewed in some circles as "the only valid basis for marriage," they found stark contrasts that led them to argue that love-based marriages were a sign of an advanced society.[15] By the 1920s, social commentators such as psychologist Naoki Sugita were arguing that "sex and love are the foundation of life, and the marital relationship rests on sex and love as the closest, most sacred, most united of all forms of human interaction."[16] Affection and even eroticism in marriage emerged as prominent themes in fiction.[17]

Love marriage entailed not only a presumed affection but also sexual equality, which was nonexistent in the prewar period. The U.S.-influenced Japanese constitution, enacted in 1947, states that "marriage shall be based only on the mutual consent of both sexes and it shall be maintained through mutual cooperation with the equal rights of husband and wife as a basis" (art. 24). Still, the language is more aspirational than descriptive.

A 1962 case shows how matchmaking continued to work (or not) in some villages.[18] Muneo and Shizuko were married in 1955. Unbeknownst to Shizuko, Muneo preferred Shizuko's sister Yoshiko, with whom he had had a sexual relationship. The sisters' mother had somehow talked Muneo out of marrying Yoshiko and into marrying Shizuko instead. After the marriage, the two sisters, the mother, and the husband lived together under the same roof.

After four or five months of marriage, Yoshiko revealed her feelings about Muneo to Shizuko. Muneo wasted no time telling his wife how he felt about the situation: "I really liked Yoshiko, but your mom split us up and made me marry you. I married you out of pity. You're cold, but Yoshiko's love was delicate and warm."

In 1959, after Shizuko had given birth to three children, the sisters' powerful mother forced Muneo to move out. Muneo turned his anger against Shizuko, saying, "You hid Yoshiko" and "Yoshiko was great. I don't want to be with you." He became violent and punched Shizuko—who was pregnant at the time—in the face.

At this point, the sisters' mother stepped in, and the mother, the two sisters, and Muneo had a family meeting. The meeting surely was awkward, but such talks are not unusual in Japan. People in the cases frequently attempt to solve love triangle crises through negotiation sessions, which often have at least four parties present: the three lovers and a parent.[19]

After this particular negotiation session, the mother decreed that Muneo would switch sisters: he would divorce Shizuko and marry Yoshiko. Shizuko and Muneo moved out. Then Shizuko had a change of heart. On behalf of the children, she tried to patch things up with Muneo. Muneo briefly returned home, but he subsequently beat Shizuko with an umbrella during an argument about money. Shizuko sued for divorce and won.[20]

Arranged marriages like Muneo's faded over time. As figure 3.1 shows, arranged marriages went from being the norm in the 1940s at nearly 70 percent to a rarity, only 6.2 percent, in the 2000s. In their place arose "love marriages," a phrase that indicates the absence of a formal arranged meeting and not the presence of love. A married couple who actually appear to be in love can be referred to by the cutesy term *rabu-rabu* (love love), a slang term used mostly by young people but not by the courts.

The love/arranged distinction is imprecise. Many couples are unable to determine whether their marriage should properly be classified as "love" (*ren'ai kekkon*) or "arranged" (*miai kekkon*). Classification would be unclear, for instance, if the spouses met through a semiformal arranged process and fell in love soon thereafter. Moreover, some people refer to any marriage not formally arranged by a matchmaker, parents, bosses, or other superiors as a "love marriage." That caveat stated, the data show that self-defined love marriages rose dramatically.[21]

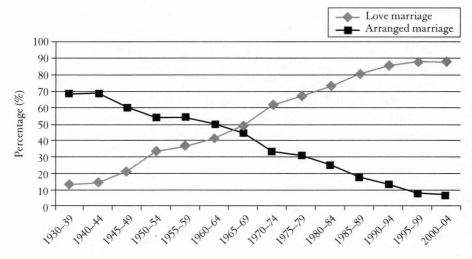

Figure 3.1. Love Marriage versus Arranged Marriage
Source: National Institute of Population and Social Security Research, Dai13kai Shusshō Dōkō Kihon Chōsa: Kekkon to Shussan ni Kansuru Zenkoku Chōsa, Fūfu Chōsa no Kekka Gaiyō [13th Survey on Demographic Trends: National Survey on Marriage and Birth, An Outline of the Results of the Survey of Married Persons] 18 (2006), available at www.ipss.go.jp/ps-doukou/j/doukou13/doukou13.pdf.

In 2006, according to government data, six percent of couples who had been married less than five years met by arrangement, either through a marriage introduction service or through the more formal arrangement process. Most couples met through a friend or a sibling (31 percent) or through the workplace (30 percent); the remainder met through school (11 percent), clubs (5 percent), in town or on vacation (5 percent), through a part-time job (4 percent), as childhood acquaintances (1 percent), or some other means (7 percent).[22] But those data tell do not reveal how men and women actually interact to become couples. I want to explore four common methods that appear in the case law of the 1990s and 2000s, each of which should be viewed in the context of a society that is heavily segregated by sex. The first two, group dating and marriage introduction services, can lead to marriage. The latter two, "girl hunting" and Internet dating, usually do not.

1. *Gōkon,* the second syllable of which comes from the English "companion," is group dating. Date parties usually happen at restaurants or bars and involve an equal number of men and women. Some formalities are often observed: men come early and women come late, seating is mixed by

sex, and toasts and self-introductions occur before informal conversation can begin.

Group dating is ubiquitous. As two Japanese sociologists explain:

> Even if a person has never participated, *gōkon* are a frequent topic on television and in magazines, and they can almost always be seen at bars [*izakaya*]. One hears rumors such as "that couple met through *gōkon*" or "that person is at that age where he can go to *gōkon* all the time." Everybody knows that they are a place at which young men and women can gather to meet in a casual setting....
>
> Everybody wants to meet someone, and nobody wants to lose. There are rules to *gōkon*. Magazines run special issues about them, experts appear, and technique books are published. These sources attempt to arouse interest by explaining how to make oneself appealing, how to draw a person's attention, or how to date someone regularly.[23]

Group dates appear infrequently in the case law. Still, in one case of sexual harassment, an assistant professor was found to be liable when, among other things, at a "second party" in a small karaoke box following the dating party, "he turned toward the customer seats and, while singing 'Love Me Tender,' gyrated his body, unfastened his shirt buttons one by one, took off his shirt, threw it to the customer seats, and took off his pants so that he was left only in his shorts." The Nagoya High Court found him liable.[24]

But for the most part, *gōkon* are safe places to meet, not only physically but also emotionally. In part that safety is based in the nature of *gōkon* as a gender-based team sport.[25] The night ends not with couples pairing up but with the male team and the female team separating to evaluate the other team.[26]

2. *Kekkon sōdansho,* or marriage introduction services, fill the third-party role played in the past by official marriage arrangers. Marriage introduction is a large and growing industry in Japan, with 600,000 "members" (60 percent male) and 3,700 to 3,900 agencies.[27] The tasks that these agencies perform are not dramatically different from those offered in the United States.

But differences can be seen in social role and in practice. In 2006, the Ministry of Economy, Trade, and Industry released a report on the marriage introduction industry. The report was designed to investigate the role of marriage services in a time in which women are choosing to have fewer children. The report, which included a 250-page data supplement, found that the services perform an important role in encouraging people to "marry and start a household," a stated policy for combating the declining birth rate. That role, the report said, was especially important because (a) many people have chosen to have love relationships without marrying and (b) chances for workplace romance have diminished.[28]

The industry has problems. A 2007 report by the same ministry examined complaints logged and consultations given at the National Consumer Affairs Center against agencies. The report found 3,409 complaints during 2005–6, or, on average, one per agency. The largest category of complaints, 42 percent, concerned consumers who had trouble getting out of their contracts. Another 10 percent were about how the business was run, including 287 cases of agencies not finding desired mates (in one case, the report states, a person specified that he or she did not want to meet foreigners, a condition the agency ignored), 146 cases of receiving too few introductions, and 76 cases of introductions to fake mates paid by the company to feign romantic interest.

Another category of complaints, with nearly 11 percent of the total, directly concerns the people who were introduced as potential partners. Consumers complained that their partners rejected them, that information about their partners was false, that their partners wanted to marry them too quickly, that their partners married them and divorced too quickly (particularly in case of non-Japanese Asian mail-order brides), and that their potential partners stalked or otherwise harassed them.[29] Most of these complaints, of course, have little to do with the agency itself. Despite the fact that the problem often lies with the potential mate, agency customers bring their official complaints against the agency.

Sometimes, as in the 1996 Marriage Service case, they sue, and courts enforce common rules of dating, whether that is their explicit intention or not. Hiroya and Sakura met through the now-defunct OMMG marriage introduction service in 1995; he was thirty-two and she was twenty-six. Hiroya wrote on his application to the service that he wanted "to create a happy household based on mutual respect and comfort." They began dating. He told her that he would marry her if she met certain conditions. He then cheated on her. Sakura sued.

Hiroya denied they had been engaged. He claimed that he never said "I love you" (*aishiteru*), one of the few times in which that expression appears in the case law. The court found Hiroya had committed a tort. It awarded Sakura $30,000 in damages.

That could have been the entire opinion: facts, analysis, decision. But that's only a tiny fraction of the cautionary tale the judges penned, and it is in those details that the substance lies. The Tokyo District Court presented the case as follows:

> On July 13, 1995, Hiroya called Sakura at her apartment and asked her out. He promised to call her on the nineteenth, but because he did not have a telephone that day, he instead called her on the twentieth and arranged to meet her at 4:00 in the afternoon on the twenty-third in Shinjuku. They met as planned for their first date on the twenty-third. Sakura gave Hiroya her business card with her work address on it, and they talked about her job at a real estate consulting firm. On this day, Hiroya kissed Sakura in the elevator, and when she asked, "So are we dating [*tsukiau koto*] now?," he answered, "Yes."

Sakura's question is understandable. Because of the way the couple met, the kiss could have led her to believe that a continuing relationship would follow. The kiss led to a second date:

> On July 25, Hiroya called Sakura at her apartment and said, "Tomorrow's your birthday, isn't it? Let's have a birthday party." On the twenty-sixth, they met at a coffee shop in Machida, had tea, and after they paid the bill, the defendant picked up a cake he had ordered. After they ate dinner at another restaurant, Hiroya said. "Let's eat the cake back at your place." Sakura liked him, and because she was on the second day of her period, she thought that she wouldn't be asked to have sex during her period, so she accepted his invitation. But at Sakura's apartment, after she blew out the candles, he began to pursue a sexual relationship. She tried to refuse him on the basis of her menstruation, but in the end, she allowed him to have sex with her. At this time, Hiroya heard from Sakura that she was on her period and also confirmed that she was bleeding.

Note that menstruation mattered, both to the parties and to the court. Sakura assumed that she would not have sex with Hiroya during her period, an idea I address in more detail later. She "allowed him" to have sex with her nonetheless (suggesting that he, at least, had no qualms). The court continued, with an oblique explanation of menstruation's significance:

> On July 29, after Hiroya met Sakura, he invited her to his apartment, and she spent the night. Because she was invited to his apartment, Sakura confirmed that Hiroya intended to date her seriously.

After that day until the end of March, Hiroya and Sakura stayed at each other's apartments and took small trips together. During that time, their sexual relationship continued, but in mid-March, Hiroya told Sakura, "I hate putting on a condom. It doesn't feel right," and they began having sex without a condom. He showed his familiarity with contraception to her by saying things like "The rhythm method is just as safe as a condom," "It's okay after your period," and "It's okay a week before you get your period," and at the same time he admonished her, "Don't you know your own body? You have to take your basal temperature," implying that if she became pregnant it would be her own fault.

Three months after their first date, and shortly after Hiroya told Sakura that he would marry her if she fulfilled certain "conditions," Sakura arrived early at Hiroya's house for a date. There she found evidence that another woman was already there (presumably she found a woman's shoes at the apartment entrance, but the opinion does not specify). Hiroya told Sakura that he was tying up loose ends with an old girlfriend and that he would join Sakura at a coffee shop later. She soon learned that the other woman was Ryōko, a nursing assistant who was a client of the same marriage agency, with whom (she discovered) Hiroya also was having sex. On the same day:

> Because her period was late, Sakura took a pregnancy test. The result was positive. When she told Hiroya, he said, "Let me talk to my friend, who is a specialist" and left to call from a public phone. When he returned, he said, "Those pregnancy tests aren't very accurate" and "I think everything is going to be okay." She later learned that the person he called on the phone was Ryōko....
>
> On October 11, Sakura went to the hospital for a checkup and learned that she was indeed pregnant and that the due date was June 4, 1996. On her way home, she bought a book about pregnancy and childbirth. That night she called Hiroya, who said things she did not expect such as, "You should have an abortion."

Hiroya eventually talked Sakura into having an abortion and told her, "Next time you can keep it." All the while Hiroya remained in contact with Ryōko, with whom he was sharing all the information. When Ryōko asked Hiroya why he did not go to the hospital with Sakura, he said, "It would just mess things up if I go down there and she starts to like me again. Please try and understand these things a little bit at a time." Hiroya continued to see both Sakura and Ryōko. And then:

> On November 19, 1995, Hiroya invited Sakura to his apartment, and while they were having dinner, Ryōko came in. It was the first meeting for Sakura and Ryōko. On that day, Hiroya and Ryōko argued, but after that, both Ryōko and Sakura spent nights at Hiroya's apartment. Ryōko left a note for Sakura and arranged for the two of them to talk without Hiroya....On the twenty-first, Sakura called Ryōko and they talked about how each of them was seriously dating Hiroya....
>
> Afterward, in the latter part of November 1995, Sakura brought her concerns about her relationship with Ryōko and Hiroya's connection to the marriage agency to a free legal counseling session. Then, after consulting Ryōko, she consulted the Tokyo branch manager of the marriage agency, and then she consulted her attorney and representative, Miura. At this point, she made up her mind to file suit against Hiroya.

When Sakura told Hiroya of her consultation with an attorney and threatened to sue him, he promised never to cheat on her again and to "allow her" (the court's words—note that Sakura controls sex during menstruation, but Hiroya controls abortions) to have a baby if she became pregnant again. They reconciled and resumed their sexual relationship, and then things took a turn for the worse. Sakura overheard Hiroya lie to Ryōko on the phone about his relationship with Sakura. The same day, Hiroya demanded that Sakura call the marriage agency and inform them that they had reconciled—again highlighting the agency's central role even after matches are made. When she refused to make the call, he yelled at her and threatened to hit her. She fled his apartment and returned home to find a message on her answering machine from him: "It's over. Give me back your key." She sued him for damages based on emotional distress.

The court analyzed Hiroya's defenses:

> On four occasions, on the second, ninth, sixteenth, and thirtieth of November, Sakura worked part-time at "Pub Club Cutie Idol." This business was a karaoke pub in which customers could view the entire body of a person who performed on a karaoke stage. Hiroya didn't like the fact that Sakura worked there, and Sakura read books with titles such as "How to Understand Men's Feelings" to try to understand him. Aside from this experience, Sakura never worked in the entertainment industry or in a restaurant....

Hiroya claims that Sakura was in the [sexual] entertainment industry from before the time that they met, that she hid from him the fact that she was a hostess, and that she continued to work as a hostess even after they broke up. But [Sakura worked only at a karaoke pub]. It is defamatory for Hiroya to use such expressions in this lawsuit as "snag customers" and to claim that Sakura worked in a fashion massage or similar entertainment enterprise that appeals directly to male sexual desires....

Hiroya claims that "at any given point in time, people keep their distance from entertainment industry women, looking down generally on people in the sex business [*mizu shōbai*], while at the same time, when referring to his own family, which is in the medical profession, he says, "My family is quite strict, and when talk of marriage emerged, of course we had an agency investigate, at which point we learned the facts of Sakura's hostess background, and marriage became unthinkable," suggesting that he believes his family's profession is elite. Moreover, when he claims that "if someone does not show up for an appointment on time, I will go home exactly when the time comes. That's what it's like to work in a trading company," it is clear that he thinks the trading company at which he works is of a high level. Looking at these facts, it is apparent that Hiroya is self-centered and psychologically immature, and it can be said that this self-centeredness underlay the way in which Hiroya related to Sakura.

There is no legal need for this language. The statute under which Sakura sued, and which I mentioned in chapter 1, is very broad: "A person who has intentionally or negligently infringed any right of others, or legally protected interest of others, shall be liable to compensate any damages resulting in consequence" (Civil Code art. 709). The statute encompasses claims for defamation, which the court addresses in the first paragraph. But the discussion in the second paragraph of Hiroya's class arrogance, self-centeredness, and immaturity is superfluous piling on. If you are not yet convinced of Hiroya's blameworthiness, here is the court's knockout punch:

Hiroya argues that Sakura dated him for sexual reasons, on the ground that she is a woman who likes to be on top and has a strong sex drive. He emphasizes the fact that on July 26, the first time they had sexual relations, even though Sakura was on her period and was bleeding, she had sex with him nonetheless, while she was on top, for an hour and a half. This is an extremely unlikely story, and the fact that he could make such statements so calmly in his deposition shows that his attitude toward this lawsuit is abnormal. He also argues that the bulk of the blame for the pregnancy falls on Sakura, stating, "It's not that I didn't like using a condom. Because I worried about infection from a condom, we decided to use vaginal contraceptive film.... She didn't use it." But when one uses vaginal contraceptive film, the risk of pregnancy from the woman-on-top position is high. It is impossible that Hiroya, if he were concerned about pregnancy, recommended vaginal contraceptive film to the "woman-on-top-loving" Sakura. When asked about this point, he revised his statement to say that when they changed from the woman-on-top position to the missionary position, he pulled out, and she put the film in place. But if that is true, his statement conflicts with his affidavit statement that says 'Sakura didn't use vaginal contraceptive film.' These false statements simply do not add up."

Hidden, or perhaps not quite so, in this paragraph are two judicial assumptions about sex (set aside Hiroya's apparent assumption that presenting Sakura as promiscuous would help his case). First, correctly or incorrectly, the court could not fathom that a woman would be on top during sex for an hour and a half. Second, the court seemed amazed that a woman would allow sex on her period for any length of time. Sakura could not possibly have been as aggressive as Hiroya claimed, so his claim surely must have been false—so false, in fact, that it represented an "abnormal," presumably casual, attitude toward the lawsuit. The court formally delivered its telegraphed judgment:

Based on [the above facts], it is clear that Hiroya used a marriage introduction service to find a partner for marriage or other relationship, began a relationship with a woman who had the intent to marry, and had a continuous sexual relationship with a woman whom he claimed he would marry if certain conditions were met. When she pressed him to marry, he would say that the conditions were not yet met, though he had no intention to marry. His plan was to pretend that he was interested in marriage, all the while continuing a long-term sexual relationship while cleverly avoiding engagement or marriage. Sakura began her relationship with him after reading his message in his introduction that he wanted "to create a happy household based on mutual respect and comfort" and mistakenly dated him thinking she might marry him. As a result, she was forced to abort her first-conceived child and so on, completely disrupting her life plan. Acts such as these committed by Hiroya against Sakura constitute a tortious invasion of her dignity rights.

The court awarded Sakura $30,000 in damages, a large amount by Japanese court standards, an amount that it stated took into consideration not only her emotional distress but also the facts that she had to retain an attorney and file a civil suit to settle the matter.[30]

The court could have based Hiroya's liability in fraud or breach of engagement.[31] It did not. Instead, it described Sakura's injury as an invasion of her dignity rights (*jinkakuken shingai*), a legal concept that allows a court considerable leeway in determining the nature and severity of the nebulous injury. With liberty to analyze, the court focused on class arrogance as well as issues like a "forced" abortion and "unusual" sex, none of which has any clear statutory basis. In effect the court seems to simply be saying that Sakura deserved compensation because Hiroya, the jerk, violated the rules of relationships.

The court's focus on the marriage introduction service suggests an importance and seriousness of such enterprises that surpasses their U.S. counterparts. Unlike online dating services, marriage introduction services are morally responsible for their choices; when Sakura learned of Ryōko, she consulted with the agency's Tokyo branch manager. The services are for meeting potential spouses and not casual acquaintances: the court specifically referenced Hiroya's application statement—"to create a happy household based on mutual respect and comfort"—and chastised him for using the service to find a woman who "had the intent to marry" when he had no such intent. Hiroya might have been allowed to string Sakura along in a relationship if he had not done so with the talk of marriage that naturally was a logical outgrowth of the use of an agency.

3. *Nanpa* (literally, "soft group," as opposed to "hard, serious group") might best be described as girl hunting (when it is performed by girls, it is called "reverse" [*gyaku*] *nanpa*), and it is one of the most visible courtship rituals in Japan. Boys hang out on the streets and at train stations and shopping arcades looking for girls, while girls hang out in the same places looking to be noticed. If a match seems possible, the boy and the girl exchange cell phone numbers, or more.

Of course, some nights end with substantial contact, and a few end tragically.[32] In one case, the defendant picked up a seventeen-year-old girl through what the court called *nanpa*. He "liked her style, decided that he wanted to have sex with her no matter what," and raped her. She was a virgin, the court said, he raped her for thirty minutes, and he took pictures of the act to blackmail her from telling on him. In the sentencing process, the court noted the severity of the act but found that, in the defendant's favor, he was remorseful, had paid her mother $10,000 as compensation, his wife and mother promised to look out for him, and he swore he would never again do *nanpa*. He received two and one-half years in prison as prosecutors requested.[33]

Note three factors specified by the court. The first two are sexual: the victim of the rape was a virgin, and the defendant attempted to blackmail her by taking pictures of their intercourse. The former suggests that virginity matters, and the latter suggests that sex, or at least virginal sex with a stranger, is shrouded in shame (more on these elements in chapter 4). The third factor is one that worked in the defendant's favor: he swore away *nanpa*. It is unclear why this factor merited mention; presumably he could meet girls through other methods and rape them. But the court's logic reflects a widely expressed fear in Japan that *nanpa* is unsafe. If he can stay away from *nanpa,* presumably he can stay out of trouble.

4. *Deaikei* are pay-to-use Internet dating sites. Most activity on the sites is conducted with cell phones, which facilitate easy and relatively anonymous meetings. The sites are a source not only for underage sex[34] but also for various adulterous affairs, perhaps because, as one court says, it is a way for couples to meet "conveniently," and "it is well-known that in order to keep a relationship going, things often are explained in ways that differ from reality" when communicating by cell phone.[35]

The advertising of one of the larger *deaikei* sites, designed exclusively for cell phone access, shows the development of a stereotypical ideal relationship between people who might use the service. A newspaper ad for Pure Ai introduces twenty-three-year-old Mana and her potential suitor, twenty-nine-year-old Atsushi. The ad, emblazoned with the headline "Find a boyfriend or girlfriend with your cell phone!" uses captioned photographs to detail the following six-hour timeline of each:

- 4 p.m.: Mana sees a Pure Ai advertisement in the subway and says, "Ah, Pure Ai." As for Atsushi, while eating in the park a late fast-food lunch consisting of a hamburger and a pint-sized carton of milk, he spots a Pure Ai ad in a sports tabloid and says, "I'll look for a girlfriend on Pure Ai."
- 5 p.m.: While relaxing outdoors, Mana turns to her cell phone and says, "I can use it for free! I'll sign up!" While busy at work, Atsushi turns to his cell phone and says, "Signup is easy and I can use it right away!"

- 6 p.m.: While eating a simple but elegant salad-and-pasta dinner at a café, Mana turns to her phone and says, "Wow, I've already got mail!" While commuting, Atsushi turns to his phone and says, "I'll e-mail this girl!"
- 8 p.m.: While relaxing in a bubble bath, [large-breasted] Mana turns to her cell phone and says, "Atsushi? He might be a good one <heart>." While smoking a cigarette and drinking a beer at a pub, Atsushi turns to his cell phone and says, "Mana sounds like a good girl <heart>"
- 10 p.m.: While brushing her teeth after her bath, Mana turns to her phone and says, "A date next week? That might be great!" After shopping at the appropriately titled convenience store "Alone Mart," Atsushi, still in his business suit, while carrying home what appears to be his breakfast for the next morning, turns to his phone and says: "I'll do it! I'll ask her out!"

They meet the following week, and by the end of their date, they appear to be a cozy couple (and Mana appears to be a bit tipsy).[36]

The ad marvelously stereotypes the differences between "masculine" and "feminine" that appear in the case law. Mana apparently has nothing to do at 4:00 in the afternoon and spends her evening in the bubble bath. Atsushi grabs lunch at 4:00 in the afternoon and loosens his tie to chug a beer on his way home. Mana appears to have her pick of men, while Atsushi seems to consider himself lucky to meet any woman at all. The company's service is free for Mana, but Atsushi must pay $5 every time he uses the service to contact Mana. Although women in the case law are often victims (as in Sakura's emotional distress case against her agency-introduced boyfriend), they are socially perceived as the sex in control—yet another example of the gap between the sexes in Japan and perhaps further evidence of why men might have a more pessimistic view of love than women.

The small print in the ad says, "The information service provided by our company is provided as a precursor to marriage. This is not a *deaikei* site. Users must be eighteen or older, and the registration of persons who are already married is strictly prohibited." That language attempts to legitimate the company by distinguishing it from those used by people for prostitution, underage liaisons, and adulterous affairs; the company wants problems neither from the law nor from angry spouses.

But of course many users use *deaikei* services precisely for those purposes. A 2005 Tokyo District Court exemplifies that prominent *deaikei* pattern. Katsuyuki and Misa married in 1991 and had a son. In June 2004, Misa posted a profile of herself on a *deaikei* site with the following text: "I'm thirty-five, married with children. Lately I can stay out later than

I could in the past, and I'd like to go out to eat at nice restaurants. I have a female friend who will do this with me, but I'd really like a male friend. If you're looking for someone like me, let's start with a text message." Two days later, she had found a male companion named Hiro. They went to dinner and exchanged e-mail throughout July. She stayed at Hiro's condominium at least one night in August.

Katsuyuki became suspicious. When he grabbed Misa's phone in an attempt to read her messages, she grabbed it back, and they wrestled over it. During the struggle, Misa had a panic attack and was rushed to the hospital. When she was released a week later, she did not come home.

Katsuyuki hired a private investigator to find her. The investigator went to Hiro's home at 8:30 one morning and knocked on the door. Misa and Hiro appeared in pajamas together. When the investigator asked Hiro why he had been living with someone else's wife for more than a month, he did not respond. Nor did he respond when the investigator asked, "When a man and a woman live in the same house for such a long time, isn't it only natural that people will have suspicions that they are living as a married couple?"

Katsuyuki sued Misa and Hiro over the adultery (I discuss the grounds for such a suit in chapter 5). Misa argued that they were not liable because Katsuyuki's violence made her leave him. The court needed to determine whether the marriage was destroyed before the affair began. To do so, it examined Misa's 2003 (pre-Hiro) e-mail to friends in which she spoke of *other* lovers. In the first e-mail, from February, Misa wrote,

> I was having an affair then with X, and before the affair was discovered, things weren't going so well, or maybe I should say that it just seemed like I was with him because it was the natural thing to do. But after the affair was discovered, I didn't feel so much distance from Katsuyuki. Things had gotten bad between us because we didn't have anything to talk about, but now we talk quite a bit. If I could see Y again, I would, but I'd feel bad for doing it to Katsuyuki. Still, Katsuyuki is so useless; he never tells me he things like "I like/love you (*suki*)," and his work is his life.

In a second pre-Hiro e-mail, from October 2003, Misa told her friend of troubles with another man she was seeing:

> Maybe it's about time that I just stick with Katsuyuki. I don't have any intention of disrupting our lives, so maybe things are OK like this. He works hard and doesn't take vacations. Being allowed to do whatever I want like

this makes my life many times better than the average person's. I bet this
will all come back to haunt me, though.

Indeed it did. The court noted that the e-mail made no mention of
Katsuyuki's alleged violence. Misa's problems, the court said, "were more
about Katsuyuki's lack of conversation and how much he worked than
about violence."

Examine closely what the court is saying. Violence is sufficient to end
a marriage; that seems uncontroversial. But the court is also saying that
Misa's expressed problems—Katsuyuki's overwork, lack of conversation,
and failure to express his feelings—were insufficient evidence of a marital breakdown. Nor were Misa's multiple affairs, during and before 2003,
sufficient evidence of a breakdown, though the court admitted that they
showed the marriage was imperfect.

If Misa's problems and affairs didn't matter, what did? Tipping the
scales against a finding of marital destruction were a supposedly happy
family trip in January 2004 and Misa's second e-mail above that stated
that she would stay in the marriage. Based on those factors and the lack
of violence, the court found that the marriage was not destroyed at the
time of Misa's affair with Hiro. The court found Misa and Hiro liable for
$11,000 in damages and attorney's fees.[37]

Deaikei sites are criticized for more than just enabling adulterous affairs
such as this one. They also are a means for various forms of fraud and other
crimes committed against both men and women who are lured into meeting strangers.[38] As the following case shows, courts seem to expect a wide
range of behavior in cases that involve *deaikei.*

In a 2009 case, a woman claimed she had been grabbed off the street,
thrown into a car, and raped by two men. Police found a suspect based
on the physical description provided by the victim and confirmed his identity through DNA testing. He was charged with rape. During the course
of the investigation, the suspect had no explanation for the DNA results,
but at trial he had a new story.

The defendant claimed he met the victim on a cell-phone *deaikei* site.
He claimed to have met thirty to fifty women through the site. The vic-
tim's listing, he said, read "Let's have sex" (*ecchi shiyō*—recall from the
Child Predator case that *ecchi* is almost always a quote). He responded,
"I can meet you now," and she replied, "I'm looking for a man with type

O blood." The defendant said, "I'm type O" and wondered if any type O man would have been acceptable.

They met at a love hotel, bathed, and had sex twice. Both times, the defendant said, the victim told the defendant to ejaculate inside her. She said, "I want to marry my boyfriend, but I can't get him to marry me. When I told him that I wanted a baby, he said he wouldn't have sex with me anymore. So I wanted to have sex with a type O man, get pregnant, and get him to marry me." She told the defendant not to ejaculate "too deep" so as to increase the chances of conception. The defendant ejaculated twice, the couple parted, and he completely forgot about her until trial.

The court found this explanation for the DNA evidence unbelievable for three reasons. First, the victim in the defendant's story never checked to see if the defendant was actually type O despite the fact that blood type was so important. Second, until the trial, the defendant didn't remember the woman despite the fact that she was the only woman, by his admission, ever to have asked him to ejaculate inside her. Finally, until the trial, the defendant didn't remember the story about type O blood. The court found the defendant guilty and sentenced him to twelve years' imprisonment.[39]

The court mentioned no other unbelievable parts of the defendant's testimony, leaving the rest of the story unchallenged. It is impossible to determine what the judges were thinking, but it seems likely that the basics of the underlying *deaikei* story—woman posts desire for sex, man meets woman at love hotel, man and woman have sex, man and woman part ways—were simply a familiar storyline. Although *deaikei* can lead to long-term relationships, encounters such as these seem more typical.

Even in these cases, love still arises—sort of. We have seen four mentions of love by courts in this section—that which lay in the hypothetical future for the facially disfigured Hanako, that which Muneo missed because he married the wrong sister, that which Misa's e-mailing husband never expressed, and that which Hiroya denied he had for Sakura, his marriage-introduction-service girlfriend. Unlike the cases from chapter 2, in none of these cases was love central to the ruling; rather, love simply arose in the facts. It is interesting, then, that the times when the court chose to insert it were times in which it was absent, when it was unattainable, or when a person yearned for it. Love in these cases is not necessarily a tragedy, but it isn't characterized as joy, as interconnectedness, or even as particularly desirable.

But let us move beyond this yearning love of courtship. It is marriage that Japanese courts call the "fundamental unit of society,"[40] so perhaps a more satisfying love is available there.

Marriage

Marriage Defined

Love*less* marriage was advocated in Japan as late as the 1970s by several influential commentators. Pediatrician Michio Matsuda's 1970 bestseller *Don't Fall in Love! (Ren'ai Nanka Yameteoke)*, pitched at teenagers, is a classic in the antilove genre. Replete with cartoons and a paternalistic tone ("You probably think that you care for your parents more than anything. But [with love], you care for someone even more! It's strange, isn't it?"),[41] the book takes aim at two related targets: premarital sex and love. After pointing out the dangers of premarital sex (namely, pregnancy), Matsuda argued that:

> Many people who think they must have a "love marriage" think they have some inner flaw. Flawed persons who enter into arranged marriages can be said to have committed marriage fraud, but if the marriage is based on love, those flaws will be revealed and accepted before marriage. Lots of girls who begin menstruating late think they are flawed. This should not be a cause for worry. [Feminist] Hideko Kageyama didn't start until she was 22. Her first period came while she was in prison. She dwelled on that fact so much that she even wrote it in her autobiography. She was able to have children and lead a family life. If you are looking for love thinking that such a thing will be accepted [by your partner] while you are in love, you are mistaken.
>
> The flaw that men think they have is small penis size. This is also an illusory problem and by no means a flaw. Masturbation is completely unrelated as well. What a foolish thing it is for a fifteen- or sixteen-year-old boy to think he is sick and lose self-confidence because he has wet dreams or otherwise involuntarily ejaculates, normal occurrences in boys that age.[42]

In Matsuda's view, then, most of the people who marry for love do so because they do not want their flaws—and note how the flaws that he lists prey on traditional teenage fears of sexual development—to cause them to be accused of fraud. Proper arranged marriage is the only cure.

Matsuda lost that battle. As we have seen, love marriage, or at least marriage that is not formally arranged, is the norm. Yet the benefits of love marriage over arranged marriage in Japan are unclear. A survey from 1965 (when the numbers of love marriages and arranged marriages were roughly equal) of married women aged twenty to fifty-nine found that only 10.7 percent of couples in arranged marriages had active sex lives, compared to 43.9 percent for love marriage, a finding which standing alone would seem to tilt the calculation toward love marriages.[43] But Robert Blood's 1958–59 survey of Japanese couples reveals a more complex picture. Blood interviewed 127 arranged-match couples and 212 love-match couples and asked them to rate their satisfaction levels. Love-match marriages had marginally higher levels of satisfaction for factors like affection, understanding, and companionship, while arranged marriages excelled in structural factors such as financial management and decision making. But when the data were aggregated, "the two systems work almost identically well."[44]

Blood's study also analyzed love in Japanese marriages. Love in love marriages peaks far higher than love in arranged-match marriages. Over time, love in both types of marriages decreases. But the trajectories differ in three respects. First, in arranged marriages, love increases dramatically from engagement until marriage. Second, after five to eight years of marriage, arranged marriages show more love than love-match marriages. But, third, by the ninth year of marriage, spousal opinion splits: arranged-marriage husbands are more in love than love-match husbands, but love-match wives are considerably more in love than their arranged-marriage counterparts. Or so they say.[45]

In Japanese courts, the arranged/love distinction is irrelevant. Marriage is defined by courts in a one-size-fits-all manner as a "mental and physical union of a man and a woman that in the eyes of society can generally be thought of as a marital relationship."[46] The translation to English is not exact: the word for "mental" (*seishinteki*) can also mean emotional or spiritual, and the word for "physical" (*nikutaiteki*) has a connotation of bodily or sexual, but the basic concepts are those of mind and body.

The definition is interesting both for what it includes and for what it omits. Note first two omissions. First, although the Civil Code (art. 739) requires the filing of a marriage registration form at city hall to effect a marriage, the judicial definition requires no filing. Many couples forget to file the form after their marriage ceremony or delay filing for a long time. In the 1910s, 16 to 17 percent of couples fell into this category; the figure now is roughly one in fifty[47] and includes many couples who refuse to file in order to avoid the Civil Code (art. 750) requirement that a married couple choose one surname.[48]

These common-law-like de facto marriages (*naien*) are treated as genuine; the Supreme Court has held that a marriage exists when a "man and a woman fail to file a marriage notification form but cooperate as a married couple in a shared lifestyle, and the relationship can be said to be one in which they share an identity and a lifestyle."[49] Societal views on common-law marriage are complex. In one study, sociologist Masahiro Yamada asked survey participants, "Can this be regarded as family?" with respect to thirty-three kinds of relationships. The data from the marriage-related relationships are presented in figure 3.2.

As the second set of bars show, only 65.5 percent of men and 57.9 percent of women view as family "a man and a woman who have lived together a long time but have not filed a marriage registration notice" (*chōkikan issho ni seikatsu shiteru ga, kon'in no todoke wo shiteinai danjo*). In practice, it might be difficult to determine which couples fall into the category, and as such respondents might have been reacting generally to the idea of unwed cohabitation and not a relationship in which the couple present themselves as married. Still, the requirement of a filing to create a family relationship by more than one-third of respondents suggests that the societal standard for what constitutes a family is higher than the judicial standard for what constitutes a legal marriage.

The survey respondents seem to value love in marriage. Only 41.4 percent of men and 34.0 percent of women viewed as a family "a married couple who live together but feel no love for each other." Contrast this result with another in the survey (not in the figure) regarding a nonmarital relationship: 57.9 percent of men and 73.2 percent of women regarded as family "a pet that is raised with love."[50] A loved pet is more of a family member than a loveless spouse.

That contrast raises the second element that is absent from the judicial definition of marriage: love. A mental, spiritual, or emotional union is required, but not love, a concept that seems just as difficult to determine as a

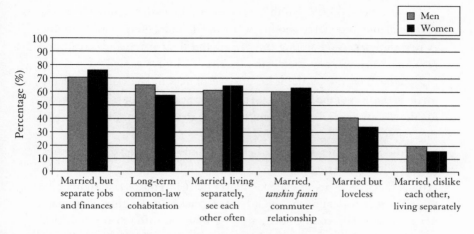

Figure 3.2. Which Can Be Considered a Family Relationship?
Source: Masahiro Yamada, *Kindai Kazoku no Yukue* [The Status of the Modern Family], 30–31 (1994).

mental union but one that Japanese law seems to reserve largely for stalkers and the damned.

Now note the elements the definition includes. First, marriage requires a mental union. Second, marriage requires a physical, sexual union. Third, marriage must be between a man and a woman.[51] Finally, *society* must view the relationship as "marital." Only three U.S. states adopt that final element; Montana, for instance, requires that the couple be "reputed in the community to be husband and wife."[52] Most states that recognize common-law marriage require cohabitation and *presentation* as a married couple, not appearance or reputation, focusing on the intent of the couple.[53]

Japanese courts focus on the last element, social appearances, as they did in the following Intent to Marry case. The case, decided in 1969, is old, but the principles set forth by the Supreme Court in the case remain the foundation of the judicial definition of marriage. Toshihide and Mie met in 1953 in their mid-twenties. They lived together and had a sexual relationship. Mie became pregnant three times but had three abortions because she did not yet have the "capability to create a lifestyle" (*seikatsu nōryoku ga nai tame*) for a child. When she became pregnant a fourth time, she consulted Toshihide, did not have an abortion, and gave birth to a daughter, Koyami. At the time, Toshihide and Mie wanted to marry, but in consideration of Toshihide's parents' objections, they did not.

On October 24, 1959, Toshihide surprised Mie with the announcement that he planned to marry another woman, Chizuko, on the twenty-ninth. A negotiation session among the parties and their parents was held, the result of which was a written oath in which Toshihide agreed (a) to marry Mie on the twenty-seventh for the purpose of making their daughter legitimate in the eyes of the law, and (b) to divorce her "a few days" afterward.[54] On the twenty-seventh, Mie submitted the marriage registration form, and the couple became legally married.[55]

Or did they? After Toshihide held his planned wedding on the twenty-ninth with the other woman, he sued to annul his marriage to Mie on the ground that he had not intended to marry her.[56] His purpose in signing the marriage registration form, he said, was to make his daughter legitimate, not to marry. Mie countersued, arguing that she suffered psychological damage, lacked the education necessary to get a good job, and would be subject to "cold looks" as a single mother—a considerable stigma would have attached in the 1960s.

Return now to the judicial definition of marriage: "a mental and physical union of a man and a woman that in the eyes of society can generally be thought of as a marital relationship." If Toshihide and Mie wed for the purpose of living as a married couple in the eyes of society, with a mental and physical union, the marriage could not be annulled. The Osaka High Court found that they were not a married couple in the eyes of society and granted the annulment.

Mie appealed to the Supreme Court. In her brief, she first pointed out—correctly—that the only relevant statute (Civil Code art. 742) said absolutely nothing about "socially acceptable" marital relationships; it said merely that a marriage "shall be void...if one of the parties has no intention to marry." But her larger argument was that marriage is a "heterogeneous and fluid institution." "Is it possible," she asked, "to draw a bright line that says 'this is a real marriage and 'everything else is not'?...In the end, a judge will simply make an intuitive decision about the questions 'what is or should be required for a marital relationship?'" Those questions, she argued, were a matter of "individual morals, ethics, and religion" and not the place for courts—who were incapable of making the decision based on "objective evidence."

The Supreme Court did not directly address any of those arguments. It held that the parties to a marriage must have "a serious desire to create a relationship that is thought to be that of the common social conception of a marriage." Like the high court, the Supreme Court held that Mie's marriage did not fit the common social conception, and again the marriage was annulled. The Court seemed confident, Mie's objections notwithstanding, that it was capable of determining both the social conception of marriage, or what it *should* be absent statutory guidance, and whether Mie's relationship fit it.[57]

Marital Duties

The social conception of marriage rests in part on spousal duties of cohabitation and cooperation. Spouses in Japan are *required* by law (Civil Code art. 752) to live together, cooperate, and aid each other. Courts have held that the duties exist "as long as a legal marriage continues" unless a spouse has an "appropriate reason" not to perform.[58] Courts in cohabitation cases do not award damages; they simply order delinquent partners to go home, cooperate, or aid.

The cohabitation duty statute was drafted as part of postwar Occupation reforms designed to democratize Japan and instill sexual equality. The concept was rooted in the 1896 Civil Code (art. 789), which required a wife to live with her husband.[59] Instead of abolishing that provision, drafters revised it to make it applicable to both spouses. No longer could a husband legally dictate his wife's abode. As an Occupation official wrote, the provision was designed to open "the door to a settlement of the question of domicile by mutual agreement of the spouses."[60]

But in practice, the cohabitation requirement has not been a tool for wives to have an equal say in where they live; that decision surely is made (or not) without the aid of the courts. Instead, courts have found in the statute the requirement of cohabitation as an essential component of marriage. As one court boldly proclaimed, the "essence" of the cohabitation requirement "derives from the trust inherent in a normal marriage, tied together by mutual understanding, love, and mutual respect."[61] Love, then, as we have seen elsewhere, is the core of a marriage—at least in the abstract. Indeed, some would take the provision further: one proposed revision of the statute would explicitly require spouses to be sexually faithful, respect one another, and protect and educate their children.[62]

The statutory duty has spawned lawsuits that have the somewhat unusual purpose of compelling a spouse to return home against his or her will. If the reluctant spouse's resolve to stay away is "particularly strong," courts usually refuse to order cohabitation even in the absence of other appropriate reasons.[63]

Crucially, cohabitation orders are not enforceable: the reluctant spouse can never be forcibly returned home.[64] So why file? A spouse might file a petition in a divorce case either as a defensive measure to prevent divorce[65] or as an offensive threat to prove malicious abandonment of three years, a listed ground for divorce. Filing statistics reflect this curious usage: two-thirds of cohabitation petitions disposed of in family courts in 2008 were withdrawn.[66]

Victory in cohabitation cases usually requires clean hands. Courts have held that a wife need not return to a paralyzed husband who is violent, a wife need not return to a house full of fighting in-laws and an untrusting husband, and a husband must return to the wife whom he forced to do housework shortly after childbirth.[67]

Consider one case in depth. Tomoko and Ikuo were married in 1968; he was twenty-three; she, twenty-two. They had three daughters. Their relationship was good until 1976, when Tomoko found condoms in Ikuo's car. He admitted only to having dinner with another woman and nothing more. Undaunted, Tomoko went to Ikuo's office to find the person she believed to be the other woman. She was right. She confronted Ikuo again, and he apologized. But Tomoko was unable to forget: whenever they had sex, the court thought it worthy to note, she would see the other woman's face.

Ikuo subsequently moved out and began a *tanshin funin* lifestyle. This "job-induced family separation," or perhaps simply "commuter marriage" situation, is not unusual: the Ministry of Health, Labor, and Welfare reports that 317,000 married people in 2004 were *tanshin funin,* and that 81 percent of companies with more than one thousand employees had a few who were *tanshin funin.*[68] The court does not tell us in this case how Tomoko reacted to Ikuo's move, but it would not be unusual if she readily consented: upon learning of a husband's transfer, 70 percent of Japanese wives hope he will go alone.[69] Most commuter marriage couples (85 percent) choose to separate rather than to move as a family in order to avoid disrupting the education of their school-age children (second place, at 39.6 percent, is taking care of the house).[70]

Ikuo came home three times a month. That frequency is roughly average: government data show that 25.6 percent of commuter husbands return almost every week, 35.9 percent return two or three times a month, and 30.8 percent return once a month.[71] The arrangement works for some couples: in one survey, 36 percent of husbands and 33 percent of wives thought their relationship (*kokoro no tsunagari*) improved while they were apart. Fifty-one percent of husbands and 47 percent of wives saw no change.[72] In Ikuo's case, the court volunteered, the couple's sex life *improved* during his absence.

But then Ikuo made what the court presented as a critical mistake in that department. He had received a vibrator at an end-of-the-year party as a gag gift. He asked Tomoko to use it as part of their sexual routine. She did not like it. According to Tomoko, when she used it, her sexual excitement decreased. She eventually did not want to have sex with Ikuo at all. Ikuo claimed that he had no idea that sex was an issue in their marriage; he claimed to have been perfectly happy with their sex life.

The couple had other problems, such as Tomoko's relationship with her live-in mother-in-law. Ikuo created tension between the two even before the marriage, when he told Tomoko not to tell his mother that she was pregnant on their wedding day. After his father died, his mother directed negative comments toward Tomoko; among other passive-aggressive barbs, she once told Ikuo in Tomoko's presence, "Since you've got a wife, there's no place for me."

The relationship worsened when Tomoko found fecal matter in the bath after Ikuo's mother had bathed. Ikuo claimed the bits of matter were the size of rice. Tomoko claimed they were as large as raisins. Tomoko asked Ikuo to approach his mother about this, and he responded by saying, "How can a person say such a thing to a parent?" and kicking her. (Eventually he relented, the court explained, and told his mother to be careful to wash very thoroughly in the shower before entering the tub.)

In 1992, Tomoko began working an hour or two a night at a barbecue restaurant. The owner was a former classmate of both Tomoko and Ikuo; he socialized with both and had a wife and two children. Soon Tomoko began to have "good feelings" (*kōkan*) about him. She thought, the court stated, that unlike Ikuo, he had a "masculine, unaffected personality" (*otokorashiku sappari shita seikaku*). Even after she stopped working there, she continued to bring flowers for display.

In 1995, Tomoko and the restaurateur went on a drive. The drive led to sex. Tomoko told the court that "it was the first fulfilling sex I ever had." Ikuo became suspicious of Tomoko's absence and confronted her. She confessed to the deed but not to the identity of her lover. Ikuo told her to "break it off with him," but she told him she could not. When she telephoned her lover to tell him of the conversation with her husband, Ikuo overheard and learned that the mystery lover was the restaurant owner. Ikuo confronted him, and the lover apologized.

Tomoko wanted to leave home. Ikuo told her that if she left, she would need to explain her departure to their children, who were then sixteen, twenty-five, and twenty-seven years old. She had hoped to stay until the youngest daughter finished high school, but she became scared of her husband when he learned her lover's identity. She left, got an apartment, and continued to see her lover for a few months until Ikuo filed suit against him for taking his wife. The two men settled out of court, with the condition that the lover never see Tomoko again.

Ikuo was left with his lung-cancer-ridden seventy-nine-year-old mother and his three daughters. He could not sleep well and became addicted to sleeping pills. The daughters were bitter. The oldest told Tomoko that "adultery is unforgivable." When Tomoko called on the telephone, the middle daughter told her, "You want a divorce, don't you? Don't call here anymore." The youngest daughter became a shoplifter: she stole pencils from the supermarket on her way home from school, an act for which her school gave her a two-week suspension.

Ikuo petitioned for an order of cohabitation. Before we examine the court's ruling, just look at these facts. With the help of the parties, the court constructed a voyeuristic, packaged account of the marriage and the affair. It started the story's clock long before Tomoko's affair and it ended it long after her departure. Many of the details—the fecal matter in the bathtub, the vibrator, the stolen pencils—seem wholly irrelevant to the holding. Yet the court provided them anyway and did not distinguish them from the seemingly more relevant facts, such as kicking one's spouse. The sense emerges that it all matters; all of it is necessary to explain the demise of the relationship. The court has no reservations about examining the tangentially related details of intimate life.

Two courts looked at those facts and came to opposite conclusions. The trial court found that the marriage was destroyed. With little legal analysis (did it need it after all those facts?), it held that Tomoko had no legal duty to return home. Ikuo appealed. The Tokyo High Court then reversed with equally sparse analysis; it seems that it simply disagreed with the district court's interpretation of the facts. In a short opinion, it ruled that Tomoko needed a rational reason to leave home and found that her husband's discovery of her adultery was not a rational reason. Ikuo, the court said, was trying to put the marriage back together, and as such it could not be said conclusively that the relationship was destroyed and had no chance of success.[73]

Importantly, the court made no mention of the quality of the relationship or the strong emotions that must have been present in the situation. The court considered many detailed facts and could have relied on them to make a statement about the quality of the marriage. But the judges chose to focus their rhetoric on the discovery of adultery. The conclusion was simple: a spouse does not have the right to leave just because his or her adultery is discovered.

The lack of legal exposition by both courts makes it difficult to determine if a universal message is intended. But if the high court is saying anything broader about relationships, it seems to be saying that a little adultery should not trump the legal institution of marriage. For a reason why, all one must examine is the insomniac pill-popping Ikuo and his family, the lung-cancer mother and the three bitter daughters, one of whom seems to be on the road to a life of crime. The lower court's analysis of those facts led to a different conclusion, but it saw some need to tell that part of the story nonetheless. Absent in the story, of course, is that which seemed important in the previous chapter: an analysis of emotion.

In any case, Tomoko must now return home.

"Marriage" Applied

To determine whether a relationship fits the judicial definition of marriage as a mental and physical union in the eyes of society, courts often examine specific factors, and sometimes they simply ignore the definition altogether and use those factors instead. Before turning to these factors, consider the social context for one factor judges *might* consider but don't, at least when analyzing particular relationships: love.

The popular magazine *Wedding Walker* lists six sample marriage vows for putatively blissful soon-to-be-wed couples.[74] One is specifically for weddings that take place when the bride is pregnant: "We promise...to strive to work together to make each of our lives better as the three of us live happily." Two other vows are said to be "original." The first: "two years ago, we met at an advertising agency, where we had a senior-junior relationship, and now we promise to succeed, basing our lives on this new project, combining our strengths to create a happy home." The second: "I, Tarō, promise to take my wife, Hanako, skiing in Karuizawa on our anniversary every year, to avoid whining and moaning the day after my favorite baseball team loses, and to moderate my weekend golf. I, Hanako, promise to save money so that we can stay in a suite in a gorgeous hotel, to greet Tarō with a smile on my face when he comes home late from drinking, and to moderate my purchases of brand-name handbags."

The list also includes three "basic" samples. In the first of the three, the couple pledges to "trust, respect, and help" one another. In the second, the couple promises to create a "bright, fun home, never forgetting to have a heart full of kindness and thanks." Only the third mentions love; the spouses agree to "continue loving so as to overcome any obstacles."

The absence of a promise to love in marriage fits well with the conception of marriage that seems pervasive in Japan. Consider first the description by feminist sociologist Chizuko Ueno:

> Japanese couples get married for the institution and not out of romantic love. [They] go into marriage with very low expectations of romantic or sexual satisfaction. They choose the institution of marriage because of the material advantages it offers them. They secure their lives financially and socially with a good match.[75]

Survey data concur. A 1990 corporate-sponsored survey asked Japanese and Americans to rate on a scale from "not at all important" to "very important" thirteen different conditions for marriage, including "being in love," "keeping romance alive," "having a good sexual relationship," and "having similar ideas on how to raise children." The data are separated by sex. The only condition that Japanese women found more important than U.S. women was "financial security" (66 percent for Japanese, 63 percent for U.S. women). The only condition that Japanese men found more important than U.S. men was "having children," and the difference was statistically insignificant (44 percent for Japan, 41 percent for the United States). Every other condition was rated as very important by a higher percentage of Americans than Japanese, suggesting that Japanese expect less out of marital relationships in general.

More striking differences emerge regarding particular characteristics of marriage. The condition of "being in love" was rated very important by 87 percent of U.S. women and 84 percent of U.S. men but only 68 and 67 percent of Japanese women and men, respectively. If those percentages for Japan still sound high given the court cases, consider that "keeping romance alive" was rated very important by 78 percent of U.S. women and 76 percent of U.S. men, but only 29 and 30 percent of Japanese. And "having a good sexual relationship" was rated very important by 72 and 74 percent of U.S. women and men, respectively, but only 38 percent of Japanese women and men.[76]

When asked in a 2005 Japanese government survey what the benefits of marriage are, "living with someone I love" came in third for both women (21%) and men (17%), behind "having children and a family" (45% for women, 33% for men) and "having a place where I can feel at ease" (32% for women, 36% for men). Fourth place was "fulfilling the wishes of my family and others" (16% for women, 13% for men), just slightly behind love.[77]

The wedding vows, the academic commentary, and the survey data correlate to judges' stated views on love in marriage. One retired Japanese judge writes that when a family court mediator decides whether to recommend divorce to a couple, the decision should be based on the basic human needs of "food" (*shoku*) and "sex" (*sei*). "Of course," he writes, "the nest, the place to live, is important too, but the foundation is food and sex." The food concern is economic: a mediator should, he writes, consider how the parties and their children will eat after the separation. As for sex, the mediator should ask, "How is the sexual relationship between the parties, and is there any chance of restoring that relationship?"[78] He mentions no other factors.

We have seen how courts define marriage to require a union of mind and body in the eyes of society. In many cases, courts ignore that definition, or pay lip service to the first element, and focus instead on specific elements of a putative marriage to determine whether it fits the social conception. Consider a case from 1987 in which a man sued the government for Japanese citizenship. The man was born in wartime Shanghai to a Japanese father (and soldier), Haruo, and a Chinese mother, Haruko. Haruo and Haruko held a wedding ceremony in December 1941, but they never submitted a marriage registration form, and they kept their marriage secret from family and coworkers whom they expected would oppose the marriage. Seven months after the plaintiff was born to Haruko in 1942, Haruo legally married a Japanese woman, Takeko.

To receive Japanese citizenship, the plaintiff needed to establish that his mother, Haruko, and his Japanese father had a common-law marriage before his father married Takeko. The court easily found such an arrangement: the wedding ceremony and the time they spent living together (secretly) thereafter established a common-law marriage. Although the couple clearly had a sexual relationship (from which the plaintiff was born), the court did not mention it.[79]

Gone is the definition from the Intent to Marry case earlier in this chapter that a couple appear to be married in the eyes of society, though perhaps the photos of and testimony regarding the ceremony and the postceremony dinner were sufficient evidence of that. Sex, the physical connection, was irrelevant or at least not mentioned (but on this point, the fact of the plaintiff's birth is informative). An emotional connection appeared nowhere, and love, of course, was nonexistent. In this case, a wedding and living together were sufficient.

Other cases, such as the following one from 1993, suggest that something more is necessary than a wedding, cohabitation, and sex to establish a marriage. Yuri was a dental hygienist living in Sendai. In 1984, at the age of twenty-three, she became involved with the Unification Church. In August of that year, she devoted her life to the church. She quit her job and began selling cosmetics for the church. Her family strongly opposed the church and even consulted the police over how they could keep her at home.

In October 1988, Yuri decided to marry in a mass wedding ceremony conducted by the church at its home base in Korea. She applied to the church for marriage, and the church matched her with the defendant, Nobuhito, a man seven years her senior from Okinawa. A few days before the wedding, each learned the other's name, age, place of birth, and blood type.

Travel snafus made Yuri late for the wedding ceremony. Nobuhito participated in the ceremony (along with 6,500 other couples) by holding Yuri's picture. The couple subsequently took a formal wedding picture, exchanged rings, and moved into a church commune in Korea in which men and women slept separately.

A month later, they returned to their hometowns in Japan. Yuri then learned of the church's requirement of a "consecration period": Yuri and Nobuhito were required to spend three to three and one-half years living separately. Yuri was disconcerted by the news but filed the marriage registration form in Okinawa anyway at the church's insistence. Legally married, the two then returned to their respective churches.

Six months later, the church told the couple they would not officially be married in the eyes of the church until they completed a three-day consummation ceremony. They went to a hotel where they had sex according to church-mandated procedures. (The court did not provide details about the procedures, but the Church's website explains that in the Three-Day Ceremony "the wife gives rebirth to her husband from the position of mother and then receives him in the position of wife. Then in the position of father, the husband gives rebirth to his wife and receives her in the position of husband."[80]) The couple then separated to continue the consecration period. A year later, Yuri left the church, and she filed for an annulment.

The Fukuoka District Court needed to decide if the parties had the intent to marry at the time that they filed the marriage registration form. Intent to marry, the court said, could be determined (of course) by the "mental and physical connection of a man and a woman that represents a marriage relationship in the eyes of society." The court also cited Supreme Court precedent that required that the parties have "a serious will to create a relationship that reflects the common social conception of a marriage" and that the relationship must be "recognized as a marriage according to social thought."[81]

To determine how Japanese society defined marriage, the court first examined the wedding ceremony. Yuri and Nobuhito's ceremony looked a lot like the Japanese version, said the court, as it included a wedding dress, vows, rings, and photographs (all things that are relatively new to Japan).[82] But the "consecration period" had no Japanese parallel. Nor were Yuri and Nobuhito living together or supporting each other. They had sex, which fits the social conception of marriage (and the judicial definition), but their sex was part of a three-day religious ritual, which had no Japanese parallel. Accordingly, the court found that the two were never married.

That ruling says nothing about a mental connection. But on the way to its conclusion, the court made a passing glance in love's direction. In its examination of the consecration period, the court noted that "because a marriage is based on the love of a man and a woman, it is only natural that feelings could change [during the period]." That the court mentions love here suggests that it easily could have included it in its analysis of marriage, and yet it did not. In fact, the court's pronouncement that it is "only natural" that feelings of love could change seems to express skepticism of love's staying power. Granted, the court is talking about a three-year period of separation. A change of feelings in that period of time might not be unusual, especially if love is expected to be the intense emotion we saw in the previous chapter. But it bears noting that the court raised the ideal of marital love only to strike it down. The social conception of marriage, then, is not (fleeting) love or (three-day) sex, but living together and supporting each other as society expects.[83]

These social expectations and conceptions are not static. Recent lawsuits that reflect changing norms have forced courts to struggle with the decision of whether to extend legal protection of marriage to relationships that vary from traditional social expectations. Consider Masao and Shizuka's case, decided in 2004. The couple met through a marriage introduction agency in November 1985, when Shizuka was a college senior. They became engaged in December and planned to marry in March.

The couple's speed from dating to marriage is not unusual for relationships that begin through marriage introduction agencies. But in this case a glitch arose. Before the new year came, the couple decided not to marry after all. The couple sent postcards to their friends to explain their situation: "Because we are very important to each other, we have decided that we will live so close that the soup won't get cold as one of us travels to the other's home, and deepen our relationship as 'significant others' [*tokubetsu na tanin*]."

In April 1986, Masao and Shizuka moved closer to each other and visited often. But as the court pointed out, "neither had a key to the other's house, neither spent the night, and their living arrangements were completely separate." Still, they appear to have been quite close in other ways. Masao wanted children, and he and Shizuka had a daughter in June 1990. They married on that day—but only for the purpose of making the child legitimate. They divorced three months later. In 1993, the couple had a son—and again, they married on the child's birthday. This time, they divorced only four days later. Masao and his mother raised the two children. Shizuka was not a major presence in their lives.

After the children were born, the couple's relationship became rocky. Once they did not see each other for six months. Masao was violent sometimes; he once smashed Shizuka's door. But the relationship continued. The couple took trips together. Masao generously gathered class materials for Shizuka, who, by 2001, was an assistant professor at a university. She taught gender theory.

Masao then met another woman and began a sexual relationship with her. He decided to end his sixteen-year "significant other" relationship with Shizuka and marry the other woman. He told Shizuka, and she sued him for $50,000. She lost in the lower courts and appealed to the Supreme Court.

The couple clearly did not have a common-law marriage under the law. They were not a married couple in the eyes of society, and as we have seen, the filing of a marriage registration form solely to establish paternity does not show intent to marry. But should the law protect their relationship, dubbed by the court a "partnership relationship," nonetheless?

In Shizuka's favor, the Supreme Court noted that the couple took trips together and had two children. But the couple did not live together, share daily lives, or share finances. The two brief marriages were conducted solely for the sake of the children, and the couple had no agreement to marry in the future. The Court expressed empathy with Shizuka; it stated that it understood Shizuka's "dissatisfaction" (*fuman*) with Masao's decision to marry someone else. But it found no legal ground on which to award damages.[84]

Note the Court's reliance on the absence of a legal factor—agreement to marry—to dismiss Shizuka's claim. The fact that the couple actually *did* marry—twice—was not considered. The children, reliable evidence of sex if nothing else, were unimportant. What mattered instead were the public partnership factors of living together, daily life, finances, and trips.

And what of love? In this case as in others in this chapter, it appears that despite the decline of arranged marriages and rise of love marriages, love and marriage remain separate. It's not that courts don't talk about love. Courts have little problem in discussing, and even determining the existence of, love, especially if it is tragic, as in chapter 2, or unattainable, as in the cases of matching from the beginning of this chapter, or the mention lacks meaning, as in the court's description of the essence of the duty to cohabitate. But in most court opinions that discuss or define marriage (or something like it) in a particular case, love is noticeably absent from the analysis. Judges have the discursive freedom to raise the issue, but they choose not to do so.

It's unclear why love or other forms of intimacy are absent in any specific case. As always, there is the possibility that the opinions merely reflect the cultures in which the judges were raised, and we have seen some evidence (such as wedding vows) that supports that correlation. But perhaps, at least in marriage, the causation is more clear: perhaps the facts of cases are so clearly governed by specific legal duties that emotions do not affect the court's decision and therefore their analysis is unnecessary. Marriage (and its demise) simply is the one expression of adult love that the state explicitly regulates, and it does so in regulatory language.

Yet two factors suggest that this explanation is incomplete if not downright false. First, we have seen emotions, even love, arise in other legalistic contexts, such as the definition of stalking. Second, sometimes love *does* arise in marriage cases. As in the Unification Church case (or in the Child Predator case), when courts speak in the abstract, they note that "marriage is based on the love of a man and a woman," strongly suggesting that love matters. But the phrase is a formulaic platitude that is not directly applied to the real people who appear in court.

The issue, then, is not that courts raise love but the way in which they raise it. The vision that emerges from the use of love in the cases is one in which closeness and mutual affection in long-term relationships are desired but unattainable. But perhaps—again—we're looking in the wrong places. Perhaps a more less tragic, more realizable emotional intimacy is connected with the physical intimacy that is the subject of the next chapter.

4

PRIVATE SEX

Hitoshi and Hanako began their arranged marriage in September 1987; it was the second marriage for each. They divorced nine months later. Hitoshi filed suit against Hanako and her mother. According to the court's recitation of Hitoshi's complaint:

> From the time of their honeymoon until their separation, Hitoshi and Hanako did not have sex even once. When Hitoshi would ask, Hanako would refuse, saying that she was tired or on her period. Her refusal reached such a level in mid-September 1987 that she raised her voice, saying, "No!," "I hate that!" and "If we have to do that, I'll break up with you! I won't do such a thing!" She stared at Hitoshi scarily and once hit him in the arm.... When Hitoshi said, "All married couples have sex," she said, "that's other people, not us." Because Hanako had had two eye surgeries and might lose her sight if she were hit, Hitoshi never was violent toward her.
>
> When Hitoshi said, "Married couples everywhere do it," Hanako scoffed, "If you know I wouldn't let you do it, would you not have married me?"

It's unclear why Hanako refused sex. This was her second marriage, so it seems safe to assume that she at least knew what the expectations would be.

Menstruation was sufficient to keep Hitoshi at arm's length for a while. But one day in January, Hanako cried to Hitoshi:

"I hate you. I want to kill you and then I want to die. But I can't do that because Mom will be sad. This marriage is my fault. So I'll cook your meals. I'll clean and do the laundry for you. You're screwed if we break up, aren't you? You want to succeed, don't you? I'll keep up appearances for you. My body just is what it is. From now on, we'll sleep separately. I don't want you to touch me at all. I can't even sleep in the same room with you. I can't love you [*mō aisuru koto nanka deninken*]," and from that day forward they slept in separate rooms and spoke only when necessary. Whenever Hitoshi tried to approach her, even if she was in the middle of watching television, she would stand up, go to her room, and yell things like, "Get out!" staring at him ominously. She would not let him in. This lifestyle was not normal for a married couple.

"Normal" or otherwise, it appears that Hanako would have been satisfied with some version of their lifestyle. It is unclear why *she* wanted to stay in the marriage, but her claim that Hitoshi would be unsuccessful as a twice-divorced man might make some sense in Japan's social system. When the Ministry of Health (which, as by now should be clear, really cares about love, sex, and marriage) asked single people ages thirty-three to forty-nine to name the positive aspects of marriage, 28 percent of men and 32 percent of women said that marriage would allow them to receive trust in society.[1] Similarly, as Merry White has noted, some employers "urge young male employees to marry as soon as possible as an indication of their own seriousness of purpose and willingness to take on adult commitments."[2] A second divorce by Hitoshi might cause him to lose social trust and to appear less mature.

Three months after they married, Hanako's mother heard the couple fighting. In earshot of Hitoshi, the mother sighed, "This is just like it was with her last husband." Hitoshi then learned that Hanako did not have sex with her first husband, either, and that he had sued her successfully for $10,000 over it. There was no physical reason for her refusal; Hiroshi learned that she had visited an obstetrician who found nothing wrong other than the fact that "considering her age, she was psychologically childish."

Hitoshi raised the issue with his mother-in-law. When he said, "I at least want to be able to show my parents their grandchildren's faces," she said, "that's just your ego talking." She continued: "Just because you don't have that in your marriage doesn't mean that you're not a couple. There are couples out there that don't do it. I know two couples like that. You just don't know many people. I didn't know that you were such a cold-hearted person."

In her defense, Hanako claimed that Hitoshi was still in love with his first wife, that his salary was inadequate, and that he became angry whenever she refused to have sex. She said nothing about the frequency or reasons for her refusal.

Writing in 1991, the Okayama District Court awarded Hitoshi $15,000, saying, "It is common sense that an important goal in marriage is the raising of children, and it follows that sex between husband and wife should normally accompany a working marriage. For the parties to have feelings of expectation of this is natural and extremely reasonable." The court denied a claim Hiroshi brought against Hanako's mother for pushing the marriage, saying that at ages thirty-one and twenty-seven, the couple's decision to marry was their own.[3]

Some of the facts of the case are odd. Perhaps Hanako had an undiagnosed illness or a traumatic past. Ignore the oddities and focus on two of the court's assumptions. First, the court ignored one feeling, Hanako's claim of Hitoshi's anger, in favor of another, the "natural" expectation of sex. It presumably gave some of the details of the story, such as the conversation with the mother, to show how strange the situation was. In so doing, it revealed its assumption that sex is a part of marriage—an entirely unsurprising assumption, but one that is at least notable given cases in the previous chapter that suggested a noncrucial role for sex in marriage. But, second, the court also assumed that the *reason* for sex in marriage is reproduction. The court could have used any number of justifications for the "common sense" notion that sex is part of marriage, but it chose reproduction.

In this chapter, I want to look more closely at these assumptions and others of the Japanese judiciary regarding consensual sex, assumptions they reveal as they carefully investigate very personal, private matters. I first examine what courts label as "common sense" notions of appropriate sexual practices, which often are conservative and almost always involve a substitution of the parties' view of appropriateness with that of the court.

I then examine what kinds of people are appropriate sexual partners. In some cases, judges find certain partners to be wholly inappropriate, findings they announce even without being required to do so. In other cases, judges protect fragile females, but they make surprising concessions to would-be suitors if those men display the requisite emotions. Finally, I look at normal, assumed birth control practices, focusing on the widespread use of abortion. In these cases, judges do not moralize; they seem completely oblivious to the underlying ideas their stories reveal. In all of these cases, judges conduct thorough investigations of sexual practices, emotions, and relationships, and they often seem less than thrilled with their findings.

Before turning to these topics, though, consider some data. In a 2005 survey (sponsored by a condom manufacturer but conducted by a prominent research firm), Japan ranked dead last—forty-first out of forty-one countries—in frequency of sex, with a self-reported frequency of 45 times per year (up from 36 times per year in 2001). The second lowest country, Singapore, was far ahead (73 times per year), and the global average was 103.[4] In another survey, the percentage of Japanese respondents who had sex once a week, 34 percent, was also last in the world.[5] The percentage of Japanese who are "satisfied" with their sex lives is 15 percent, far below every country in the survey.[6] The first sexual partner for more than half of men over 30 is a prostitute,[7] and 13.1 percent of Japanese men report having been to a prostitute in the past year.[8]

Perhaps judges base their "sense of society" on data such as these. The lack of sex as seen in the data is at least consistent with the picture that emerges of consensual sex in court opinions, especially in marriage: it is a shameful, male-dominated, puritanical duty. That's not a very exciting conclusion, but that's part of the point. Courts routinely and matter-of-factly decide issues of intimate life, areas we might ordinarily think to be beyond the law's reach. When they do so—when they distinguish the normal from the abnormal—they implicitly express a vision of Lovesick Japan.

Normal Sex

Which sex practices are acceptable in Japan, and which are not? May a spouse refuse sex? How should a court handle a fetish?

Answers to these questions appear in two kinds of Japanese court opinions: opinions about nonconsensual sex, and opinions about divorce. I have divided the cases into those areas of law instead of types of sexual activity in part because what a judge describes as normal in one legal context (marriage) might be abnormal in another (rape). But as we will see, judges often compare cases across contexts, blurring the lines.

Lessons From Nonconsensual Sex

The Japanese Supreme Court has not yet reached consensus regarding what a man finds, or should find, sexy about a woman, but it has framed a case in such a way that the question arose. In a 2008 case, a thirty-one-year-old Self-Defense Forces member stood accused of taking eleven pictures of a twenty-seven-year-old fully clothed woman's buttocks with his cell phone camera. He took the photos from several meters away in a shopping center. A Hokkaido ordinance specifically prohibited "peeping" at or taking photos of underwear and the like. The ordinance also prohibited "obscene [*hiwai*] conduct" in a public place that would cause another person "extreme embarrassment or unease."[9] Obscene conduct is "acts or words that violate sexual morality in the eyes of society."

The defendant prevailed at the district court but was convicted in the high court and fined $3,000. He appealed to the Supreme Court.

The result was unexciting: the Court found that his conduct was obscene, and he lost. But a lone dissenting justice, Mutsuo Tahara, had a competing view that was less grounded in the statutory language. According to Justice Tahara, a person might have nonsexual reasons to photograph a woman's buttocks. A person might, for instance, admire the beauty of the lines of a woman's body, or he might look at the muscles of a woman's buttocks if she were an athlete. Besides, the Justice reasoned:

> In a Japanese dictionary (*Kōjien,* 6th ed.), "obscene" is defined as "being filthy and indecent; being vulgar or dirty," and it is understood to mean rudeness or coarseness with respect to sex or excretion. If one considers that [the victim] was clothed, the "buttocks" [*denbu*] themselves are far less sexual than a crotch or a woman's breasts. Also, they are not directly connected to excretion.[10]

There is much to unpack there. Most fascinating for our purposes, Justice Tahara has unwittingly provided a list of various body parts ranked by their sexiness: crotch, then breasts, then—far lower—buttocks. (Is he also implying that the order might differ if the victim disrobed?) He might have derived these examples from the typical surreptitious photography scenario in which those body parts are often a target. But there was no legal or rhetorical basis for the statement. Many people might agree with his sexy ranking, but did this vision of normality need to be revealed in an official statement of the country's highest court?

That case of nonconsensual sexual activity is somewhat unusual in that it involved no physical contact. Compare abnormal nonconsensual photography to nonconsensual hugs and kisses, which arise in sexual harassment cases. In a 1997 Tokyo High Court case, the defendant "tried to embrace [the victim], putting his arms around her shoulders." The court held that the "touching was not persistent and we cannot say that this was an illegal act that exceeded socially acceptable norms." Why? Because even though the victim "felt displeasure," she "casually broke free" of him.[11] The Tokyo District Court reached a similar result in a 2004 case. Although that court found that the defendant boss sexually harassed his victim by slow dancing with her on a karaoke outing, it ruled there was no harassment when, as practice for a work-related trip to Europe, he placed his hand on her back to demonstrate that a hug [*hagu*] is a form of greeting in Europe (but not in Japan).[12]

If a European hug is fine, how about a kiss? Yotarō picked up Hiroko in his car. He put his left hand on her right shoulder (the steering wheel is on the right in Japan). When she did not resist, he pulled over, put his right hand on her left shoulder, and "pressed his lips to hers for a few seconds," after which he pulled away. She got out of the car. Prosecutors charged Yotarō with "indecent acts" undertaken by "violence or threat" (Penal Code art. 176). Supreme Court precedent states that an act is indecent if it would "cause an ordinary person sexual embarrassment or shame and violate healthy sexual morals."[13]

Yotarō was convicted under that standard. He appealed to the high court, lost again, and appealed to the Supreme Court. Presumably in the name of uniformity, the Court, writing in 1975, conducted a thorough analysis of three high court opinions that had found kisses to be indecent acts. It found that those cases had four common elements: the lack of a preexisting relationship, irresistible force, lack of consent, and an underlying theory that the lack of those factors would make a kiss "decent" in light of all the circumstances. It was those factors that distinguish an "indecent" kiss from "a kiss between parent and child, or between children."

The court applied those factors to Yotarō's case: he already knew Hiroko, he kissed her only briefly in such a way that she was able to resist further contact, and she showed signs of consent by getting into his car and letting him hold her hand. In such a situation, the Court pronounced, an ordinary person would not feel sexual embarrassment or shame. It overturned Yotarō's conviction. The Court also editorialized about consensual kissing in general:

> In a situation in which a man and a woman share a kiss for purposes of sexual satisfaction, even when the woman gives tacit consent, resistance may arise to some extent based on her shyness or embarrassment. To overcome the resistance, the man will of course [*tōzen*] use some degree of force by the very nature of the act. It therefore cannot be said that every such case is an indecent act that is contrary to a healthy sense of society. Especially given the relatively short history of the custom of kissing in Japan as an act for sexual satisfaction, such cases are likely to be numerous.[14]

Kissing indeed has a short history in Japan. Before the "kiss debate" that began in 1947 over the appropriateness of the act, kissing was considered by many to be "unhygienic, unaesthetic and culturally inappropriate."[15] Kissing became more popular following the Allied Occupation, as authorities encouraged kissing, most visibly in films, as a way of promoting democracy and its underlying ideals. Kissing was a sign of love, an indication of the decline of the patriarchal household system, and a romantic subtext that contrasted starkly with wartime ideology.[16]

I don't know how much osculatory experience these particular judges had, but a timeline offers some clues. The youngest judge on the panel, Justice Shigemitsu Dandō, was a criminal law scholar born in 1913. According to his autobiography, his 1940 marriage was deftly arranged: a former Supreme Court justice and criminal law scholar introduced him to his wife, Yoshiko, whose grandfather, unsurprisingly, was also a criminal law scholar.[17] In 1947, then, the year the national "kiss debate" began and a year after the first Japanese on-screen kiss,[18] Dandō was a thirty-four-year-old full professor at the University of Tokyo who had been married to Yoshiko for seven years. The other four justices, on whom we lack personal information, were between six and seven years older than Dandō, putting them in their forties during the kiss debate. These justices would have been too old to make effective use of the Occupation's dating lessons described by Mark McLelland:

> [A]lthough in the American context, young men and women would gradually have learned the body language and emotional cues appropriate to dating and making out through trial and error from their low teens, in Japan in the early postwar period, young men and women had to have practices such as dating, walking arm in arm, kissing, petting and other techniques of love making explained to them in detail.[19]

Despite the fact that the judges came along a bit too late to get the lessons, or perhaps because of the fact that they might have lacked experience, they seem to have a specific kissing scenario in mind. It is natural for the woman to resist a bit. It is natural for the man to press forward anyway, as she really does not intend to resist; she is just shy. And it is natural for kisses to be difficult to interpret. The court's narrative voice assumes away all other possibilities, all the joys and awkwardness and playfulness of a kiss, into a story in which men use a bit of force—a theme that extends past the 1975 ruling.

Hugs and kisses, then, seem to be acceptable even if the hugee or kissee does not fully consent. If the recipient consents, hugs and kisses would surely be seen as normal. But what if the parties proceed further, to nonconsensual intercourse?

The Japanese Penal Code's rape provision (art. 177) states that "a person who, through violence or intimidation, has sexual intercourse with a female person of not less than thirteen (13) years of age commits the crime of rape and shall be punished with imprisonment at forced labor for a limited term of not less than two years. The same shall apply to a person who has sexual intercourse with a female person under thirteen (13) years of age." Supreme Court precedent requires that the violence or intimidation must be such that it makes it "remarkably [or significantly] difficult" for the victim to resist.[20]

Some urban myths about when sex is not rape—all false and with no discernible source in the law—have arisen in Japan. One common myth is that a man cannot be prosecuted for a sex-related crime if, when he kisses a woman, her back is not physically touching a wall. Another is that rape does not occur if a man places a handkerchief under the woman. And in a 2006 rape case, the defendant based his actions on another myth when he incorrectly informed his rape victim that "if I put it in, it's a crime, so *you* put it in."[21] These myths correlate with a legal regime that looks primarily at the degree to which a woman can resist violence: a woman can easily resist if her back is not against the wall, if she allows the man time to lay down a handkerchief, and if she is in charge of penetration.

Japan's force-based rape regime stands in sharp contrast to the U.S. system, in which rape historically has been defined as "carnal knowledge of a woman forcibly and against her will."[22] With exceptions to be sure,[23] the modern trend is to focus on nonconsent and downplay the element of force. Some jurisdictions go so far as to require an affirmative expression of consent. Japan, however, has no consent-based standard, and in its absence courts must find ways to measure whether violence or intimidation "is remarkably difficult to resist."[24]

To see how that standard works, consider a 2008 Osaka District Court case involving a fourteen-year-old girl and a twenty-four-year-old male defendant. The victim's age is a nonissue; as the statute above shows, statutory rape does not apply to a fourteen-year-old girl.

The court explicitly stated that the girl did *not* consent to sex. Instead of looking at consent, the court (properly) interpreted the statutory language. To determine whether the defendant's violence or intimidation were "remarkably difficult" to resist under the law, the court examined the facts both before and after the date during which the rape allegedly occurred. It noted that the girl "prior to this incident, had experience dating men, and had experience kissing," and that before the date she "applied make up, changed clothes, and took a bath." It stated that during the date, "the defendant asked her if she would date [*tsukiau*, a question that is frequently a prerequisite for physical contact] him. She agreed, and accordingly it would not have been unnatural for the defendant to think that sex was allowed." Immediately before intercourse, "in order to lower her resistance, the defendant told her 'I won't go all the way and put it in' [*ireru made ha seehen*]," which indicated that her resistance was lowered by means *other* than force—it was lowered by his *words*. Finally, the court opined that the girl "did not cry either before or after the intercourse," "said, 'Stop' [*yamete*] in a voice loud enough only for the defendant to hear and not in a shouting voice to show resistance," and "held on to her pants loosely when they were removed and did not hold on to her underwear when it was removed."

The court determined that the violence was not sufficiently difficult to resist. It found him not guilty, despite the acknowledged absence of consent. It offered a final bit of moral education, though: "it is clear that as a human being the defendant should reflect deeply" on his "socially inappropriate acts" [*shakaiteki ni ha fusōtō na kōi*] of "having sex in a parked car on a public road with a fourteen-year-old junior high school student who he just met the previous day."[25]

I have no argument with that. But what is curious is the way in which the court determined that the force was remarkably difficult to resist. Some of the cited facts are amazingly irrelevant to the ruling. The girl had kissed—perhaps unusual for a Japanese fourteen-year-old but certainly not a fact relevant to the rape. Taking a bath seems of marginal relevance at best. A lack of tears tells us little about rape. And yet to this court, these bits of information mattered, as a victim of nonconsensual sex presumably should be a pure, upset stranger.

Absent a consent standard, in determining a victim's ability to resist, courts sometimes take an odd tack: they compare the facts of the rape to actions that may occur during typical consensual sex. In so doing, the court provides information on what "typical" sex is. Consider three cases that made such a comparison.

In the first case, the defendant, a Mr. Tsutsumi, met his alleged victim at a seaside resort and volunteered to walk her to the train station. He put his hand on her shoulder for fifty to sixty meters of the walk, and she did not resist. She walked with him through the forest for three hundred meters.

The court examined the hand and the walk through the lens of consent. It found that her actions "defied common sense" and that it "would not be unnatural to believe that she gave tacit consent to intercourse" through her actions.

But that was only an introduction to the statutory analysis of resistance. Once in the forest, Tsutsumi tried to hug the victim, grabbed her by the neck, and shoved her to the ground. He pulled off her underwear, mounted her, and had intercourse with her. Her injuries to her arm, back, and anus required three days to heal.

The court found that the victim's statement of these actions was "a vague, abstract description of a level of activity that would normally accompany intercourse." More specifically, "Mere grabbing by the neck, pushing down, mounting, and pulling off underwear are things that occur during regular intercourse and do not always rise to the level of rape." Tsutsumi was found not guilty.[26]

That 1959 case admittedly might reflect dated views, but it remains representative of the ways in which courts compare consensual sex to rape. Ten years later, the Hiroshima District Court provided more commentary on what acts occur during "regular" intercourse. In that case, the defendant knew the victim because they stayed at the same long-term hotel. One night, he came to her room, asked, "Aren't you lonely?" and entered the room without her consent. They had sex, and she claimed it was rape.

The court first noted that the woman did not scream; the walls were thin, so someone would have heard her if she had. Her resistance thus was insufficient for rape. But more important, "the defendant embraced her, pushed her down, pressed her right arm with his body and held her left arm, pulled off her underwear and so forth, and mounted her. However, it can be said that [such actions] may not only be part of rape, but also generally [*ippanteki ni*] accompany sexual intercourse."[27]

In a subsequent Hiroshima High Court case, the defendant ran a newspaper sales office where the alleged victim worked. One night around 8 o'clock, he called her from a pay phone and told her to come for a business meeting. She at first declined, as her son had a school entrance exam the following morning, but when he claimed that the meeting would require only thirty minutes and volunteered to pick her up, she accepted.

He drove her to a sand dune on the coast. He confessed: "I'm sorry I lied. I've had feelings for you for a long time. I wanted to let you know that today." After his confession, he quickly reached the chapter-2 doom stage of love, saying, "It's OK if I die. Will you die with me?" After thirty minutes of conversation, the woman asked to be taken home. He asked, "Will you go out with me the next time I call?" She responded, "I'm not sure."

The court said that at this point the defendant realized that this would be his "last chance" to have sex with the victim. He said, "I'm begging; I want it [alternatively, "I want you"; the sentence has no object]" and put his left hand on her shoulder. He pulled her close to kiss her. He mounted her, pulled her blouse up, and "sucked" on her breasts. She began to cry and said, "Stop it. Take me home." He unzipped her pants, pulled them off with her underwear, took off his own clothes, and had sex with her. She claimed that he told her, "If you try to run, I'll kill you." He then took her home. She took a bath and ran, in tears, to her brother's house.

The standard for such a case, again, is force, as determined by resistance. In this case, the victim did not try to run. Before sex, the defendant told her, "It's OK to open your mouth" as he tried to kiss her, and "I can't get hard if you keep saying 'take me home,'" statements the court said suggested "peaceful sex." When he mounted her, she said, "Wait, that hurts," and he adjusted his body position for her. During sex, she hit her head against the door as he thrusted, and he was kind enough to shift her body. The court held that his actions, including the hand on the shoulder, the pushing down, and the pulling off of clothes, were all things that happen during consensual sex, and therefore there was no rape.[28]

In each of these cases, the judges blatantly reveal at least as much about consensual sex as they do nonconsensual sex. Each defendant in the rape cases—and even in the kiss-and-hug cases—was acquitted at least in part because the woman's conduct was normal, an element not mentioned in the applicable statute. The victims are expected to play a patterned role of a female sex partner: submissive, passive, no protests. A chaste woman, courts assume, behaves differently when confronted with rape. That notion can be found in U.S. law as well,[29] but Japanese courts, with their direct comparisons to consensual sex, seem to be saying more.

If a woman vigorously defended her chastity, a Japanese court likely would convict her attacker. But what if the woman's behavior can be interpreted as *sexually* aggressive? Consider a 2002 rape case.

The defendant broke into a twenty-seven-year-old woman's apartment at 1:30 in the morning. He put his hand over her mouth and pinned her down. He told her to be quiet and began touching her breasts as he tried to remove her clothes. She resisted strongly, flailing her arms and legs. He continued to threaten her, and she saw no escape. She decided, the Tokyo District Court stated, to do anything she could to avoid rape. Here is the court's presumably careful choice of words:

> The defendant told the victim, "Take off your clothes" and attempted to pull them off. The victim thought that she should do everything possible to avoid rape and that he would leave her alone if she could satisfy his sexual

hunger by causing him to ejaculate. She removed her pajama top only, keeping her t-shirt on. She then manually stimulated the defendant's penis and performed oral sex on him. To dissuade him, she said, "I've got a disease that makes me itch" and "It hurts when I have sex."

This is shaping up to be relatively difficult prosecution under Japanese law. The court's story began with the man pinning down the resisting woman, but now the court cites no evidence that the victim performed manual and oral sex directly as a result of the defendant's force. Still, she showed obvious resistance to penetration:

When the defendant asked the victim to show him her genitals and tried to take off her shorts, she thought if she removed her clothes, she would be raped. In order to evade him, with her underwear still on, she moved her body above his head and let him lick her nipples and toy with her genitals. Even still, the defendant asked her to show him her genitals. In order to put her body in a position that would make rape difficult, she put her genitals in the defendant's face in the so-called "sixty-nine" position. To attempt to make him ejaculate, she continued to stimulate him manually and orally, and he touched and licked her genitals.

The defendant became tired, lost his erection without ejaculating, and he lay on the futon next to the victim. He talked about himself to the victim, and in order to prevent him from harming her, she pretended to empathize with him and talked to and listened to him. During that time, the defendant touched the victim's nipples through her t-shirt and said things like "I'm really into making nipples erect." He eventually regained an erection and said, "I'm hard again" and asked the victim to touch his penis. The victim did as she was told, and the defendant once again asked her to show him her genitals.

The victim wanted to do anything she could to get the defendant to leave. She said, "If you see it, will you go home?" He agreed, and she once again removed her shorts and put her genitals in his face. The defendant licked her genitals and looked at them using the light of his cell phone. After that, the defendant received the victim's cell phone number and left around 4:30 in the morning.

Three hours had passed. A few days later, he called her to ask her out on a date to see a fireworks show. She agreed, he kept the date, and police arrested him.

At trial, the defendant argued that he had abandoned his attempt to rape and as such deserved a penalty lower than the penalty he would have received for attempted rape. He had entered the apartment merely to look at the victim's face, not to rape her, he claimed. The court disagreed, noting that he had broken into the apartment without permission and had held the victim down. The defendant claimed that the two had become friends, but the court found that they were not; the victim merely was a "method for fulfilling his sexual desires." The court anticlimactically found him guilty and sentenced him to two and one-half years' imprisonment.[30]

I have glossed over a word in the opinion. Yes, in the first paragraph of the longest quote, the court said "sixty-nine" (*shikkusu nain*). Importantly, the court did *not* say "mutual oral sex" or "mutual oral stimulation." It used the language that has the same kind of common, decidedly nonclinical connotation that it has in English, and it used the word four times. The first time, it said "the so-called [*iwayuru*] 'sixty-nine' position." The second and third times, it dropped the "so-called" language but kept the word sixty-nine in quotes. By the fourth time, the word no longer had quotes.

English loanwords for sex acts are common in Japanese. Although Japanese words exist, courts use English words for sex (*sekkusu*), petting (*pettingu*), penis (*penisu*), clitoris (*kuritorisu*), kiss (*kisu*), anal sex (*anaru sekkusu*), fellatio (*fuerachio*), and vibrator (*baibu*). (Noticeable in its absence is "vagina," which courts always render in Japanese.) Virtually the entire Japanese sex industry exists in English, using Japanized versions of English words like porno, adult video, hostess, soapland, love hotel, cabaret, fashion health, delivery health, and so on. It is not the use of English, then, that made the choice of "sixty-nine" in the opinion unusual.

Nor is the crudeness rare; courts do not shy away from vulgarity in some contexts. Blowjob (*shakuhachi,* the same as the woodwind musical instrument), for instance, appears with some frequency in forced-sex cases and even fuck (*fuakku*) makes an appearance.[31] But courts use those words when quoting testimony, not as part of their own narrative. The applicable rape statute required merely a showing of sexual intercourse through violence or intimidation. If the court had agreed with the defendant's abandonment argument, it might have been using the word to suggest that the victim was a willing participant in an act that was somehow dirtier or sexier than "mutual oral stimulation." But the court ruled against the defendant, making the word's appearance more curious.

So what is different here? Maybe cunnilingus. This case is one of only three that I can find in which the act appears (the other two also were in attempted rape cases), and it is the only one in which it seems particularly relevant.[32] In each case, courts describe the act but do not name it (if they did, it would be *kunniringusu,* as there is no more appropriate Japanese word).[33] Cunnilingus is prominent in Japanese cultural history: it is a common theme of *shunga* (erotic woodblock prints),[34] in which men are often depicted performing oral sex on prostitutes, a situation that Chizuko Ueno cheekily describes as the oddity of a "man paying to give a woman pleasure" (she quickly notes that he benefits from the experience as well).[35] But in court cases, it is rare.

Consciously or otherwise, the court seems to have been expressing panic over the act and the victim's explicit sexuality.[36] Using "sixty-nine" four times suggests that the court just might have been transfixed by the woman, amazed by her, fascinated that what they might have seen as a dominating woman who would take such an abnormal action. It is unclear if the abnormal sex affected the defendant's guilt or sentence, but it does shed light on how the court viewed the incident—even though it offered no purposeful commentary—and suggests how the court thinks people should behave.

Marriage

Japanese courts in 1960s breach-of-engagement cases frequently found that a couple was engaged to marry if they had had sex.[37] But by 2005, more than a quarter of all marriages were *dekichatta kekkon,* marriages in which the bride was pregnant.[38] More than half of women who marry between the ages of twenty and twenty-four, and four out of five women who marry between the ages of fifteen and nineteen, are pregnant on their wedding day.[39]

We have a mountain of data on sex and marriage—much of it, naturally, courtesy of the Japanese government. Table 4.1 shows that an increasingly large percentage of people in Japan agree with the statement that "sex is acceptable before marriage if a man and a woman love each other."

As sex before marriage has increased, sex *after* marriage has become an increasingly prominent social issue. Table 4.2 shows the frequency of marital sex in Japan by age group.

TABLE 4.1. Attitudes toward Premarital Sex between Partners Who Love Each Other, 1992–2005

Year	Strongly agree	Agree	Disagree	Strongly disagree	No answer
2005	27.6	49.6	12.2	3.2	7.4
2002	29.9	48.1	14.4	3.8	3.7
1997	23.2	46.6	20.0	6.3	3.9
1992	14.8	41.1	28.1	13.8	2.3

Note: Data are percentages of survey respondents.

Source: National Institute of Population and Social Security Research, Dai13kai Shusshō Dōkō Kihon Chōsa: Kekkon to Shussan ni Kansuru Zenkoku Chōsa, Dokushinsha Chōsa no Kekka Gaiyō [13th Survey on Demographic Trends: National Survey on Marriage and Birth, An Outline of the Results of the Survey of Single Persons] 18 (2006), available at http://www.ipss.go.jp/ps-doukou/j/doukou13_s/Nfs13doukou_s.pdf.

According to the Japan Society of Sexual Science, an otherwise healthy person is "sexless" (*sekusuresu*) if he or she has a partner but has not had sexual contact, including holding hands or kissing in a month.[40] Using that standard, a 2006 Ministry of Health survey found that more than one third of married couples under the age of 50 were sexless.[41]

The Ministry of Health cares about all of this because of Japan's shrinking birth rate: if the birth rate is to rise, people must have sex. In part because of the government shaping and selling of the concept, the word *sexless* is bandied about in Japan as if it were both a physical and social disease. With the designation of sexlessness as a disease comes the possibility that the statistics are skewed by respondents who do not wish to admit to its contraction—but the concept remains nonetheless.

But sexlessness might not be much of a problem at all. Sociologist Yuko Kawanishi notes that many sexless couples "say they do not mind this situation, as otherwise they get along with their spouses perfectly." Nearly 90 percent of surveyed husbands, she adds, do not find a sexless marriage problematic. She goes on to speculate that these attitudes might simply reflect an inability or lack of desire to deal with fundamental issues in the relationship.[42]

Still, most people in Japan find connections among love, sex, and marriage. In a 2006 survey conducted by NHK, Japan's national public broadcasting corporation, 68 percent of female respondents said that sex is *necessary* for love to bloom—without sex, there can be no love.[43] When a 2002 survey asked "What is sex to you?," 73 percent stated that it is "an expression of love," suggesting that judges at least have other options from which to choose when they announce reproduction as the reason for sex in

TABLE 4.2. Frequency of Marital Sex, by Percentage and Age Group

	20s	30s	40s	50s
More than twice a week	23	9	6	3
More than once a week	23	20	18	3
Two to three times a month	25	25	22	25
Once a month	18	20	18	23
A few times a year	9	15	16	13
None this year	2	11	20	33

Source: Fūfu no Sei 100nin ni Kiku [1,000 Surveyed Re Marital Sex], *Asahi Shinbun,* July 4, 2001.

marriage. Number two was "communication" (47%), and number three was "reproduction" (35%) (respondents gave multiple answers). But other responses diverged; among the more interesting, 14 percent of women in their forties, 16 percent of women in their fifties, and 26 percent of women in their sixties described sex as a "duty."[44]

How strong is the duty? When respondents to another NHK survey were asked whether a husband has a "right" to ask for sex, 26 percent of respondents said yes, 46 percent said no, and 23 percent declined to answer or didn't know. When asked whether a wife has a "right" to refuse, 49 percent said yes, 20 percent said no, and 25 percent either declined to answer or didn't know. Two-thirds of women in their twenties and thirties thought a woman had a right to refuse, but only 44 percent of women in their fifties and sixties thought so. The percentages for men were lower.[45]

A rough summary of all of these data is that sex with love is up, sex in marriage is down, and sex that occurs in marriage is seen as a duty unrelated to love. The dutiful nature of sex in marriage is clear in the case law. Marital rape cases in Japan are virtually nonexistent. A standard criminal law treatise penned by a Supreme Court justice states the scholarly commentary succinctly: "In a legally valid marriage, because the husband has the right to ask the wife for sex, even if he has intercourse with her by use of threats or violence...the crime of rape does not arise."[46] The three exceptions to the rule in the case law, in which husbands were found guilty of rape—a 1955 case in which the couple may or may not have been in a common-law marriage,[47] a 1986 case in which an angry husband and his friend raped the wife together after the marriage was "destroyed,"[48] and a 2004 case in which the spouses were living separately and the husband was under a restraining order[49]—suggest that convictions are unlikely to emerge soon.

Divorce cases underscore the dutiful nature of marital sex. As we will see in chapter 6, the standard in many divorce cases (and in all of the following sex cases) is whether a spouse can show a "grave reason that makes continuing the marriage difficult" pursuant to the Civil Code. Courts have interpreted that bland statute to cover claims based on problems in marital sex—and their analyses extend far beyond the statutory text.

One case holds that "It is clear that marriage brings certain responsibilities because the parties to a marriage consent to living together. The law does not allow a party to evade his or her responsibilities simply because one party falls out of love [*aijō*], with no further reason."[50] Another finds that "it is not illegal for a husband to force sex upon his wife, and the wife has no right to refuse . . . [unless,] for instance, the husband *has* an unusual body, or if he requests sex with abnormal frequency, or if the husband has another woman, or if the wife is in poor health."[51] The court did not provide examples of an "unusual body."

These cases do not differ significantly from U.S. divorce law on frequency of intercourse, or at least when compared to the days when a showing of fault was required. A 1954 New York court, for instance, granted a divorce after a year and a half of "withdrawal from sexual intercourse."[52] A 1973 Arizona court similarly affirmed a divorce decree when the suing husband testified to a lack of sex for five years.[53] And as in Japan, an 1889 Illinois court and a 1908 Kentucky court found "excessive" intercourse to be grounds for divorce.[54]

The differences between the Japanese and U.S. cases emerge in the detailed facts and decision-making processes. In the 1986 case of Shinobu and Seiko, for instance, the two began an arranged marriage in 1984; he was thirty-two and she was twenty-nine. They went to Hokkaido on their honeymoon. They did not have sex on their wedding night, during their honeymoon, or during the following month that they lived together. In fact, the court explained, they did not even "kiss or otherwise touch" (*seppun nado no sesshoku*). Shinobu never explained why he did not want to have sex. They do not appear to have talked much at all.

Seiko left Shinobu and returned to her parents' house. On the same day, Shinobu visited a urologist to undergo an operation to "cure" his phimosis. Phimosis is a condition in which the foreskin of the penis does not retract. Despite the clinical language, the condition in Japan usually does not require a "cure," as it usually is not a medical problem. The widely advertised surgical correction in Japan for phimosis is a cosmetic circumcision undertaken because an uncircumcised penis—which most Japanese men have[55]—is said to be "not popular" and "impure," while a circumcised one is "cleaner" and "looks better."[56] But the problem, as anthropologist Laura Miller explains, is about more than just aesthetics:

> [Some] ads say that clients will turn into "cool men" (*ikemen*) and have good relations with their girlfriends if they have the operation. Male worries about this aspect of the penis may stem from international pornography, in which the circumcised foreign penis is available for emulation, but more important is the prevalence of media commentary from young women who openly discuss penile qualities. For instance, an uncircumcised penis is often derogatorily referred to by women as an "eyeless stick" (*menashibō*) or "mud turtle" (*suppon*).[57]

Depending on the degree of Shinobu's phimosis, he could have experienced physical discomfort, so it is at least possible that his operation was not cosmetic, but Miller's descriptions suggest that his problems probably were psychological. Seiko learned of Shinobu's surgery. She maintained that she "had no confidence in their future together." She filed for divorce and asked for $30,000 in damages (a tort suit and a divorce suit may be brought simultaneously).

The Yokohama District Court described Shinobu as "a Christian with a nervous personality who had no sexual experience before his marriage." Shinobu had claimed in testimony that he had had sex with a prostitute, but the court did not find this testimony credible. He was in perfect health, the court said, and, apart from his phimosis, his sexual function was normal (by implication, his phimosis was abnormal). Shinobu claimed that he had resisted his urges to have sex with Seiko because she was not feeling well. The court did not find this testimony to be credible either; because Shinobu never even kissed or touched Seiko, the reason must have been his embarrassment over his uncircumcised penis. Had he informed Seiko about his condition as he should have, the court admonished, she would have been spared worry and might have been able to help him.

The court seems to think these words were at least a partial explanation for Shinobu's behavior: "he was a nervous Christian with no sexual experience and shame over his penis." By labeling him as nervous (*shinkeishitsu*) and a Christian, the court seems to have been attempting to explain that his sexual reticence and embarrassment were not normal. But note that the court offered no comment on or explanation of Shinobu's implicit calculation that the stigma of male virginity was worse than the stigma of intercourse with a prostitute.

The court then delivered its opinion on the couple's sexual activity: "because marriage is a union for the purpose of reproduction, sex between spouses is very important.... For newlyweds not to have sex for such a long time is extremely unnatural and abnormal." Seiko was granted a divorce and $10,000 in damages.[58]

The case is interesting, among other things, for its glimpse into Shinobu and Seiko's life, for the implicit commentary on sexual inhibition and prostitution, and for the court's pronouncement—again—that sex in marriage is about reproduction, not an expression of love as seen in survey data. At least as interesting, though, is the court's more basic assumption: it took for granted the idea that newlyweds have sex, for to do otherwise is "unnatural and abnormal." That outcome may seem wholly unsurprising, but in fact some other court opinions, such as the following one, suggest that newlyweds should not rush into sex too quickly.

Kiyoe and Nobuya met in November and married six months later. Kiyoe, the Kyoto Family Court made a point of saying, liked Nobuya for his educational record and his "self-confident personality." Nobuya liked Kiyoe's "bright, extroverted personality."

Nobuya and Kiyoe had problems from the start; he became angry with her during their honeymoon when she lost a pamphlet. They argued about expenses, and, the court said, they were never "warm newlyweds." Kiyoe left Nobuya a month later, and Nobuya petitioned the court for a cohabitation order.

The court said the couple never had the "love and respect" that a typical married couple has and then dropped the unusual bombshell that love and respect, at least in an ideal world, are "prerequisites for married life." More centrally, Nobuya did not respect Kiyoe's "pain and shame" and "embarrassment" over sex after their honeymoon. The court found that Nobuya filed the action not out of love but out of combativeness and the fear that his social reputation would suffer if Kiyoe divorced him. His petition was denied.[59]

The court did not say what kinds of acts might cause "pain and shame" or "embarrassment." Some insight into the kinds of behaviors the court might have had in mind comes from survey data that indicate which sexual practices are conventionally understood to be normal. One study finds that only 5.7 percent of Japanese married couples have sex with "regular lights" on, while 18 percent turn off all the lights. (Those data fit with other evidence; men's dating guides equate lights-on sex with pornographic videos and encourage men to turn them off so as not to embarrass the woman.)[60] The same survey found that 39.9 percent of women married to managerial workers, and 43 percent of women married to "regular" workers, "always" have sex with their pajamas on.[61] Perhaps Kiyoshi left the lights on? Maybe he asked Nobuya to disrobe? Were those the kinds of actions that led to her embarrassment?

A Tokyo High Court case offers additional hints as to what activities might embarrass a woman. The court granted a divorce to a wife and then compared the transgressions of the husband and the wife to determine whether the wife should receive damages. As for the husband, he threw things, hit, and kicked his wife, causing the couple to lose their "love" and "trust." But the wife, said the court, was too puritan in her attitudes toward sex. She disliked sex and began to avoid it. This, the court stated, made the husband crave sex more. He had to work nights, which meant that he "even" wanted sex with her "in the daytime." She continued to refuse him, and accordingly she bore some blame. The court awarded her no damages.[62]

Set aside for a moment the court's views of sexual and marital relations and focus on the court's view of a proper sexual schedule: sex is a nocturnal act. Normal sex happens under cover of darkness, for the protection of the woman, if for no other reason.

The case also seems to stand for the point that a wife must have sex with her husband even if he hits and kicks her, a point we have seen before. But this case adds an additional wrinkle: the wife was to blame for making the husband want sex even more than usual. Did he have no other method of dealing with his sexual desires?

Perhaps he did not: in a 1993 divorce case, the Fukuoka High Court ruled against a husband who masturbated while viewing pornography. In the first five months of their marriage, the couple occasionally had sex, but eventually the sex stopped. The husband admitted that he masturbated but said that he did so only during his wife's pregnancy and that she had never complained.

The court ruled against the husband: "They had sex at the very low frequency of two or three times in the first five months of their marriage, and have not had sex since 1990, yet [husband] masturbates to pornographic videos. His attitude toward sex life, when viewed from the perspective of a normal married couple's sex life, can only be called abnormal."[63] It is not that the husband's activity disrupted the marriage or that it displeased his wife—it was abnormality that caused the husband to lose the suit.

In a similar case from the Urawa District Court, a wife filed for divorce, claiming that her husband cheated on train fares, stole items from the trash, and gave used gum to their children, all acts that worried her. But more centrally, the husband refused to have sex after the birth of their children. Instead, he bought pornographic magazines and masturbated behind closed doors. With no elaboration, the court found the wife's assertions to be credible and granted her a divorce.[64]

The lack of analysis in these two cases makes it difficult to determine precisely what was wrong. If the issue were simply the husbands' lack of sex, whether because of inability or refusal, the courts could have granted divorces based on that ground. The focus on masturbation, which seems superfluous to the legal analysis, suggests something important about that particular act.

Still, I find no cases in which masturbation, with no other factor, was sufficient for divorce, suggesting that the courts' language on self-pleasure might simply be commentary on Lovesick Japan and not central to the ruling.[65] Was one of the issues in the cases, then, the use in marriage of *pornography* for masturbatory purposes? Three non-masturbation-based Tokyo District Court opinions from mid-2005 (each with different judges) suggest otherwise. In the first case, the defendant husband watched pornographic DVDs and visited adult internet sites on the computer in his study, where he kept DVDs and magazines that included scenes of orgies, violence, and rape of underage girls. His wife claimed that these materials were "extremely abnormal," but the court found that "regardless of how such tastes should be evaluated from the standpoint of wholesome common sense...for the defendant to have such tastes does not rise to the level of grounds for divorce."[66]

In the second case, the divorce-seeking wife argued that the defendant husband kept pornography, including child pornography, in the house. The court found that he kept pornographic comics that featured underage girls and stored pornographic pictures on his computer, but it found no proof that the pornography included "child pornography in which a child is raped by an adult." The court found that such pornography was not sufficient cause for divorce.[67]

In a third case, the court granted the wife a divorce but did not recognize her claim for damages: "The plaintiff requests damages on the basis of the facts that the defendant played at clubs, bought Viagra for his own use, had adult and 'entertainment' [*fūzoku*] magazines in the house, and that there were empty Viagra bottles found in the house. But even if this is true...there is no evidence that these things are anything more that the defendant's hobby or fancy [*shumi, shikō*]."[68]

So if neither masturbation nor pornography is independently sufficient for divorce, why does the combination merit divorce? An Osaka District Court case suggests the issue is not categorical or formulaic, but rather is simply deviation from ad hoc court-created, judge-specific conceptions of "normal" sex. The case is from 1960 and therefore might be discounted a bit, but the themes and the court's decision-making criteria continue to resonate in the case law. Hikaru and Sakiko had an arranged marriage; he was thirty-six and she was twenty-seven. They stayed in an inn on their wedding night, but, the court states, they did not have sex that night because Sakiko was menstruating.

This issue has arisen so frequently in the case law that we have seen that it requires a closer look. Menstruation at various life stages is seen differently in Japan than it is in the United States. When girls in Japan begin to menstruate, the event historically is celebrated with red rice (*sekihan*), a practice that would seem to be more than a bit embarrassing in the United States. Mature working women are protected by the Labor Standards Law (art. 68), which explicitly excuses women's absences from work during menstruation.[69] As women age in Japan, menstruation takes on a broader meaning as a symptom of *kōnenki* or, more recently, *menopo-zu,* words that translate to English as menopause but that refer to a broad range of midlife changes both social (the "end of one's prime as a woman") and physical (the most common complaint is shoulder stiffness; "hot flashes" are rare in Japan) over a period of time that can last ten or more years.[70]

In the cases, menstruation often emerges in a specific way: as we have seen, courts take for granted the fact that refusing sex during menstruation is normal or acceptable and not an abrogation of duty. Sex during menstruation has long been taboo in Japan, where menstruating women ate and slept separately from their families in huts or isolated rooms as late as the early 1900s.[71] Modern sex guides for men encourage abstinence during menstruation because "during menstruation, the walls of the vagina are very fragile and can easily be injured."[72] Sex during menstruation has even played a role in courtroom procedure: in the 1936 Sada Abé strangulation case from chapter 2, the presiding judge (according to his memoirs) found himself sexually excited while reading the court documents. He scheduled the trial around the menstrual cycles of the other three judges' wives, so that they would have "the proper means of relieving their excitement."[73]

The menstruation prohibition appears frequently even in cases of nonconsensual sex: attempted rapists often abstain when they learn that their victims are menstruating (and for courts not to question the action),[74] and in a sexual harassment suit, "she protested because she was on her period, but he did not listen.... He put his hand in her skirt, but either because of her resistance or because he felt her menstrual pad under her underwear, he stopped."[75]

Back to Hikaru and Sakiko and the taboo on their wedding night. Although they missed their wedding-night sex because of menstruation, they did have sex during their honeymoon. Before the honeymoon, Hikaru had told Sakiko to bring two pair of shoes so that her feet would not become tired. She did so. When they arrived at the inn, Hikaru wrapped the shoes in newspaper and took them to the bedroom (presumably the newspaper was to protect the tatami mat floor from damage).

The first time the couple had sex, it became clear that the second pair of shoes was not intended to keep Sakiko's feet from becoming tired. Hikaru took the shoes out of the newspaper, placed them on the bed, and had Sakiko wear them. Then, "with the lights on," said the court, they had sex, and Hikaru "ejaculated while looking at her."

When the couple began their posthoneymoon married life, Hikaru continued to "require" (not "request" but "require") Sakiko to wear shoes for sex. The court found that Hikaru had "more of a sex drive than the average person; when they are at home, he will not leave her side. He always has to touch her, regardless of the time of day or night, and he asks for sex several times a day."

The court then looked specifically at the shoes: "[Hikaru's] sexual activities, especially the act of forcing the plaintiff to wear shoes on the bed during sex for the purpose of sexual excitement, is a very abnormal sexual method, and it cannot be said to fall within the range of normal sexual activity." The court granted the divorce.[76]

The court's factual presentation offered many clues that Hikaru's behavior was improper. He looked at his wife while ejaculating, a statement that suggests either sexual overexcitement for Hikaru or embarrassment for Sakiko. He had sex with the lights on. But in the end, it was the "abnormal" shoes that finally went over the line.

U.S. courts, mostly in cases over forty years old, opine on the normality of sexual acts as well. The Mississippi Supreme Court, for instance, affirmed a divorce in a 1967 case in which a husband asked his wife "to have unnatural sexual relations with her, proposed that they whip each other without clothing, and tried to choke her."[77] In a 1965 Texas case, a wife "testified to many unnatural and immoral ways that appellant demanded that she would receive him. Little would be gained...by detailing these sordid and revolting acts."[78]

The U.S. and Japanese words sound similar, but the analytical lens differs. In the Mississippi case, the court focused not on unnaturalness but on the wife's emotional and physical pain. It explained that the wife "ran out of the apartment in an hysterical condition" and later was hospitalized after "another peculiar sexual incident." In the Texas case, the court focused not on immorality, but on the wife's health. It noted that the sex, which occurred when the wife was pregnant, "endangered both her health and the life of the baby" and that "she was physically hurt many times to the extent that she would lie in bed and cry."

In Japan, by contrast, Sakiko's consent or (emotional) harm seems largely irrelevant to the judgment. The court mentioned that she avoided and disliked (*kihiken'o*) the activity, but it did not discuss actual consent or (emotional) injury. What mattered was a factor external to Sakiko: as in the comparisons of rape to consensual sex, as with masturbation, and as with newlywed sex, the important factor was whether the act was *normal*. At least according to the court, it was not.

Underage Girls and Other Appropriate Sex Partners

With whom should a person have "normal" sex? In a 1980 case, the defendant had violently raped a sixty-seven-year-old woman and strangled her to death as she resisted. He claimed that he suffered from alcoholism, he was drunk (intoxication is a valid defense), and therefore he could not be held criminally responsible.

Some evidence suggested that the defendant was unaware of his actions because of alcohol. He fell asleep after the incident and seemed to have no memory of it, though he did seem to recall that he had had sex. But in analyzing the rationality of his drunken decision making, the court looked at an additional factor: the victim's age. The Tokyo District Court noted that "a normal, healthy young person like the defendant would normally never have a sexual interest in a sixty-seven-year-old woman or make her an object of sexual desire." The Tokyo High Court clarified the statement on appeal, noting that the defendant did not necessarily have intercourse knowing the woman was old, but that his judgment simply was so impaired that he could not determine if she were an old woman or not. Both courts rejected criminal liability, in part for this reason.[79]

The court's framing of a sixty-seven-year-old rape victim as unusual reveals two assumptions. First, despite the statutory standard that focuses on violence, rape in Japan seems to be about sex, not violence (more on this in the next chapter); if it were otherwise, the sexual attraction of young to old would not merit mention. Second, if sex with a sixty-seven-year-old is unusual, there must be some age at which a sexual partner is of appropriate age or an age difference between partners that is appropriate. Either sixty-seven is too old for a woman to have sex, or sixty-seven is too old for a woman to have sex with a "normal, healthy young person." In either case, the discussion suggests a possible outcome not on the face of the statute: that the defendant might have been convicted had he chosen a younger victim.

How young? At the extreme end of the appropriate-partners spectrum are young virgins (who, as the Japanese urban legend goes, are identifiable by their pink labia, which intercourse has not yet darkened).[80] The underlying logic of proper partners is the reverse of the rape victim's story: sixty-seven-year-olds are not proper sexual partners for young men because they should not be an object of sexual desire, but virgins merit special protection because they are expected to be objects of sexual desire. A virgin is a proper sex partner, or perhaps the ultimate sex partner, not for a rapist, but for a special someone. Of course, virgin means *female* virgin; as we saw in the phimosis case, a man would rather admit to paying for sex than to his virginity.

The issue of virginity arises in two types of cases: those in which courts award special protection to virgins and those in which courts give diminished protection to nonvirgins. As for the former, in a 1993 case, the defendant, armed with a knife and wearing a stocking mask, entered the apartment of a "woman living alone." He demanded money and attempted to rape her. Because the victim "vigorously resisted actual rape, he forced her to perform oral sex and other obscene acts. His criminal acts can be regarded as nothing other than truly vicious." The court continued: "The victim is a single woman *with no sexual experience* [emphasis added]. She will never forget the fear and humiliation that she endured as a result of the criminal act, and her mental suffering is unfathomable."[81]

In several cases like this one, courts have found, or at least strongly implied, that sexually experienced victims should react differently than virgins to sexual assault. In a 1972 case, the defendant took the victim to a love hotel (she claimed that she thought it was an ordinary hotel), where he told her that if she did not kiss him, he would rape her and keep her captive until morning. When she kissed him, he then told her that petting was required to avoid the same fate. Using that strategy incrementally, he eventually had sex with her. The court twice specifically noted that "if she was really a virgin [as she claims]," she would have resisted more. The defendant was found not guilty.[82]

In a 1992 rape case with a similar theme, an eighteen-year-old girl visited a love hotel with two men she had just met. She disrobed, took a bath, climbed into bed, and then refused to have sex. The men forced her to have sex. The court found that "it cannot be denied that such a situation completely clashes with common sense of an ordinary woman. But in this modern age of increasing sexual freedom, it is conceivable that a woman might go to a love hotel to have sex with multiple men."

Yet even in the "modern age," twenty years after the previous case, the "greatest problem" (*saidai no mondai*) to the court was the woman's sexual history: it noted three times that "the victim was an eighteen-year-old college student who was a virgin" and that the experience was especially shocking and psychologically damaging because she "had no sexual experience." The court found this status to be highly problematic, and it convicted the defendants. Still, it suspended their sentences because of their remorse and the difficulties that they, as "young men with vigorous sexual desires" (*wakaku seiyoku mo sakanna dansei*), must have faced when the victim told them no.[83]

Finally, a 1994 rape case involved a twenty-nine-year-old "event companion" and "party companion" whom the Tokyo District Court said "enjoyed going to discos." The woman claimed she was raped after a night of tequila-soaked drinking games with several boys. The court wrote:

> A-ko . . . told her lawyer that "because of this rape, I lost my fiancé. I'll never be able to get married now" and so on. According to A-ko's testimony, F was her fiancé . . . but even though F testified on her behalf, he said, "A-ko and I talked about marriage, but we were not engaged. We broke up because our personalities didn't match, not because of this incident." He also testified that the two of them had sex the second time they met (the first time they were alone together). We have no reason to doubt F's testimony, and [A-ko's statements to lawyers] were merely attempts to try to make her case sound more tragic. In addition, it must be said that her chastity is questionable.[84]

The court, then, found her testimony unreliable and acquitted the defendant. The court did not spell out precisely what it was that made A-ko's testimony unbelievable, but it hinted: A-ko was the kind of woman who would go to discos and have sex "the first time they were alone together," a timing the court thought worthy of note.

In these cases (and many others),[85] then, virgins, or women who credibly claim to be, are protected more than experienced women. Perhaps courts are protecting a perceived fragility. But given the untouchable sixty-seven-year-old, it at least seems plausible that virginity is protected because a virgin is, as one commentator puts it, "the ultimate erotic experience, a sort of sexual Holy Grail. . . . A virgin is a blank screen upon which to project one's fantasies of sex and of virginity itself."[86]

Or perhaps the issue underlying virginity simply is youth. Consider an indecent exposure case from 2009 and three rape cases from 2010 in which youth seems to have been the issue. In the first case, the Hiroshima District Court determined the fate of a public school teacher who had been dismissed from his post after publicly exposing himself. The court noted that he had exposed himself not to a young woman, but to a fifty-six-year-old woman, and that "he had a taste for slightly older women over young women." The court found that his dismissal violated the sense of society.[87]

In a 2010 rape case the Shizuoka District Court made particular note in its sentencing analysis that the defendant had searched for "places in which *young* women would be present."[88] In a similar case, the Osaka District Court specifically noted that a defendant accused of rape preyed on "*young* women between the ages of 18 and 27" as it sentenced him to life imprisonment.[89] And another decision by the Shizuoka District Court (by different judges) noted that the defendant raped "three *young* women whom he did not know."[90] Perhaps "young" didn't matter in these cases. But if not, why mention it? Would exposing oneself to young women or raping women who were not young have been different, legally or otherwise?

And yet youth is not problematic in the right context: sometimes courts excuse sex with minors. In a 1979 case, the defendant was charged with violating the Niigata Prefectural Ordinance for the Protection and Healthy Upbringing of Young People. Article 20 of that ordinance provides that "no one shall perform an indecent or sexual act upon a young person [under the age of eighteen]."[91] In this case, the male defendant was eighteen; the girl was sixteen. Inside a parked car, he kissed her and fondled her breasts.

The court began by noting that the ordinance was not intended to prohibit relations "of mutual love [*aijō*] or those involving close human ties.... Even if the relationship is not conditioned on marriage, it is not appropriate to prohibit actions in which the parties have love for each other, do the actions for personal interaction, or express themselves sexually within appropriate limits." Love, then, seems to legitimate otherwise improper sexual behavior, at least behavior that lies "within appropriate limits," which implies a lack of intercourse.

But in this case, both the boy and the girl had told investigators they were *not* in love. The court then switched gears from the ideal to the specific case: "whether the relationship can be called love or not, the existence of mutual affection was obvious, and in the context of such personal interaction, it cannot be said that kissing and caressing [*aibu;* alternatively, fondling or petting] breasts are 'indecent acts' under the ordinance." "Mutual affection," then, was sufficient to insulate the defendant from criminal liability.[92]

The scope of that case seems limited. The boy was only two years older than the girl, and there was no sex. What if a couple has intercourse? Six years later, courts faced that set of facts, this time as part of a challenge to a

Fukuoka prefectural ordinance similar to that of the previous case.[93] The adult defendant had consensual sex at a love hotel with a girl who was twelve days past her sixteenth birthday. He was convicted and fined, and he appealed. The Japanese Civil Code sets the minimum age for marriage at sixteen for a girl and eighteen for a boy.[94] The defendant argued that because the girl was sixteen and therefore he *could* have married her and by so doing avoided any criminal penalties, the prosecution of the ordinance against him violated his constitutionally guaranteed rights to liberty, to assemble, to associate, and to think freely. All he was doing, he said, was trying to express his "love" (*ai*) for her.

The appellate court first noted that the ordinance was designed to protect girls from sweet-talking men. But then it announced a test similar to that of the Niigata Family Court in the previous case: if a couple is planning to marry and is in a serious "love affair" (*ren'ai kankei,* alternatively, "romantic relationship"), conviction is unconstitutional. The court then applied its standard to the defendant's case. When the couple first met, the girl was still in middle school. The couple frequently went on drives up the coast. They had sex at least fifteen times, usually in the car. The court stated that at this stage, they might have had the intent to marry. The record does not make clear what changed in the relationship after that point, but the court said that as time went on, the relationship became more coital than marital. The court found that the defendant was simply "playing around" and continuing the relationship "simply for his own satisfaction." Because the couple was not serious or planning to marry, the conviction would stand.

The defendant appealed to the Supreme Court, protesting the ruling that their relationship was "simply for his own satisfaction." The Court undertook an analysis similar to that of the high court, focusing on the word "indecent" in the ordinance and establishing a clear precedent for future courts that trumped previous rulings. The word "indecent," the Court said, does not apply to every sexual act with an underage person. Rather, it refers to intercourse or similar sexual activity that occurs as a result of "seduction, intimidation, deceit, or causing confusion to an inappropriate degree in an undeveloped mind and body" or to "intercourse or similar activity that is determined to have occurred only because the young person is being used to satisfy one's sexual desires." To hold otherwise, said the Court, would make illegal the "sexual acts of a young person who is engaged to be married or between young people who are in a similarly earnest [*shinshi*] relationship," acts that would not be punished "according to the general sense of society [*shakai tsūnenjō*]." In applying this engagement-or-earnestness standard (which obviously makes no mention of love or affection), the Court held, the situation should be judged according to the age and sexual experience of the parties and from the perspective of an "ordinary person" (*ippan shakaijin*) exercising "common sense" (*jōshiki*).

Engagement or earnestness, then, can turn illicit underage sex into licit.[95] (In the United States, normally nothing short of legal marriage is sufficient.[96]) For the defendant, that is a generous result to extrapolate from an ordinance that simply states that "no one shall perform an indecent or sexual act upon a young person." The engagement or earnestness elements stand in stark contrast to the suffering that we have seen elsewhere as evidence of love; in fact, the Court seems to be searching for an *absence* of love and passion. Too much passion, too much uncontrollable emotion, shows a lack of earnestness.

The Court then analyzed whether the man was serious enough to meet its newly announced earnestness standard. He was not; like the high court, a majority of the Supreme Court's justices determined that the defendant was merely playing around and "fulfilling his own sexual desires." Four justices dissented, including one who argued cleverly that "*all* sex is for the satisfaction of sexual desires."[97]

A 2010 case highlights the continued significance of this 1985 Supreme Court precedent. Katsu, a thirty-one-year-old assistant manager in a Nagoya restaurant had an affair with A-ko, a seventeen-year-old part-time worker, a senior in high school three months shy of her eighteenth birthday. As in the previous cases, an Aichi Prefecture ordinance prohibited indecent acts with minors.

Katsu was prosecuted in Nagoya Summary Court. The court found that the couple met in February 2006, had their first date in April, and began visiting love hotels in June. They went on "drive dates," went to movies, and made plans to go to Disneyland together. Katsu was married, had a child, and his wife was pregnant. He was aware that the A-ko was underage. The court noted specifically that the relationship was not leading to marriage (because the defendant was already married), but it held nonetheless that the couple "was in an earnest [*shinshi*] relationship that cannot be said to be purely for sexual satisfaction, and as such there is no crime." The court found Katsu not guilty.[98]

Katsu did not stop there. In an extremely rare move, he sued the local and national governments for illegal prosecution (among other things) in Nagoya District Court, claiming $50,000 in damages. The standard in such a case is whether as an objective matter there is a reasonable basis for prosecutors to expect a guilty verdict when they prosecute.[99] That is quite a hurdle for Katsu to overcome: to oversimplify, if the state can show there was a reasonable basis to believe that a thirty-one-year-old man was having sex with a seventeen-year-old for purposes of sexual satisfaction, the man loses.

In its analysis, the district court first discussed (in a lengthy exposition) the gist of the 1985 Supreme Court ruling: in an underage sexual relationship, the sex needed either to be preconditioned on marriage or part of an earnest or serious relationship and not merely for fulfilling one's own sexual desires. It then conducted a detailed examination of the facts. In addition to the facts cited by the lower court, the court noted that Katsu and A-ko exchanged e-mail, kissed several times, and told each other of their feelings (*sukida*). Whenever they went to hotels, "they watched television and talked for half an hour before having sex, had sex for an hour, and then again had idle conversation, left the hotel, and had dinner together on the way home." In fact, "[w]ith the exception of the fact that the defendant was married with a child and had no intention of divorcing his wife to marry A-ko, their relationship did not differ from that of boyfriend and girlfriend [*koibito dōshi*]." Furthermore, the court noted, Katsu explicitly told investigators that "we had feelings of love [*ren'ai kanjō*] for each other" and "it is wrong to say 'I did this to satisfy my own sexual desires.'"

The court found that Katsu met his high burden. The facts not only evidenced earnestness, they constituted such clear evidence of earnestness that prosecutors could not have reasonably expected a conviction. The court ruled in Katsu's favor and awarded him $10,000 for his illegal eight-month prosecution.[100]

I'm leaving out a likely reason why police pursued the case in the first place: it appears that A-ko's mother filed the criminal complaint against Katsu only after his company refused to pay her off. But the court only hinted at that motive, focusing instead on the nature of the "boyfriend-and-girlfriend" arrangement (and ignoring Katsu's marriage). The court gave significant clues about what constitutes an "earnest" relationship: it is not only dating, but kissing, telling each other feelings, and waiting a few minutes to have sex after arriving in a hotel room. All are of such great evidentiary value that prosecuting a case in which they exist can be illegal. With underage girls, then, the court takes issue not with a dispassionate, calm relationship but with excessive sexual activity, lust, and other overwhelming feelings.

Sometimes, however, no amount of earnestness can legitimate a sex partner—even an adult. The Threesome case from 2000 involved one man and two women who lived together. The man had sexual relationships with both women. They were not married, so there was no question of bigamy. Nor was there any mention of a lesbian relationship, though one should not draw conclusions from the court's silence on the issue.

The man and Woman A sued Woman B after she allegedly defamed Woman A, punched the man in the side of his head, and refused to observe their verbal agreement to share living expenses. The court dismissed the defamation and violence claims for lack of evidence, and the opinion focused on the contract claim of shared expenses.

That seems like a straightforward case. Either the parties had an agreement or they didn't, and if they did, the court's job would seem to be interpretation of that agreement. But the court did not go near those issues. Instead, after stating the facts of the case in one paragraph, the court said:

> According to [the evidence and testimony], the agreement on which the appellants base their claim for the shared responsibilities of living expenses in this case is not merely one of shared expenses that result from living together. It was an agreement among the parties to share expenses to maintain a joint lifestyle between one man and two women premised on sex.

The court extended its gaze past the contractual agreement and into the parties' lifestyle. It had some statutory authority for the inquiry: the Civil Code (art. 90) provides that "a juristic act with any purpose which is against public policy is void." The court did not cite or quote that statute (or any other), but presumably it had it in mind when it analyzed the relationship:

> The relationship of marriage or common-law marriage in which a man and a woman live together is essentially based on love and trust, and should be one in which each person's personality is respected. Accordingly, that joint

living arrangement is respected as the fundamental unit of human society. Based on this evaluation by society, [marriage] is respected by law and codified. It is impossible for the essence of respect for mutual human love, trust, and respect of personality to arise in multiple heterosexual relationships. In the relationship at hand among the appellant and the appellees, even supposing that all parties consent to the arrangement, it is based on curiosity and sexual love [*seiai*]. It is a momentary, hedonistic lifestyle that will give rise to mutual human conflict, tumultuous relations, and mutual injury. Moreover, family and third parties will be victimized by this lifestyle. Accordingly, this lifestyle of the parties before the court, two women and one man, must be said to be a violation of wholesome sexual morals and an antisocial violation of custom. It is not something to be encouraged by either society or law.

The court, then, began with the familiar cliché that love is important to marriage. It then found that the parties in the case lacked that love. Public morals trumped the parties' private agreement, despite the fact that the sexual aspect of the relationship presumably took place privately.

The court analyzed the agreement a final time before ruling:

It is precisely because this relationship is not based on love and trust that the parties need an agreement to share expenses to curtail each person's freedom, to manage their income, to maintain and continue their abnormal living arrangements, and to prevent any of them from leaving their joint lifestyle. It would be impermissible for this court to use the name of the law to support actions that are contrary to public morals and socially and legally unacceptable by accepting the claims in this appeal and validating the agreement on which it is based. Accordingly, even if the facts as presented are true, the agreement to share expenses on which the lawsuit of the appellants is based is contrary to public morals and therefore void. This rule holds even if the appellee has attempted to leave the joint relationship. There is no need to investigate the point any further, and the appellants' claims for reimbursement are denied.[101]

Although consensual engagement in "abnormal" sex was tangential to the lawsuit, the court stretched to it and found it completely unacceptable— the court seems almost angry. The arrangement was problematic not because of religion or politics as one might expect in the United States, but because of its tendency to cause conflict, tumult, and injury. Precisely how that differs from more traditional relationships, or how it was that the court determined that the parties had no love, is unclear. But to the court, these nontraditional relationships, these nonmarital, sex-and-curiosity charged, unacceptable relationships, were characteristic of Lovesick Japan.

Serial Abortions (for the Man)

What are normal birth control methods in Japan? Until Japan approved the pill for contraceptive purposes in 1999, it was the only country in the United Nations in which it was banned.[102] For more than thirty years, government officials maintained the ban, citing fears about sexual morality, hormonal imbalances, the low birth rate, a reduction in condom use in an era of AIDS, and even "the possibility that pill users' urine, when released into the environment, might cause hormonal imbalances in animals and humans."[103] But when the male erectile dysfunction drug Viagra was approved in less than six months, proponents of the pill gained new momentum, as they were able to argue that all the government fears should have applied to that drug as well. The Ministry of Health relented and approved the pill.[104]

Still, only 1.2 percent of women in Japan use the pill for birth control. In the United States, 26.9 percent of women use it. Eighty percent of Japanese women who do not use the pill base that decision on concerns about side effects.[105]

If not the pill, what? According to one study, about 75 percent of Japanese adults rely on condoms for contraception.[106] Historically condoms were available only in pharmacies. Customers are said to have been shy about asking for them. To alleviate the embarrassment, Okamoto, a company that claims half of the Japanese condom market share, began a campaign in the 1960s in which it encouraged customers to request condoms from the pharmacist simply by making the "OK" sign with the thumb and forefinger. Pharmacists confused the sign with another Japanese sign that means money and thought customers were begging for change. The campaign never took off.[107] Slightly more successful were "skin ladies," older women who sold condoms door to door in the 1960s and 1970s.[108] But purchasing in the privacy of one's own home surely left some buyers red-faced.

With the rise of vending machines, purchasing condoms became less embarrassing. But despite widespread availability, about 50 percent of surveyed respondents who use condoms also rely on early withdrawal as a birth control method.[109] A 2006 government survey of married women tells a similar story. When asked their method of contraception, 78.5 percent said condoms. Another 4.4 percent relied on basal temperature, 3.3 percent used the rhythm method (known in Japan as the Ogino method after the Japanese doctor who promoted it as a means of *increasing* the chances of conception), and 1.1 percent said the pill. And 17.8 percent responded positively to the single joint category of "abortion/early withdrawal."[110] Yes, the government lumped abortion with early withdrawal as a method of contraception, and perhaps that's appropriate: 40 percent of Japanese women who use early withdrawal have had abortions.[111]

How many abortions are actually performed in Japan is difficult to determine. Official figures based on forms submitted by doctors put the number around 350,000, but private estimates are at least three times as high,[112] suggesting a figure roughly equal to the number of abortions performed in the United States, which has twice Japan's population.[113] That figure would also mean that about half of all pregnancies in Japan end in abortion, compared to one-third in the United States. Even relying on official figures, 22.6 percent of women have had an abortion. Disaggregated, the pregnancies of 68.9 percent of women under age nineteen, 34.4 percent of women aged twenty to twenty-four, and 62.2 percent of women over forty end in abortion.[114] One in four women have multiple abortions.[115] If those data are combined with the data we saw earlier on the low frequency of sex in Japan, it appears—with some crudely estimated math on the crude data—that approximately one in every 1,500 Japanese couplings ends in abortion. The same loose math applied to U.S. data yields one abortion for every 8,000 couplings.[116]

We have limited data about how women in Japan make their decisions to terminate pregnancy. In response to one survey, 40 percent of women said they decided on their own to have an abortion. Twelve percent said they made a joint decision with the father. And 33 percent had an abortion based on "the will of the partner."[117] In other words, between 100,000 and 300,000 abortions each year in Japan are performed for the man, presumably against the would-be mother's will.

There is no Japanese *Roe v. Wade;* there is no political debate on abortion in Japanese courts. Instead, it is this concept of abortion, and often multiple abortions, based on "the will of the partner" that is illuminated by the cases. Two cases among many show the typical pattern.[118] As in Sakura's Marriage Service case from the previous chapter, the courts in these two cases find themselves closely policing social norms of abortions. A little coercion by the man is allowed, but too much, too often creates liability.

First, consider the case of Teruo and Mari, who met at work in August 1998. Teruo proposed marriage the following month, and Mari accepted. He gave her a ring from Tiffany and they planned to marry in April in Saipan. The court specified the brand of the high-profile jeweler, which has seventeen stores in Tokyo alone. Consciously or otherwise, by dropping the name, the court seems to be implying that Teruo was no slouch; he was generous, or maybe wealthy, or at least middle class or higher.

The couple had sex in December. The timing here is worthy of note. The parties agreed to marry after they knew each other for only a month. They had sex for the first time two months after becoming engaged.

Mari soon learned two important pieces of information. First, shortly after having sex, Teruo told Mari that he was already married but that he was in the process of divorce. Second, the following month, January 1999, Mari learned she was pregnant. When Teruo first heard the news, Mari claimed, he seemed happy about the baby and their impending marriage. But in March, Teruo's in-laws told him they would never let him divorce their daughter. Teruo called off the wedding and asked Mari to have an abortion. She did. She then sued Teruo for emotional and physical damages she sustained from the abortion and the breach of engagement.

Teruo told a different tale. Mari, he said, knew he was married from the very beginning (he was in divorce proceedings, but he never told her so). Teruo told her that contraception was important, and she told him not to worry, as they were having sex on a "safe day." He was never excited about the baby, but Mari had an abortion because her parents asked her to do so, not because Teruo did. The parties agreed, then, that the decision was not Mari's.

The court found that Mari had suffered but that Teruo had done nothing illegal. According to the court, Mari wanted to go to Saipan with Teruo even after she learned of his family's opinion, so even if she were mistaken about his being single and had sex based on the mistake, she seemed not to have cared very much. The relationship ended because of parental opposition, as the court concluded that Teruo had not "forced" an abortion.[119]

Consider next the Doctor's Abortion Case. After graduating from nursing school, Natsumi moved to Tokyo to be near her boyfriend, who she was "dating on the assumption of marriage. She had sexual relations with the man, but [a year after moving to Tokyo] they broke up." She was working as a nurse in the same hospital as Tetsuo, who was a newlywed doctor. Natsumi and Tetsuo began a secret relationship.

Tetsuo frequently told Natsumi that his marriage was failing and that he wanted to marry her, but he never followed through. After two years of a relationship that appeared to be going nowhere, Natsumi decided that "considering the way that their relationship had gone, in addition to the fact that she was turning thirty years old, she decided to break off the relationship. . . . After the two took a final ski trip together, Natsumi called Tetsuo's wife and told her of their relationship." And then:

> After Natsumi and Tetsuo spoke on the phone, Natsumi and Tetsuo and his wife met to talk at the Keio Plaza Hotel. . . . At that meeting, Tetsuo revealed his intent to break off the relationship with Natsumi, and at the same time, he acted as if he and his wife were going to separate, when in fact he had no such desire and was only trying to placate Natsumi.
>
> Shortly thereafter, Tetsuo informed Natsumi that although he had said that he and his wife were separating, they could not separate because his parents opposed the separation. Natsumi and Tetsuo continued their talks, and as a result, at Natsumi's request, they signed a letter (which Natsumi calls a memorandum of understanding), which stated "I deeply apologize for the mental distress that I have caused you as well as the three abortions that you endured over the past four years. In consolation, I will pay a total of $30,000 in $700 monthly installments, to be paid by the 10th of each month." On March 1, Tetsuo wired $1,500 [as a down payment] to Natsumi's bank account.

The narrative raises many interesting facts on which the court offers no additional comment. First, the fact that Natsumi had three abortions in four years suggests that she and Tetsuo—a nurse and a doctor who surely understood the mechanics of reproduction—were relying on abortion as their contraceptive method. Perhaps they deserve a bit of leeway for the fact that contraception is not taught in Japanese medical schools, but the lack of caution is still surprising.

Second, Tetsuo's parents apparently have considerable decision-making power in his relationship with his wife. Perhaps he was lying to Natsumi about their influence in order to shift the blame. But even if he were lying, Natsumi seems to have accepted parental opposition to separation as a legitimate reason for staying in a marriage.

Finally, the memorandum of understanding is curious. Neither an apology nor a lump-sum payment seems to have been sufficient for Natsumi. She wanted a three- to four-year alimony-like contract. But after signing the contract:

> Two days after the payment, Natsumi learned that she was pregnant with Tetsuo's child. On the third of the month, she wrote a letter that said "My due date is October 27. I plan to tell the hospital about my pregnancy and my relationship with you, and quit my job. I will have the baby at xx hospital, and you will allow me to call you at work at the hospital as well as at your home. The child that I am bearing is a treasure to me, and I plan to pressure you, you coward, all my life." She placed the letter under the driver's-side windshield wiper of Tetsuo's car....
>
> Natsumi and Tetsuo spoke on the phone, at which time Tetsuo acted as if Natsumi could take whatever action she pleased. But in the middle of the month, Tetsuo's father learned of Natsumi's pregnancy, became angry, and wanted Natsumi to have an abortion. On the twentieth of the month, he strongly requested that she have an abortion.

Natsumi had the abortion, her fourth, and then sued Tetsuo for damages. The court recognized that Natsumi entered the relationship freely but found that "Tetsuo knew that Natsumi wanted to have Tetsuo's child, but to avoid the birth, he acted as if he wanted to split with his wife, revive his relationship with Natsumi, and marry her, when in fact he had no such intent." The court ignored the $30,000 contract, finding $25,000 to be the appropriate amount to compensate Natsumi for her psychological pain. It offered no commentary on the abortions or on Tetsuo's strong requests (not to mention his father's).[120]

Sex practices in Japan as elsewhere cannot be summarized in a few sentences, but a few broad themes, none of them terribly symbolic of endearment or necessarily even passion, run through the judge-told stories. Male-dominated sex is the norm. Aggressive women are a bit perplexing. Sex in relationships is an act for procreation, not pleasure or love. Sex acts should stay within normal bounds, and courts determine when acts exceed those bounds. Abortion, a widely used method of birth control, is often decided by the man.

These themes once again provide evidence of a lack of separation between "law" and "nonlaw." These are not cases of judges deciding large-scale constitutional disputes. They are simple cases of contracts, torts, criminal law, local protection-of-minors ordinances, and divorce. Courts in these cases venture deeply into private lives. That they do so in these sensitive areas is no surprise, but their examination is far more extensive and intrusive than we might expect. Judges decide what sexual activity is legally appropriate—down to the shoes—without examining consent. They suggest that virgins and nonvirgins are different, no matter their age, a judgment that they were never asked to make. And here again courts are arbiters of emotions that sneak in: just as courts examined love in chapter 2, courts in this chapter attempt to crawl into the mind of a man who sleeps with an underage girl to determine whether he is earnest. They seem to trust their ability to do so.

5

COMMODIFIED SEX

A delivery health (*deriheru*) service is a legal business in which women are dispatched to meet men in their homes or hotels for any sexual activity except intercourse. The following 2002 case involved one of those establishments. The defendant shop owner told his store manager, who was in charge of hiring, that he wanted his workers to be over eighteen, to be drug-free, and to abstain from vaginal intercourse with clients. The defendant and the manager never asked prospective employees for proof of age. When Hideko applied for the job, she volunteered that she was only sixteen. The manager, who faced a shortage of "health girls" (*herusujō*), said, "Let's keep that a secret," and listed her age as eighteen. The defendant sent Hideko out on jobs just as he did any other employee, and Hideko had oral sex with her customers. She was seventeen at the time.

The defendant was prosecuted for violating child welfare laws ("no person shall...cause a child to commit an obscene act").[1] Although the defendant did not actually know that Hideko was under eighteen, the court held that he should have checked her age, and found him guilty. The court sentenced him to probation and one year in prison, suspended for four years. It explained the sentence:

> The defendant was heavily involved in the establishment of a so-called delivery health business in which he dispatched women to customers' houses and hotel rooms to perform oral and manual sex, and he played a substantial role in management....
>
> The defendant once ran a *hotetoru* [hotel Turkish bath] in Fukushima Prefecture, and on February 7, 2000, he was found guilty of violating the Prostitution Prevention Law, for which he received a sentence of one year and six months, suspended for four years. The defendant committed this act while under a suspended sentence, and for that he should be heavily condemned for his lack of a law-abiding spirit. As the prosecutor noted, after autumn 2001, the defendant stopped paying the victim child the money he had promised when he caught her dozing when she was supposed to be servicing a customer. The defendant faces jail time, and he should reflect seriously on his actions.
>
> However, in the background behind the defendant's failure to check the victim child's age is the former store manager's disloyalty; the defendant had told the manager not to hire women under eighteen, he prohibited the "health girls" from having intercourse, and he required customers to sign an oath when they were introduced to a girl.... At the time of the incident, he had already decided to wash his hands of the sex entertainment industry, he shows genuine remorse, and his wife has sworn that she will assist with his rehabilitation.[2]

Two factors seem to have hurt the defendant. First, the court criticized him for not paying his child prostitute her due for her sexual services, implying that if he had paid the seventeen-year-old appropriately, he might have been less culpable. Second, the court condemned him for his lack of a law-abiding spirit, a factor that presumably increased his light sentence. Despite these criticisms and condemnations, the court refrained from disparaging the defendant for running a pseudo-brothel in which women are paid for oral sex. To this court, the morality of the business, like its legality, seems to have been a given.

Two other factors seem to have helped the defendant (leaving him with no actual jail time). First, he showed remorse, a factor commonly cited in Japanese sentencing but especially interesting here for the fact that the defendant's wife had sworn to help him (what if she hadn't?). Second, the court credited the defendant for his requirement of his customers of a signed oath (presumably prohibiting intercourse and violence, among other things) of questionable enforceability. The court gave the defendant points for running a contractually sound pseudo-brothel.

In this chapter, I explore three areas in which Japanese courts rule and comment on commodified sex. The first two are clearly commercial: prostitution and other kinds of neon-lit sex-for-money transactions, and pornography. In these two areas, in contrast with the conservatism of private sex, a wide variety of sexual services are clearly legal. Courts generally enforce the law strictly, but their commentary is inconsistent: although they never approve of commercial sex, sometimes they are unexpectedly silent, sometimes they are critical, and sometimes they are ambiguous. Finally, I look at a middle ground between commercial and private, a set of cases in which courts find monetary value in private sex that, while not founded explicitly on love, has a similar emotional or "real" component. In all three areas, courts tacitly allow or actively enforce the commodification of sex and the emotions that may accompany it.

The Prostitution Industry

A 1997 survey found that 51.7 percent of men over the age of twenty-five had paid for sex or sex-related acts such as manual stimulation. (Unlike the survey of sexless spouses, it's unlikely that these numbers are overstated.) The survey asked that 51.7 percent why they paid for sex. More than half said they did so for one of four reasons: "seeking stimulation" (16.4%), "because physical desire is only natural (15.0%), "because someone is selling it" (13.4%), and the remarkable "because I don't want to destroy my family" (9.4%), which suggests that some kinds of extramarital sex differ from others.[3]

Like the men who gave those responses, the law assumes the availability of prostitution. It is not illegal in Japan for a man to pay a woman for sex. The Prostitution Prevention Law (art. 3) declares that no person "shall prostitute or be the client of a prostitute," but violation of that provision carries no penalty.[4] The law prohibits and penalizes public solicitation and advertising,[5] serving as an intermediary, contracts to prostitute, supplying a venue, capital, land, or buildings for prostitution, and compelling a person to stay in a house of prostitution—but not prostitution itself.[6]

The definition of prostitution in the Prostitution Prevention Law requires "sexual intercourse." Any sex act that is not sexual intercourse is not prostitution, and the above prohibitions of public solicitation and the like do not apply.

This law was never expected or intended to shut down the prostitution business. Enacted in 1956 and enforced in 1958, the law's stated purpose is to protect women. One of the law's drafters (who eventually became a Supreme Court justice) writes that at the time of the law's enactment, he argued that "most of these woman are from farming villages in places like the Tōhoku region, and they are to be pitied. Our policy should be to help them, not punish them."[7]

The law passed in part because prostitution became a "women's issue" in another sense: Japanese mothers portrayed the business as harmful to their children. Yet after the law passed, as Sheldon Garon notes:

> The women's movement failed, above all, to transform the morality of a society that tolerated prostitution as a normal sexual outlet for husbands and single men alike. This fact of Japanese life, in turn, enfeebles efforts to destroy the resilient sex industry. According to one official survey, more than two-thirds of the proprietors forced out of the prostitution business in 1958 simply converted their operations to restaurants, inns, cabarets, bars, cafes, and other establishments in which prostitution probably continued.[8]

The legal requirement of vaginal penetration for prostitution left a wide range of other sex-for-hire possibilities for those restaurants, inns, and the like, many of which are regulated by the Entertainment Law.[9] Enacted in 1948 and frequently revised since, the Entertainment Law sets forth specific categories of sex-service enterprises and requires them, among other things, to be licensed, to keep certain hours, and to locate in certain areas. The law contemplates several categories of sex-related businesses:

> In this law, the term "immovable sex-related entertainment special enterprise" shall apply to the following enterprises:
>
> (1) An enterprise that is a bathhouse facility that provides private rooms, in which said rooms serve the purpose of providing contact to a customer

of the opposite sex (excluding those enterprises regulated as public bathhouses under article 1 of the Public Bath Law [Law number 139 of 1948]);

(2) An enterprise that provides private rooms, in which said rooms serve the purpose of contact to a customer of the opposite sex for the purpose of responding to customers' sexual curiosity (excluding enterprises to which the previous article applies);

(3) An enterprise...that is wholly designed to show the human form after the removal of clothing for the purpose of arousing sexual curiosity.[10]

In addition to these brick-and-mortar stores, the law also regulates "moveable sex-related entertainment special enterprises," which are businesses in which a person's "residence or a facility used for a person's lodging serves the purpose of providing contact to a customer of the opposite sex for the purpose of responding to customers' sexual curiosity, which is operated by method of dispatch in accordance with customer orders."[11] Since 2002, the law also regulates so-called "telephone clubs" (*terekura*), defined as either a bricks-and-mortar or a moveable "enterprise that introduces persons of the opposite sex through the provision of an opportunity for conversation (including audio messages), with an unknown person of the opposite sex, for interaction (including conversation) that temporarily satisfies sexual curiosity to satisfy the wishes of a person."[12]

The specificity of the law is intriguing on two levels. First, the law is relatively clear as to what is allowed—and much is allowed.[13] Second and crucially, the law did not create these categories of sex businesses; rather, it simply described and regulated those that were in existence, banning none of them. The law presupposes the existence of the enterprises and attempts to control the relatively minor issue of how they are operated in much the same way that strip clubs and adult video stores are regulated in the United States.

Pursuant to the contextless legalese of these Entertainment Law provisions, the enterprises function in practice as follows. Category (1) of immovable businesses in the statute are soaplands (*so-purando*). Formerly known as Turkish baths, or *toruko,* until a Turkish exchange student complained in 1984 (either directly to the Ministry of Health[14] or through the Turkish embassy,[15] depending on whose story you believe), soaplands offer nude massages, oral and manual sex, and usually illegal intercourse. In a soapland, a customer pays the owner a bathing fee, just as he would in a legitimate public bath. He then meets a woman inside. The Prostitution Prevention Law requires that intercourse take place with an "unspecified" woman, but the woman the man meets arguably is "specified," just as if she were a long-term acquaintance. He pays her a separate fee, thus insulating the bath owner from criminal liability, and then he and the woman have sex.

Prostitution activity at soaplands is difficult to prove but not impossible. In a 1994 case in which customers were charged $70 for the bath and $130 for sex, a court found liability under the law for financing a soapland, as "it must be said that it was generally common knowledge" that all soaplands in the area "without exception" offered prostitution services.[16] But most soaplands operate freely with little intervention from the authorities, perhaps because of the difficulty of prosecution.

Category (2) enterprises in the statute are "fashion health." "Fashion" refers to the costumes that women wear (and which are used in "costume play," or *kosupure*); "health" refers to the ostensible purpose of the activity. A fashion health offers a full range of sexual activity with the sole exception of intercourse.

Category (3), "an enterprise...that is wholly designed to show the human form after the removal of clothing for the purpose of arousing sexual curiosity" is commonly referred to as the strip club category. But for two reasons, strip clubs in Japan have a slightly different meaning than the statute suggests. First, courts apply the statute broadly; for instance, a court used the statute to regulate an adult video rental store that featured individual rooms where customers could watch their rented DVDs on site (the court also specifically noted the sale of tissue and lotion at the store's counter and in vending machines, without mentioning the purpose of those amenities).[17]

Second, the focus in the Japanese version of the strip club is neither stripping—the act of removing clothing—nor the naked body. In one strip club case from 1988, a defendant was accused of violating the Worker Dispatching Law[18] by recruiting women for strip clubs. The law (art. 58), which was designed to protect against abuse by "labor bosses" who farmed out workers into poor and sometimes dangerous working conditions,[19] sets forth penalties for the dispatch of workers "to engage in work injurious to public health or public morals." The court found the defendant recruiter at fault because he sent the women to a strip club even though he knew that the women, as strippers, would have to "expose their genitals, have sex with customers, and otherwise participate in an obscene show."[20] A similar 2001 case was even more specific, finding a strip bar to be a place where a woman, "on a strip stage, becomes naked in front of customers and exposes her sex organs, has her body touched by customers, and, further, at a customer's request, commits acts of prostitution and so on."[21]

In both cases, the Japanese judges did not directly examine the dance, the tease, or the nudity, factors that would have been central under U.S. standards.[22] Instead, the cases focused in part on the exposition of genitals— and that is the focus in the strip clubs as well. In a Japanese strip club, there are no g-strings but much audience participation. The clubs, as described by three different authors, "feature special acts in which gentleman can inspect a dancer's female anatomy with a flashlight or a magnifying glass,"[23] where "men peer intently at the brilliantly illuminated holy of holies; its rosy glow is reflected in their glasses,"[24] and women "slowly move around, crablike, from person to person, softly encouraging the spectators to take a closer look, [after which]...several men produce handkerchiefs to wipe the sweat off their heated brows."[25] Perhaps the attempted rapist's inspection of the victim's vagina with his cell phone light in the sixty-nine case in the previous chapter was not so unusual after all.

If this form of recreation is too public, a man can turn to "moveable" enterprises. In the moveable category, a delivery health (abbreviated in Japanese to *deriheru*), as seen in the beginning of this chapter, is the same as a fashion health, except for site of the activity; the woman visits the male customer at his house or in a love hotel. Although vaginal intercourse is illegal, enforcement is lax.

Similarly private are telephone clubs or date clubs, places (in the bricks-and-mortar version) in which men wait for phone calls from unknown women. Women call the club, talk to the men, and the men pay for services ranging from conversation to sex. The women are often teenagers; one survey found that 34.6 percent of high-school girls had called a telephone club.[26]

Each legal category has variations; "image clubs" (*imekura*) devoted to the "image" of sexual fantasies such as train groping or sex with a girl in schoolgirl uniform, "touch pubs" in which men touch women in pubs, and "pink salons" in which oral sex is offered in an open room of thinly shielded booths.[27] All are legal and licensed. According to official police statistics, which label the enterprises by their common names and not their statutory categories, in 2005 there were 1,306 soaplands, 1,021 fashion health, 439 strip clubs, 794 telephone clubs, and an astounding 25,727 (cheaply run) delivery health.[28]

There also are ways for *women* to receive sexual contact, though it would be hard to argue that any of them are mainstream. Love commentator Sanae Kameyama claims that many Japanese middle-aged women who say that they prefer male masseuses and hair stylists do so because they regard that physical contact with a man as a sexual act.[29] If that contact is insufficient, a woman may choose to become a client at one of hundreds of spas that unabashedly offer "sexual massage" (*seikan massa-ji*) especially for women. In most sexual massages, both the male masseuse and the female client are naked, and the focus is erogenous zones. A typical enterprise, B-Pleasure, advertises on the Internet that its sexual massages can "make your skin look younger," "return your estrogen to normal levels," or "put some excitement into your life," all for $200 per ten-minute period (plus hotel charges for "delivery sexual massage").[30] Intercourse is not advertised as an option, but other specialties, such as "aromatherapy sexual massage" abound. Finally, less commonly advertised but nonetheless available are male sex "volunteers" who are hired explicitly to meet with women, have sex with them according to their desires, and leave. They split the restaurant tab, and no money is otherwise exchanged. The service is not as socially visible as sexual massage, but it is legal.[31]

Also legal are sadomasochistic (*SM* in Japanese) clubs, one of Japan's more extreme sex enterprises. The following case is one of the more outlandish stories to emerge from that industry, but it hints at broader themes. In a 1998 Osaka High Court case, the male victim, age twenty-nine, became heavily involved in "extreme S&M play." He regularly frequented S&M businesses, and frequently chose the same woman for his "hitting play." The victim had the defendant dominatrix wear black leather gloves when she entered his apartment and punch him with her fists while he was naked with his back against the wall. As she did so, he said things like "Hit me harder" and "After you hit me, keep pressing into my stomach," words duly noted by the court.

After several months of this kind of "play," the victim decided he wanted more extreme action. He had watched news stories about the stabbing of an Aum Supreme Truth cult leader, and he decided that he wanted to die in the same way. He promised the dominatrix $80,000 if she would stab him. She turned him down, but he continued to request that she do so. After six months, his begging intensified: he told her that if she did not kill him, he would kill himself in such a way that she would be implicated in his death. He also promised to pay her $3,000 up front and give her the key to a train station locker that contained $83,400 that she could access upon his death. He gave her the $3,000, which she immediately used to pay off a shady loan.

After asking repeatedly if death was really his desire and receiving affirmative answers, she agreed to kill him. The next morning, the victim placed on a table in the middle of a room in his home duct tape, a survival knife, his wallet, and the key to the coin locker. He asked her again to kill him. She tied his hands with duct tape, put a towel in his mouth to silence any cries, and helped him stand up. She asked, "Are you sure it's OK"?, he grunted yes, and she stabbed him in the abdomen and sliced upward. He died from blood loss. (For what it's worth: when she went to the coin locker, she found it empty.)

The court found the defendant guilty of aiding the victim's suicide—but not the more serious charge of murder. If the court's facts, taken from the defendant's testimony, are to be accepted as truth, that seems like the correct result. As the court noted, even if the victim did not fully understand the consequences of what he was asking, the defendant had a reasonable belief that she was following his plan and had no separate intent to kill. She received a four-year sentence, a punishment the court said balanced her apology and regret with the tragedy and influence on society of the case.[32]

The incident is unequivocally abnormal. But to see why it matters nonetheless, compare it to a 2010 U.S. Supreme Court case of unequivocally abnormal behavior, *United States v. Stevens.* In *Stevens,* the Court considered the constitutionality of a statute that punished the creation, sale, or possession of depictions of animal cruelty. The statute was aimed primarily at "crush videos":

> Crush videos often depict women slowly crushing animals to death "with their bare feet or while wearing high heeled shoes," sometimes while "talking to the animals in a kind of dominatrix patter" over "[t]he cries and squeals of the animals, obviously in great pain." Apparently these depictions

"appeal to persons with a very specific sexual fetish who find them sexually arousing or otherwise exciting."[33]

The defendant was indicted for violations of the statute based on dogfighting videos that he sold. He claimed that the statute was overbroad and thus invalid under the First Amendment. The Supreme Court agreed.

The place in the law in Japan and the United States of these two definitively nonmainstream acts—S&M-based suicides and crush videos—differs. Although the legal issue in the U.S. case was statutory breadth, the Court highlighted the "great pain" of the animals (unnecessarily, as the issue was statutory breadth) and spoke of "the intentional torture of helpless animals"; in his dissent, Justice Samuel Alito additionally noted that these were "horrific acts of animal cruelty" in which animals experience "excruciating pain" and that the videos were "a form of depraved entertainment that has no social value." By contrast, the Japanese court did not editorialize on the S&M business; even its presentation of the bizarre facts was banal. True, the practice was not a legal issue in the case, but since when does that inhibit Japanese judicial commentary on "abnormal" acts?

Despite the silence in this case, in many other sex-related areas of the law, Japanese courts rule conservatively and offer conservative commentary. In constitutional cases, courts regularly uphold on social morality grounds the regulation of soaplands by local governments.[34] In employment cases, courts find that businesses licensed under the Entertainment Law to offer oral and manual sex nevertheless can "cause harm to public morality" with their services.[35] Similar expressions emerge in contract cases: in a 2007 case brought by a real estate developer against a tenant in one of its commercial buildings, a court held that if the public learned that the space was used as a sexually transmitted disease clinic for sex workers, it would "generally cause strong feelings of wariness and disgust, raising questions about the business of the owner of the building, and delivering a huge blow to the company's image."[36] From torts: when television announcer Airi Ryūen sued publishers of the tabloid *Shūkan Gendai* in 2001 for reporting that she worked in a "lingerie pub" called "Cutie Honey" in her student days, the Tokyo District Court found that the story was untrue and defamatory because it "lowered her social status."[37]

In other legal contexts, judicial sermons on commercial sex are more ambiguous. Consider an unorganized form of sex-for-hire: "compensated dating" (*enjo kōsai*), a practice by which underage girls "date" men in exchange for money. These relationships are not necessarily sexual; though most compensated dates involve sexual activity, some simply involve dining together. A Japanese study based on interviews of girls who engage in the practice found that the relationships can be complex and involve love and role play of romantic couples and of father-daughter relationships.[38]

It is unclear how common the practice is, but a 1996 survey found that 4.4 percent of high school girls had had at least one compensated date and 25.2 percent had been approached for one.[39] The demand certainly exists: when a 1993 magazine survey asked 100 white-collar workers (*sarariiman*), "If you had the chance, would you like to buy a high school student?" 40 percent said no, 47 percent said yes, and the remainder were in the somewhat odd category of being "not sure."[40]

David Leheny's thorough study of compensated dating, its social context, and legal attempts to curtail it shows that at one time or another the practice has been blamed on materialism, moral relativism, a lack of sex education, greed, moral breakdown, male dominance, and of course, more concretely, the men and the girls.[41] The judicial assessment of blame is less complicated: courts usually speak of the man's acts in a compensated dating transaction in the condemning rhetoric of prostitution. When a man served as a pimp for young girls who introduced themselves to men through *deaikei* sites, a 2003 court labeled it "prostitution" and additionally explained that compensated dating, in case there was any doubt, means "the receipt of compensation for sex."[42] When a man sexually abused his stepdaughter and sent her out on compensated dates to pay the bills, a 2009 court said he was sending her out into "prostitution" and causing her to view herself as nothing but "a tool for sex."[43] When a man picked up girls for compensated dating and then beat, robbed, and raped them, a 2009 court accused him of acts of "child prostitution."[44] When a man picked up a twelve-year-old girl for compensated dating, handcuffed her to keep her in his car, and she fell out of the car to her death, a 2002 court was clear that he engaged in a form of "prostitution called compensated dating."[45] And to stretch things one step further: when actress Aimi Nakamura sued the male-run, male-audience tabloid *Bubka* over an article that implied that she had been engaged in compensated dating, a 2003 court explicitly labeled the practice "girl prostitution" (*shōjo baishun*), the only time that particular term appears in the case law, and awarded her $22,000 in damages for the lowering of her social status.[46]

The blame implications in the first two cases are more a product of the legal context than the judges' mindset. The men in those cases were prosecuted under the Prostitution Prevention Law and the relatively new Child Prostitution/Child Pornography Law (1999),[47] each of which explicitly references prostitution, and each of which places blame on the man. But the remaining three cases were *not* about prostitution. The first two were prosecutions for rape, assault, unlawful confinement, and homicide; the third was a civil case of defamation. Framing compensated dating as prostitution in those cases helps the judges legally not at all—and yet they raised the issue, presumably to highlight the men's blameworthiness.

But courts do not always blame the man. Japanese courts usually do not frame as prostitution the man's role in compensated dating if the girl is somehow blameworthy. In a 2003 case, for instance, the defendant was said to have drugged an eighteen-year-old victim in order to rape her. The victim claimed the drugs made her groggy and unable to resist sex. The defendant told a different story: the two had agreed on a price of $500 for intercourse, conditioned on the defendant's ability to perform (he had difficulty achieving and maintaining erections). He—and the court—gave elaborate details about their automobile-based sexual encounter, including positions, actions, and even a thrust count; no one shied away from the facts. The court found the victim's testimony not credible and found the defendant not guilty, in part because "if he had the intention to rape, there would not have been need for a lover's contract [*aijin keiyaku*] or a promise for compensated dating."[48] The court used the phrase "compensated dating" fourteen times. And yet with all the details of the sex and the acknowledgment of a "lover's contract," it never once spoke of prostitution or used other keywords for commercialized sex. The contract was not condemned; it was simply evidence of the defendant's lack of guilt of the rape charge.

Curiously, I found no case in which courts editorialize about compensated dating as a *social* problem. Judges have had plenty of chances to explore the reasons why girls or men enter the transactions or to elaborate on evils or dangers—but they don't, even after the legislature has given them specific statutory tools off of which to improvise. Other aspects of sex, love, and marriage merit additional evaluation, but apparently teenage prostitution does not.

But courts' silence, as we have seen, is not unusual in commercial sex cases. Political debates on the morality of the industry apparently are not worth raising, and despite judges' penchant for sermonizing, they do so little here. When they tip their hands as to their feelings on the matter, they acknowledge "strong feelings of wariness and disgust," "harm to public morality," and a lowering of social status, but the topics rarely provoke morality speeches. And when underage girls sell sex to "innocent" partners on their own accord, judges don't call it prostitution. Maybe things aren't so bad?

Fetishes and Pornography

The second major realm of Japan's legal sex industry is pornography. As noted earlier, the Worker Dispatching Law (art. 58) penalizes a person who dispatches a worker "to engage in work injurious to public health or public morals."[49] In a 1994 case, the defendants had scouted for adult video actresses. They "dispatched" the women to film sites where they would perform acts of "sexual intercourse and oral sex" with male actors. The defendants argued that adult videos were legal, they were in compliance with the rules of the Japan Ethics of Video Association, they were not sold to minors, and they were sold in regular bookstores, all of which showed that their enterprise was not one that caused harm to public morality. The defendants argued further that sexual intercourse was "based on a basic human need" and as such did not cause "harm."

The Tokyo District Court disagreed. Although the product itself might be legal, the court said, the dispatch of workers to make the product was not. "Sexual intercourse and oral sex" in the enterprise, the court noted, could not be equated with "sex behind closed doors [*hitome no nai*] between two people who love each other [*aishiau*]." The court found the defendants guilty.[50]

The court's basis for finding "harm" as required by the statute is unclear. It did not raise issues of obscenity or protection of the women who were filmed. Is the "public morals" problem with sex (especially oral sex?) in pornography the fact that it lacks love, as the court implies? Perhaps so; one court found that the statement "love and sex are different matters entirely" (*ai to sekkusu ha betsubara*), made by a production staff person about a porn star during the filming of one of her gangbang videos, was insulting to the porn star (although one would expect her to have little difficulty separating the two).[51] But other cases suggest that the problem that courts find in loveless pornographic sex is deeper.

Three cases show how Japanese courts explicitly link adult videos to the harms of rape and other deviant sexual behavior. In a highly publicized 2002 case mentioned in the previous section, the defendant met a sixteen-year-old through a telephone club and paid her $300 to go with him to a love hotel on a compensated date. After they had sex, he sprayed her with mace, handcuffed her, beat her with a pipe, and stole the $300. He later met a twelve-year-old through a telephone club, sprayed her with mace in the car while driving to a love hotel, and handcuffed her. She tried to escape and died from the skull fracture she sustained when she fell out of the car and onto the highway. The court found the defendant guilty of unlawful imprisonment and determined the source of his actions: "the defendant watched rape-based adult videos and decided to fulfill his desires by handcuffing and raping a female high school student, just as in the videos."[52]

In an assault and kidnapping case from 2006, the defendant kidnapped an eighteen-year-old high school student by pretending to help her get a job interview. He took her to his home, where he committed an act "to satisfy his peculiar [*tokui*] sexual appetite": he prepared a bucket, gloves, and sleeping pills, and then stuck his finger down her throat to make her vomit. The court found the defendant guilty and sentenced him to four years in prison.[53] But how did the court conclude that for the defendant, forced vomiting was sexual and it satisfied a "sexual appetite"? The defendant, the court found, was addicted to pornographic videos, and in particular to a genre in which women vomit after performing oral sex on men. Without the videos, the court strongly implied, the crime would not have occurred.

In another 2006 case, a policeman lay in wait nightly, carrying a knit cap, lotion, and a vibrator, and "looking for women to rape." He tried to rape five women on five separate occasions over a ten-month period. Twice he was successful, and three times he failed: once when the woman cried out and neighbors responded, once as police approached, and once he "could not achieve his objective because the woman was menstruating" (exemplifying again the no-sex-during-menstruation rule). The court sentenced him to seventeen years in prison and noted that although he was supposed to keep the neighborhood safe, he "decided to rape after watching rape-based pornographic videos...to satisfy his sexual desires."[54]

The court found not only the cause of the rape (pornography) but motive: the crime was undertaken to "satisfy his sexual desires." Japanese courts routinely present rape as a result of the absence of consensual sex.[55] Conversely, if a man can have consensual sex, he does not need to rape. In a 1997 Tokyo High Court case, the defendant appealed the life imprisonment sentence he had received for brutally raping and killing a woman with a butcher knife. After detailing the defendant's troubled childhood and lengthy criminal past (including a 1978 rape), the court turned to his family life. According to the court, the defendant met his second wife in a bar. After they married, he gave her his monthly $4,000 paycheck, saving only $400 to $600 for himself, which he used on pachinko and gambling on horses. And then:

> Despite the fact that [*ni mo kakawarazu*] the defendant and his wife had a happy marriage, with no particular problems in their sex life, the defendant could not forget the abnormal sexual feelings that he had when, in November 1986, at the age of twenty-two, he gagged, bound, and raped his victim. He began to embrace this desire to rape, and in order to fill his abnormal sexual appetite [he committed the acts for which he was convicted].

The court has set up an interesting contrast: the defendant raped *despite the fact* that he had a happy marriage and a good sex life. The court affirmed the life sentence.[56] It is unclear if the outcome would have been different if he had a bad sex life, but if his sex life had been unsatisfactory, the court probably would have thought that fact so obvious that it would not have warranted mention.

Courts' criticism of adult videos is not absolute. Some cases suggest that outside of the rape context, even underage fetish videos are not so problematic. In a case from 2006, the comedian, actor, author, and film director Hitoshi Matsumoto brought suit against a tabloid that printed pictures of him purchasing a pornographic video. The article contained statements by the owner of the store, who claimed that "on that day, around 11:00, he drove up in his Jaguar, looked over the S&M tapes, and in the end bought one that featured girls in high school uniforms."

That sounds, as the article stated, "embarrassing," and most Japanese people would agree. A Japanese academic study found that Japanese adult video renters deal with their inevitable embarrassment by avoiding a busy checkout counter or one staffed by a woman, renting nonpornographic videos at the same time, and avoiding a video store after recently renting from the adult list.[57] The same study showed less embarrassment among experienced renters, and perhaps Matsumoto was one of them. But on a television program that aired before the incident, with comedian Shinsuke Shimada, he had the following exchange:

SHIMADA: It's embarrassing to go into those places. You can't rent anything, right?

MATSUMOTO: I'm not so shy about that stuff.

SHIMADA: You go into those places and rent stuff alone!??

MATSUMOTO: Yeah.

SHIMADA: You go into the adult video corner by yourself and just glance over the shelves?

MATSUMOTO: That's exactly what I do. I even go into sex goods shops by myself.

SHIMADA: All by yourself? You buy things?

MATSUMOTO: Sure. You know those ping-pong balls with the hole in the middle, the ones for S&M, that you stick in your mouth? If somebody said something to me about buying one of those, I'd think it was perfectly normal.[58]

He was joking, of course, but he also was speaking publicly about his purported sexual preferences. The court nevertheless found the tabloid article violated his right to privacy, in part because the article revealed his particular favorite genre. As the court stated, "detailed evidence regarding an individual's sexual proclivities, including the specific genre of adult videos that a person enjoys and purchases, is extremely personal, private, and secret." The court awarded $9,000 in damages. It offered no further commentary on the purchase of clearly legal sadomasochistic high-school-uniform porn.[59]

These high-school-uniform porn and rape videos are indeed entirely legal as long as the actress is of age and as long as genitals are not shown. As in strip clubs and in prostitution, the focus is the vagina, which played a starring role in the 2006 Pornstar Privacy case. Kaoru Kuroki was Japan's first high-profile adult video actress. A former Yokohama National University student, she became famous in the mid-1980s for S&M films, her unshaved underarms, and her formal, educated-sounding spoken Japanese. She played a leading role in only three films but produced five nonfiction books, all about sex and relationships, over the course of ten months in 1987. She retired from public life in 1994 after a fall from a Tokyo hotel that some called a suicide attempt.[60]

In 1999, the weekly tabloid *Shūkan Asahi Geinō* ran an article about Kuroki that discussed her pre-1994 exploits, including the alleged suicide attempt, her family life, and her adult video career. Kuroki claimed the article invaded her privacy and defamed her. She brought suit in Tokyo District Court.

Among other things, the article described Kuroki's genitals and sexual practices as each had appeared in an unedited underground video. Legal videos use mosaic technology for blurring genitals (and courts have found that the provision of software for unscrambling the mosaic genitals violates obscenity laws).[61] Sometimes the intercourse in those videos is entirely simulated, as reality would be difficult for a viewer to discern. Underground videos, allegedly made for the foreign market, ignore such restrictions, and the intercourse is real. According to the court's 2006 opinion:

> Moreover, the defendant claims that its presentations of particular aspects of the underground video in [the article] were not illegal. But that article contained descriptions of genitals and related parts that are not shown in edited videos, such as "the man's shaft is swallowed down to its base," "the well broken-in mouth to her hole into which many different objects have been inserted," "a man puts his middle finger in her wide-open gap. He toys with her with his thumb and finger-bangs [*yubipisuton*] her," "slowly, the shaft sinks into her hole, glistening with love juice," "in an instant, the shaft glistens with her juices," "into her mushy hole go two fingers," and "two fingers become three, they enter the base of her hole and spin intensely." Accordingly, the defendant's claims that these passages do not differ from [what can be seen in unedited] legal videos has no merit.[62]

I have not translated that passage in a deliberately provocative way. If anything, the English sounds slightly more restrained the Japanese. The terms for genitals in the Japanese opinion are those that are reserved for erotic novels, and although "shaft" (*nikubō,* literally "meat stick") and "hole" (*nikutsubo,* literally, "meat pot")" convey the right tone, the dissonance of erotica in a court opinion is not quite the same.

The applicable law in this case is a statute we have seen before: "A person who has intentionally or negligently infringed any right of others, or legally protected interest of others, shall be liable to compensate any damages resulting in consequence" (Civil Code art. 709). To determine liability under that statute, the court needed to discuss the substance of the article.

It needed to give a few examples to convey to its audience the extent of the damages to Kuroki's right to privacy, which it valued at $22,000. But, to be blunt, in its application of the statute, could the court not have ended its narrative at one or perhaps two fingers? Their focus on Kuroki's vagina in the passage, not to mention their ruling that a porn star's right to privacy was invaded by a description of her vagina, suggests an awed yet prurient reverence for the forbidden.

Although Japanese pornography shows no genitals, male or female, anything else is fair game: clothed crotch shots of apparently underage girls, "tentacle porn" in which tentacles substitute for the penis, and any other figurative representation of the sex organs are all legal.[63] This is the crux of the difference between U.S. and Japanese pornography regulation: under Japanese law, it is only genitals that are problematic.[64]

Consider a direct comparative example. In a 2010 Iowa case, manga comic collector Christopher Handley pleaded guilty to possession of obscene visual representations of the sexual abuse of children and to mailing obscene matter. Handley had ordered seven books from Japan. Those books, according to the stipulation of facts attached to his plea agreement, contained "cartoon drawings of minors engaging in sexually explicit conduct. Each book contains obscene images, with one book containing images of bestiality, including images of sex between a male pig and a minor human female, and images of a minor human female engaging in oral and genital intercourse with a male dog."[65]

Handley received a six-month jail sentence for the first count and five years' probation for the second. But set aside the outcome of the case; the interesting aspect is what facts are legally significant. The relevant statute criminalizes the knowing possession of a "visual depiction," including a "cartoon," that (a) "is obscene" and "depicts a minor engaging in sexually explicit conduct" or (b) "lacks serious literary, artistic, political, or scientific value" and "depicts an image that is, or appears to be, a minor engaging in graphic bestiality, sadistic or masochistic abuse, or sexual intercourse, including genital-genital, oral-genital, or oral-anal, whether between persons of the same or opposite sex."[66] Accordingly, the prosecution's sentencing brief in the case focused not on genitals but on acts, with descriptions such as "tied up with her arms behind her back," "masturbate and digitally penetrate," "being penetrated from behind," "sitting up with her legs open," and so on.[67]

In Japan, the depicted acts would not have been relevant.[68] The books Handley received are legal and widely available in Japan,[69] an argument the Iowa court ignored.[70] The prosecution stated repeatedly in its brief that the books showed genitals, but blurred genitals, strongly suggested genitals, lines instead of labia, phallic objects instead of the real thing—all are legal in Japan. In Japan, manga publishers face criminal penalties only when they cross an imaginary line of genital recognizability: in 2004, the publisher of the erotic manga comic *Honey Room* (*Misshitsu*) was convicted of obscenity charges because a reader could "generally grasp the condition of the genitalia."[71]

Handley, then, would not have been prosecuted or convicted in Japan, a result that highlights a paradox of Japanese obscenity regulation. Act-based materials like videos and "images of sex between a male pig and a minor human female," which judges in Japan find lead to rape and deviant behavior, remain legal if they show no genitals. But the mere presentation of Kaoru Kuroki's vagina, even without the sex acts the court painstakingly described, would have violated Japanese law, despite a relative lack of judicial commentary on its social ills.

The Japanese Supreme Court has relaxed the rules for presentation of genitalia in recent years, moving Japan closer to the U.S. regime. In 1999, publisher Takashi Asai landed at Narita airport with a copy of Robert Mapplethorpe's 384-page photography book *Mapplethorpe*. Because the book contained twenty objectionable photos of male genitalia, customs agents seized it. Asai sued. The Tokyo High Court stated his argument and countered:

> Now in Japan, representations of genitals and pubic hair in photographs and magazines are publicly displayed, distributed, and available on the Internet. Anyone can easily peruse images of exposed genitals and pubic hair in foreign countries, and regular people no longer feel opposition to photos and so on that display genitals and pubic hair. In this environment, the definition of obscenity itself is undergoing dramatic change. The appellant argues that in contemporary Japan, the photography book at issue cannot be said to be obscene given the sense of society....
>
> Although it is true that photographs of exposed female pubic hair, called "hair nudes," are presented in books and magazines that are publicly for sale, those are not pictures of exposed genitals. And although it is true that images of exposed genitals and sex acts can be accessed on the Internet through

sites located in Japan, those photographs that directly represent genitals and sex acts, [society does not approve.] Accordingly... the photographs numbered 1 through 20 are obscene given the sense of society.[72]

The court focused on exposed genitals and carefully distinguished "hair nudes" (*hea nu-do*). The display of pubic hair was banned until 1991, when police enforcement changed to allow the presentation and sale of so-called hair nudes.[73] Until that time, censors regularly scraped out pictures of genitals and every single pubic hair from *Playboy* and similar magazines imported from abroad. Mapplethorpe's representation of genitals obviously far exceeded pubic hair, the outer boundary of what was permitted to be shown.

Asai appealed to the Supreme Court. In 2008, the Court overturned the high court decision, finding that the book had artistic merit, the pictures did not "directly represent sex acts," and only 19 of the 384 pages (one of which had two photographs) were objectionable. The opinion suggests a focus away from genitals alone, a development that might give lower courts interpretive space in future obscenity cases. But Justice Yukio Horigome's partial dissent shows how central sex organs remain:

> It cannot be denied that a judgment as to whether an object is obscene changes with changes in the sense of society. But a determination of whether a photograph is obscene must at the very least find that a photograph is obscene when it directly shows the exposed genitals of a man or a woman concretely in the center of the image.... It cannot be denied that the 20 photos are obscene.[74]

For Justice Horigome, then, as with judges of the high court in the case and countless others, as long as sex organs remain hidden, social morality will be preserved. Their exposition by Mapplethorpe is a sign of continued social decline.

Commodified Private Sex

A spouse in Japan may bring suit against his or her adulterous spouse's lover (and the spouse). The suing spouse must prove adultery and that the lover knows or should have known of the spouse's marital status.[75] These "alienation of affections" actions commodify sex in a way that is both similar to and the opposite of prostitution: a person, usually a woman, pays another woman for the commodity of sex with the woman's husband. Strictly speaking, these cases are not about commercial sex; they are not sex for sale via prostitution or pornography. But the law's treatment of this form of private, noncommercial private sex is similar to that which is available in the marketplace, except for one thing: courts often add a vague emotional requirement to the sex. As in the cases of "earnest" underage sex, it is unclear what that emotion is, but courts require the relationship to somehow be based on genuine feelings and not sexual desires. If this "realness" is coupled with sex, the court orders that money change hands.

My focus here is bar hostesses, common defendants in alienation of affections actions. It is not clear why they are so often sued. Perhaps they have money to pay damages, perhaps wives are especially enraged by them, perhaps they are frequent adultery partners, or perhaps there is no single pattern.

A hostess, according to Shōichi Inoue's encyclopedia of sex terminology, is a woman who, "at a cabaret, nightclub, bar, or other facility services and entertains customers for a living."[76] What exactly a hostess is and does depends on the particular bar, club, or "snack" that employs her and its location, its price, and its clientele. Hostesses usually are under thirty years old, except for the "mama," an older woman who runs, and often owns, the club. In general, the job of a hostess is to entertain men, who often come in groups after working hours. Hostesses must be attractive—and it is for that reason that one plaintiff hostess successfully sued her salon for $2,400 after her stylist cut off too much of her hair, one of her "appeal points," and miscolored it.[77] For the same reason, courts specifically note a hostess's occupation when she sues over botched acne scar surgery or automobile accidents that result in facial damage.[78]

For most men, as Anne Allison explains in her study of hostess bars, "the hostess *acts* as if she were sexually and romantically interested in the man, and since there are always stories of hostesses becoming involved with customers, a man may assume that he has a chance."[79] He often does not have a chance, even if the club permits the relationships, for at least at the high-end clubs, a relationship with a hostess is an expensive proposition. The man pays not for an encounter but for an ongoing relationship.

In the cases, hostesses differ in two respects from regular sex workers. First, although legal commentary suggests that a sex worker (*fūzokujō*) would not be liable to a wife in an alienation of affections action because her sex act is not undertaken "completely at will,"[80] hostesses, who have more freedom to choose their sexual partners, may be, and are, held legally liable.

Second, considerably less stigma attaches to a hostess club relative to explicitly sexual enterprises, a logic revealed in a 2004 Tokyo District Court decision. The court in that case held that an allegation that a lawyer who appears frequently on television visited a cabaret (hostess) club was not defamatory—but an allegation that he was "immersed in" or "crazy about" (*hamarichū*) clubs was.[81] In other words, it is acceptable to frequent hostess clubs as long as one doesn't make a habit of it. The lack of stigma appears in survey data as well. When women ages fifteen to twenty-two were asked what occupation they would like to try, hostess was cited by 20.5 percent of the respondents, making it twelfth on the list. Actress/model was number one. Lawyer was number thirty-five.[82]

When a hostess (or anyone else) is sued in an alienation of affections case, the relevant statute is the same one seen in the Pornstar Privacy case: "A person who has intentionally or negligently infringed any right of others, or legally protected interest of others, shall be liable to compensate any damages resulting in consequence" (Civil Code art. 709). From that broad statute, which clearly says nothing about sex, love, or even marriage, Japanese courts have framed the cases in three different ways.

The first view, the Natural Love View, comes from Kōji and Hisako's case. Ten years after the two married, Kōji fell for a hostess in Tokyo's Ginza district. Kōji and the hostess planned, said the court, "a fling" (*uwaki*), but it soon turned into "love" (*aijō*). The pair had a child seven years later, and Kōji began living with her three years after that. Kōji's wife Hisako brought suit against the lover.

The Tokyo High Court found no liability for the lover. The court first noted that the lover could support herself financially and that it seemed as if "she would not object if he went back to his family." The lover "was not even asking him to live with her, so she has no direct responsibility." There was nothing "illegal" about the relationship. But most significantly, the court noted that the two "fell in love naturally [*shizen no aijō*] and had sexual relations."[83]

The court did not elaborate on what love means; it is the *naturally* that matters here. If a couple falls in love naturally, there are no ulterior motives, no gold digging, no jousting for power. And if the love is natural, as we saw in chapter 3, it is impossible to combat—it is an uncontrollable emotion that eliminates liability, for no person could avoid it. Why would a court dare to interfere with the natural, primal order of human emotions?

Hisako appealed to the Supreme Court. Writing in 1979, the Court nixed the lower court's Natural Love View in favor of a Strict Liability View. It noted that the lover worked at a Ginza bar and accepted no money from the husband; accordingly, their relationship was based on natural love. But the Court ignored the lower court's romanticism and instead announced a different standard: "When a third person has a sexual relationship with a married person, whether deliberately or by mistake, regardless of whether that person lured the other or the love [*aijō*] arose naturally, the rights of husband and wife are infringed, the act is illegal, and the third party has a duty to compensate the spouse for mental anguish."[84] The Supreme Court, then, found the lover liable, and completely removed love from the lower court's equation.

A flood of conflicting scholarship from family law scholars about the 1979 case followed, most of it questioning whether the Strict Liability View had or should have exceptions.[85] Seventeen years later, the 1996 Supreme Court, surely conscious of this debate, resolved the conflict with a new standard: the Destroyed Marriage View. Katsuyumi and Mitsuko were married in 1967. They had personality conflicts and frequently fought over money. Katsuyumi started his own business, and Mitsuko opposed it. Katsuyumi became a corporate director, and Mitsuko opposed the appointment on liability grounds.

Katsuyumi filed for divorce mediation in 1986. Mitsuko failed to appear, and Katsuyumi dropped the matter until spring 1987—about the same time that he met Kimie, a bar hostess. Kimie and Katsuyumi began having sex in the summer, and she moved in with him in the fall. They had a child in 1990.

Mitsuko sued Kimie. In her court papers, she claimed that the love between her husband and Kimie did not arise "naturally," using the Natural Love View the Court had disregarded in 1979. The Court rejected that argument by completely ignoring it. The Court then announced a different standard that runs throughout Japanese marriage law: liability depends not on the quality of the adulterous relationship but on whether the *marital* relationship is destroyed. If the marriage is destroyed at the time of the affair, there is no affection to alienate, and the affair is not the third party's fault. Only if the third party disrupted the "peace" in the marriage is she liable. In Mitsuko's case, with no discussion, the Court determined that the marriage was already destroyed at the time of the affair, and accordingly Mitsuko received no damages. It distinguished its 1979 Strict Liability View, clarifying that in that case, the affair occurred before the marital relationship was destroyed.[86]

Each of the three approaches is a bit odd. Although easy to apply, the Strict Liability View would allow a spouse to receive damages in some cases regardless of any quantifiable loss. Both of the exceptions to the rule, the Natural Love View and the Destroyed Marriage View, require courts to take on the seemingly impossible task of delving into the particulars of the relationship to determine whether one of the relationships was in some sense natural or at least an ongoing concern—just as we have seen courts determine whether parties are in love for purposes of suicide or whether a relationship is earnest for purposes of underage sex.

As in those areas of law, there are no specific tools with which courts can determine when a relationship is "destroyed." Courts often apply the Destroyed Marriage View purely objectively. As we saw in the *deaikei* case of Katsu and Misa in chapter 3, courts tend to look not at feelings, but at factors like family trips and a lack of violence. But in some cases, courts seem to search for emotional content. Consider a 1998 case that is somewhat rare because the husband was the plaintiff and the defendant his wife's lover.[87] Kenji and Hanako married in 1985; she was twenty-two and he was thirty-eight. Hanako gave birth to a son nine months and seventeen days after the marriage. Kenji worked hard at a manufacturing company, returning home at ten or eleven o'clock every night. They spoke little and did not have sex after Hanako became pregnant. Hanako, the court said, became lonely.

Beginning in 1990, Hanako began going out with her female friends to bars and karaoke boxes to combat her loneliness. The court explained: "Kenji thought these things made her feel better, so he let her do as she pleased. Hanako did not like to drink, so her stress relief came from drinking oolong tea and singing karaoke."

In 1991, Hanako met Jun, a construction manager, at a bar called Peace. Hanako and Jun became fond of each other, and each soon learned that the other was married. In 1995, they began having sex. Jun divorced in 1996. A few months later, Kenji learned of the affair from Hanako's mother. Hanako then asked Kenji for a divorce.

Kenji requested and received a negotiation session at the karaoke box La La House with Jun, Hanako, Hanako's mother, and Hanako's brother-in-law. They were unable to reach an agreement. They met three days later at the karaoke box Turkey, where Kenji told Jun, "If you keep seeing her, I'm going to sue. If you break up now, sign an oath to never see her again, and give me a signed apology to apologize for all you've done, I won't sue. If you don't take this offer, I'll sue you as much as it takes to get compensated."

Kenji's words on his relationship, as presented by the court, are somewhat contradictory. On one hand, Kenji is speaking of his wife as a compensable commodity. But on the other hand, Kenji seems to be a sentimental romantic, as he would give up his monetary claims if he could only have his Hanako back (and an "I'm sorry"). In any event, Jun refused, telling Kenji, "If you'd like to sue me, be my guest." He did.

Pursuant to the Supreme Court test, the Tokyo District Court first examined whether Hanako and Kenji's marital relationship was destroyed at the time the affair began. They had not had sex in more than a decade. The court noted it was "at the very least not normal for Kenji to have not asked Hanako for sex even once in the ten-year period since their son's birth, when Hanako was twenty-two, even considering the fact that Hanako was diabetic [and was once hospitalized for it]." Still, the court found that that fact alone did not necessarily mean the relationship was destroyed.

After examining the negotiations between Kenji and Jun, the court said it "harbored doubts" as to whether Kenji was simply suing because Hanako was his wife and not because he had any feelings (*kimochi*) for her—explicitly searching for emotional content and not finding it. Still, the court noted, if Kenji were to lose Hanako, "Kenji's peaceful household," which included his first-grade son, "would completely collapse," and as such, it would "be unjust for Jun not to be held responsible for his tortious act." The court set damages—the price Jun was to pay for Hanako—at the relatively low price of $10,000, perhaps because of its harbored doubts.[88]

What if there is clearly absolutely no emotional content to the relationship? A 1996 case involved Akiko, who was pregnant when she quit high school to marry Jōji in 1984. They had two children. By 1988, Jōji had become a twice-a-week regular at a bar called Kitayan. From October 1989 until March 1990, he spent only one week per month at home. The rest of the time, he slept in a room on the second floor of Kitayan with his girlfriend Sachiko, a hostess at another bar.

Sachiko and Jōji's passion soon faded. But in September 1990, Jōji began a relationship with Mika, the divorced owner of Kitayan. When Jōji first invited her to a love hotel, she refused. He then confessed: "the only person I think about is you. I want to be with you. I'm thinking very seriously. I want to divorce my wife." At around the same time, Akiko, aware of Jōji's infidelity, told him that she planned to divorce him after her brother's upcoming January wedding.

Two weeks later, Mika entered the hospital for treatment of a pancreatic illness. Jōji visited her in the hospital and announced, "I'm breaking up with my wife. It's not your fault. You don't need to worry about our marital problems. I want you to be with me." He added, "Let's recover together. I'll do my best to help you recover." They had sex. In her hospital bed.

In October, Jōji told Mika that Akiko had agreed to the divorce. Jōji and Mika moved in together and made plans to marry. But on December 1, Akiko learned Mika's identity. She visited Mika and Jōji's house for a three-party negotiation. She demanded a cash payment of $50,000 in exchange for her husband—in effect, a settlement of a potential alienation of affections action. Jōji and the two women negotiated all night, but Mika refused to pay.

The following night, Jōji visited Kitayan as usual. He waited until the last customer left, then approached Mika about the $50,000. He wanted Mika to pay, he said, so that he could divorce Akiko and be with her. She refused. He violently grabbed her breast, put his hands around her throat, and punched her in the stomach.

Three days later, Akiko visited Kitayan. In front of customers, she yelled at Mika, "You wanted a man? I told you $50,000, and you still haven't brought me a damn thing" (*otoko hoshikattanka. 500man iuten, mada, motte keehennoka*). Mika refused. Three days after that, Akiko returned to the bar, this time with Jōji in tow. Jōji appeared to have switched allegiances. As he stood smirking by Mika's side, saying, "I've got nothing to do with this," Akiko threatened her. Mika called the police, and Jōji and Akiko left.

Akiko sued Mika. The Supreme Court discussed at length Akiko's threats and attempts to sell her husband. It held that because of these actions, her suit was an abuse of her right to sue. It dismissed her claim.[89] Had she negotiated more fairly for the price of her husband, perhaps she would have been successful. Or would she? Although the court does not explicitly say so, the logic that seems to underlie the abuse of right determination, coupled with the stark presentation of the facts, is that there was no emotional content to any of the sex. None of the relationships was "real," and compensation was unnecessary.

This particular love-for-sale view of adultery is gone from U.S. courts, from which alienation of affection cases have vanished.[90] The action disappeared in the United States in part because of difficulties of proof, in part because such suits were shunted to divorce litigation when adultery became a ground for divorce, and in part because the commodification of love was viewed as unseemly in an age of natural romantic love.[91] Japanese courts—which, at least at the Supreme Court level, could change or abolish the doctrine—seem to find the commodification of love, and the compensation for the loss of what the Tokyo District Court explicitly labels "love profits" (aijō rieki), less problematic.[92]

The commodification and contractualization of love in Japan runs deeper than the legal ties of marriage or even of common-law marriage.[93] In a case of a one-year dating relationship, Yasuko, a hostess at the Ginza bar Monte Carlo, dated Shinji, whose occupation the court did not mention. Shinji became a frequent customer. According to the Tokyo High Court:

> They had sexual relations at hotels and Japanese inns in the city and at her house. Around May or June of 1975, she became pregnant with Shinji's child. On July 19 (at the beginning of the second month of her pregnancy), she aborted the child at the [Clinic] in Shibuya, Tokyo. Although Shinji denied that the child was his, he paid her $1,000 as compensation.

He loaned her his ATM card [kyasshu ka-do]. She used it to buy a kimono, and he acquiesced in the purchase. She made several deposits to his account using the card. And then:

> Seeing that his wife would return to her parents' home at the end of the year, Shinji invited Yasuko on a three-night-four-day New Year's trip to

the Nagoya area. They continued their sexual relationship. They stayed at the Nagoya Miyako Hotel on the night of the thirty-first, stayed at the Yunoyama hot springs Toraya Hotel on the night of the first, returned to Tokyo and spent the night of the second in the Hotel Okura, and spent the night of the third at her home. When work began on the fourth, Shinji left for work directly from her home. Since they met in December 1974, they had had sexual relations at least twenty times.

The court is paying particular attention to the number of the couple's sexual encounters, presumably to highlight the intensity of the relationship. Yasuko, the court suggests, was not merely a hostess but a frequent travel and sexual companion.

The dissection of the relationship continued:

In the middle of January 1976, Shinji carelessly gave Yasuko a roll of film and asked her to have it developed and printed. The roll included a picture of him with a woman who appeared to be his wife, and Shinji's lie about being single became obvious. Yasuko immediately checked the family registry at the ward office and telephoned his home on the twenty-third to confirm that he was married. She was furious and suffered great psychological shock.

Here the court emphasizes even more strongly that Yasuko's relationship with Shinji was emotional and not merely that of hostess-customer. Yasuko's reaction upon learning of Shinji's marriage was not to confront him in rage but to check his records, a sign of seriousness or even earnestness. Only then did she feel the expected painful emotions of love. And after that:

Then, on the twenty-fourth and the twenty-sixth, she withdrew in cash almost the entire balance of $27,700 from the savings account at issue. After applying $2,104 to his charges for food and drinks at the Monte Carlo, she kept the remaining $20,595 for herself. She then returned the ATM card and announced that she would have nothing more to do with him.

Shinji sued for return of the money.

Three Civil Code provisions were applicable. The first, article 709, we have seen frequently: "a person who has intentionally or negligently infringed any right of others, or legally protected interest of others, shall be liable to compensate any damages resulting in consequence." The second, article 549, is about gifts: "gifts shall become effective by the manifestation by one of the parties of his intention to give his property to the other party gratuitously, and the acceptance of the other party thereof." The third, article 703, is about unjust enrichment: "a person who has benefited from the property or labor of others without legal cause and has thereby caused loss to others shall assume an obligation to return that benefit, to the extent the benefit exists."

I quote the three dry statutes to show the contours of the legal analysis that lay before the court. But the court did not even cite the statutes. The court concluded that there was no tort and no unjust enrichment, using the following analysis:

> Men give women ATM cards with the right to withdraw freely only when in a harmonious relationship. Once that relationship disintegrates, her right to withdraw funds stops. When such a nonmarital relationship ends, the man, who generally has greater economic resources, frequently pays the woman, who has less, a termination fee [*tegirekin*] for damages or as consolation payment. It is wholly natural given this sense of society [*shakai tsūnen*] that a woman would see the possession of an ATM card as collateral against that termination fee. Accordingly, when a long-term relationship ends, absent an agreement to the contrary, it should be understood that a woman has the right to use an ATM card to withdraw from the man's savings account a termination fee in an amount that she considers reasonable.

Because Yasuko withdrew a termination fee that she considered reasonable and in accordance with the sense of society, the court dismissed Shinji's case.[94]

In its decision, the court not only gave the government's seal of approval to termination fees, it also gave license to the woman—a woman in an emotional, noncontractual arrangement—to determine the amount. It did so not pursuant to any particular statute but based on the sense of society regarding contract-like expectations of dating. It is unclear exactly what commodity the $20,000 purchased—genuine affection, sex, an absence of emotional pain, the right to end a bad relationship—but the court found that the rules were so clear that the expectation of that payment was wholly natural.[95]

The cases suggest four judicial conceptions of sex, none of which seems particularly conducive to compassionate interpersonal relationships.

Private sex is for reproduction, the missionary position is preferred, the lights should be off, it should not take place during menstruation, and a partner might wear less clothing on the beach than in bed. By clothing, I mean pajamas, which are acceptable, not shoes, which are not (and in a marriage of people under fifty years old, there is one in three chance that sex will not happen at all). If a woman becomes pregnant, the man can cause her to have an abortion. Underage sex is acceptable if the man is earnest, but heterosexual threesomes are not (and homosexuality doesn't exist).

The other three conceptions of sex commodify it. In the *sex trade,* a broad range of state-sanctioned market-based sexual options appears, all of which are legal as long as there is no intercourse and the girl is of age— and if she is underage, courts do not even consider it prostitution. These anything-goes (except *that*) options stand in stark contrast to the strict world of private sex. Courts are relatively tolerant of these activities, perhaps because they have little choice, though they sometimes express some misgivings.

Another option is *violent, nonconsensual* sex, the world of rape (and vomiting), sex that is framed as an implicit possible consequence of an inability to have sex that falls in one of the first two categories above. The depiction of this kind of sex is legal, but it is harmful to society, and actual sexual activity of this sort is unacceptable unless it is purchased.

Finally, there is *commodified private* sex, which might seem private (money does not change hands) but shares many aspects with the sex trade (it is given a price). These sexual relationships, which often involve hostesses, include some sort of "realness" component that has nothing to do with intimacy and does not quite reach the level of suffering love. Courts explicitly put a price on the relationship if its terms are violated.

At least as fascinating as the judges' views is the extent to which the law permeates sexual life in Japan. We expect certain laws that pertain to sex: abortion, strip clubs, rape, and public indecency are highly regulated. But Japanese courts incorporate sex acts, the emotions of sex, and the consequences of sex in ways that we might not expect from a country that has low litigation rates and is said to favor norms over law, and privacy over publicity. Japanese courts have no problem waltzing into bedrooms and brothels in ways that are not essential to deciding the case at hand. What they find there rarely seems to please them, and the areas in which they refrain from commenting are sometimes disconcerting.

6

Divorce

In immediate postwar Japan, fewer than one out of ten marriages ended in divorce. Divorce gradually became both more accepted and more common.[1] In the 2000s, four out of ten Japanese marriages end in divorce, a figure neither unusually high nor unusually low among developed countries.[2] As we see in this chapter, many judges seem to long for the golden days when couples stayed together—despite a clear absence of the emotional connection that judges use to define marriage in other contexts.

Before exploring judicial views, consider some evidence of spousal views on one particular question of divorce: why? The purported causes of divorce in Japan are as intriguing as the fact that the Japanese government assumes they can be accurately determined and recorded. A spouse who files for divorce in court is required to specify on a form his or her "motivation" for filing. Approximately 70 percent of filers in any given year are women, a ratio that has held for at least the last half-century. The form lists fourteen possible options, with instructions for the spouse to circle all that apply and to double-circle the *most* applicable option.

There is no U.S. counterpart to this Japanese example of meticulous record keeping; there are no forms that ask a party who wants a divorce in the United States to circle a reason (as opposed to legal grounds) from a list of preselected options. The data in Japan might be intended to help mediators get to the heart of the marital problems quickly, but if so, the aggregation and publication of those data seem unnecessary. The question might simply suggest a detail-oriented bureaucracy, but it is still interesting that bureaucrats chose to gather responses to this particular question, as if knowing the aggregate motivations for divorce might somehow help policymakers better understand the issues or devise solutions.

The 2008 data, with a total of 48,041 responses for wives and 18,436 for husbands, are in figure 6.1.[3]

The frequency with which motivations are checked on the form varies by sex. Men seek divorce because of personality clash and adultery. Women want divorce for those reasons but also for violence, psychological abuse, and the husband's unwillingness to provide money.[4] It is difficult to tell how accurately the data depict real life. A person seeking divorce might come to court, be presented with the form, and check with abandon all the

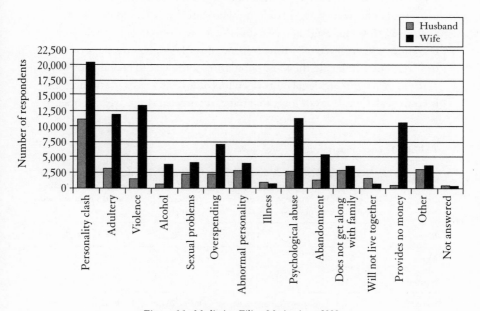

Figure 6.1. Mediation Filing Motivations, 2008

annoying things about his or her soon-to-be ex-spouse, without thought as to the true "motivation," whatever that means.

But the form itself is as interesting as the responses because of a possible motivation that it omits: loss of love. The listed factors might simply be reasons why people fall out of love, and bureaucrats who designed the form might simply have felt uncomfortable with such a nebulous category. Still, the category appears in other official statistics: in the suicide context, bureaucrats list "loss of love" as a possible motivation on a form on which police must record the details of each incident.[5] Perhaps loss of love did not make the divorce motivation list because it is simply not a sufficient reason for divorce in the bureaucratic mind, or in the collective mind of this particular division of the bureaucracy.

Other evidence suggests that loss of love is relevant to the divorce decision. A 1995 academic survey asked college students in eleven countries two questions, presented in table 6.1 along with the results for Japan and the United States.

In response to both questions, Japanese respondents were *more* likely than their U.S. counterparts to find divorce appropriate in loveless marriages. Still, two issues make conclusions from the data suspect. First, all of the respondents were college students, who statistically would be about a decade away from marriage and two decades away from divorce. Perhaps they become less starry-eyed over time. Second, note the high percentage of "neutral" responses in Japan: the most popular response was to take no position.

Evidence from pop legal culture on loss of love as a basis for divorce also is equivocal. Questions of love, marriage, divorce, and sex arise frequently

TABLE 6.1. Love, Marriage, and Divorce Survey

	Q1. If love has completely disappeared from a marriage, I think it is probably best for the couple to make a clean break and start new lives.		Q2. In my opinion, the disappearance of love is not a sufficient reason for ending a marriage and should not be viewed as such.	
Response	Japan	U.S.	Japan	U.S.
Agree	41.1	35.4	26.4	36.8
Disagree	17.1	34.7	27.9	40.3
Neutral	41.9	29.9	45.7	22.9

Source: Robert Levine et al., Love and Marriage in Eleven Cultures, 26 *J. Cross-Cultural Psych.* 554, 563 (1995).

on the popular Nippon Television program *Gyōretsu no Dekiru Hōritsu Sōdanjo,* or The Legal Consultation Office That Is So Good That People Queue Up. Viewers send in questions and a panel of four lawyers answers them. One question was "Can a couple divorce if the marriage exists only in public and the husband is cold and loveless?" In the factual presentation, as acted on television and as presented as a comic strip in the book version of the show, a twenty-eight-year-old woman who has "finally found her happiness" marries a thirty-three-year-old "elite city banker." He buys her whatever she wants but spends no time with her; he suggests that they sleep in the same room only once a week because he wants children. He says that he does not like humanity. The bride bursts into tears, realizing that he has no love for her or for anyone else.

The four lawyer-panelists split as to whether the bride would be allowed to divorce. The first said no: "If lack of love were a reason to divorce, 99 percent of couples would be divorced." (Laughter.) The second said that it was very unlikely that a divorce would be granted, as it would be "difficult to prove lack of love." The third said yes, divorce would be allowed in this case because the couple never had love in the first place: it would be unreasonable to subject the wife to the husband's never-ending coldness. The fourth said yes, divorce would be allowed, as the situation was one in which the marriage was destroyed beyond repair.[6] Those four opinions represent significant disagreement on the seemingly basic issue of whether a spouse may leave a loveless marriage over the other spouse's objections.

Why would a spouse choose to remain in a loveless marriage? Reasons abound, and the phenomenon obviously is not unique to Japan. But in Japan, at least, law and economics play unmistakable roles in keeping couples together. Yukiko Tsunoda, an attorney, scholar, and women's rights activist, described to me one of her divorce cases:

> One of my clients is being sued for divorce by her husband. She tells me that she has not even a scrap of love [*aijō*] for her husband, and yet she says she will never divorce him. She says that if she were to divorce him, she could not put food on her own table, and she would not be able to continue to live in the house that is in his name. She says that if it turns out that she has to divorce, she at least wants to take as much time as possible so that she can save some of the monthly living expenses (which were decided in mediation) that

she receives from her husband. In court, I have no choice but to argue that the marriage is not destroyed.

In cases like this one, then, the language of love necessarily takes a backseat to the wife's economic needs. The asset distribution system is set up such that if the wife agreed that the marriage was destroyed, she would lose economically. Love had nothing to do with it, either to the spouse or the judge. But as we will see in a broad range of cases, the official take on the relation between divorce and love and other emotions is more complex.

The divorce process is relatively simple. A spouse who wishes to divorce in Japan has three legal options: negotiation, mediation, and adjudication. Negotiated divorces, which comprise 90 percent of all divorces in Japan (of which there were 253,000 in 2009)[7], are remarkably simple. In a negotiated divorce, the spouses reach agreement privately and submit a divorce registration form, duly stamped by each party and two witnesses, to a local government office. This is true no-fault divorce in a sense far beyond that of the United States; there is absolutely no need to give any reason or excuse for the action and no decision-making role for the state. The government's sole function in a negotiated divorce, also referred to as a "paper divorce,"[8] is record keeping.

If a spouse contests the divorce, the spouse who wishes to divorce must petition the family court to mediate the dispute. Nine percent of divorces are mediated. Three mediators sit on a panel: a judge and two laypeople between the ages of forty and seventy, usually one man and one woman, who serve two-year terms. Although mediator techniques and motivations vary, the prime directive for many seems to be to keep families together, especially if children are present.[9] About half of divorce petitions are successfully mediated, and 80 percent of those successes are divorces.[10]

If (and only if) mediation is unsuccessful, a spouse may file for adjudicated divorce in district court. Only one percent of all divorces reach this stage.[11] To obtain an adjudicated divorce, a spouse must prove one of five grounds: adultery, malicious abandonment, disappearance for three years or more, mental illness with no chance of recovery, or a "grave reason that makes continuing the marriage difficult."[12]

Japan, then, allows divorce if spouses consent to it or a court awards it after finding fault. Such regimes have their critics. A *New York Times* editorial, for instance, argues that the requirement of fault for divorce requires litigants to spend "thousands of dollars in unnecessary legal fees," involves "a ridiculous use of judicial resources," and "cannot rescue irretrievably broken marriages."[13] More troubling, economists Betsey Stevenson and Justin Wolfers found that the introduction of unilateral divorce lowers female suicide by 8 to 16 percent, reduces domestic violence by 30 percent, and results in a 10 percent decline in women murdered by their partners.[14]

Anecdotally, at least, the Japanese regime creates acrimony and leads to false accusations as spouses search for grounds. Many people in unhappy marriages in Japan navigate these issues through private investigators. Investigative agencies in Japan are easily found; they have multiple branches and national toll-free numbers. For a fee, an agency will do more than investigate; they can help a person break off a relationship, begin a new one, or break up another couple. But an additional core agency service is the gathering of evidence of grounds for divorce through "adultery investigations" (*uwaki chōsa*).

Cases abound. In a *deaikei* Internet dating case from chapter 3, we saw how investigators hired by a husband found a wife living with another man (and they answered the door together in their pajamas).[15] In a 2006 case, a wife hired an agency to conduct an adultery investigation on her husband. The agency found the other woman, opened her mail, and set up a video camera outside her apartment to monitor her activities for three days. The Kyoto District Court found that the agency's actions violated her right to privacy.[16] In a 2005 case, a wife learned of her husband's infidelity when she searched the house for a photograph of her husband to give to the agency. She found instead a photo of him with his girlfriend, which made the agency's work easy.[17]

The agencies have a prominent social presence. The Splash Agency, for instance, advertises its ability to conduct "American-style" adultery investigations for about $100 to $150 per hour (the United States is said to be a "developed country" in terms of private investigations).[18] The GNC Group advertises its ability to provide photographs of lovers entering hotel rooms or copies of love letters or e-mail specifically for the purpose of proving grounds for divorce and reminds potential customers that even common-law spouses can receive tort damages for betrayal.[19] The Gulu Agency reminds its clientele in its promotional materials that the statute of limitations for an adultery-based tort claim is three years.[20]

Even if a court finds a basis for divorce, it may still refuse to grant a divorce if it determines that the marriage "should continue" in light of "all the circumstances." Such denials, as we will see, are common. One example from 1955: the Tokyo District Court, in an arguably romantic moment, refused to grant a wife a divorce despite her husband's numerous affairs because her husband still loved (*aijō*) her, he pledged to remain faithful, and she, then fifty years old, simply wanted to move on with "the remainder of her life" instead of forgiving "as she should."[21] As we will see, the court's words continue to resonate.

The government's role in adjudicated divorces in Japan, then, differs significantly from that of negotiated divorces. In a negotiated divorce, only the opinions of the spouses matter, and the government is irrelevant. In an adjudicated divorce, although courts sometimes consider the opinions of the parties, they need not do so. A court can freely determine on its own that a marriage should continue over the protests of a spouse who wishes to divorce even if grounds are proven.

Courts thus have significant power to shape marriage and divorce. The system they have created is characterized largely by rules that require the less-than-happy marriages of the sort we have seen throughout the book to continue over the objections of a spouse who wants to leave. Two specific aspects of judicial divorce regularly trump spousal desires: statutory "grave reason" grounds for divorce and court-created rules against at-fault divorce. In both cases, love occasionally arises, but it is largely irrelevant.

Grave Reason

As late as 1966, New York's divorce law, written by Alexander Hamilton in 1787, had only one ground for divorce: adultery.[22] By comparison, since 1947, a relatively progressive Japan had five grounds in its Civil Code, including the catch-all "grave reason that makes continuing the marriage difficult." That broad provision appears to give judges significant authority; it requires no allegation of fault, and it is facially similar to "irreconcilable differences" in the United States. It predates the U.S. no-fault divorce revolution (in which states adopted rules by which a spouse need not allege fault to obtain a divorce) by more than twenty years.

The "grave reason" provision sounds as if it might have been penned by a liberal U.S. New Dealer during the Occupation, but its origins are far deeper. During debates over the family law provisions of the Civil Code in the 1890s, Baron Nobushige Hozumi, who had studied abroad and whose face eventually would grace a postage stamp, proposed a system under which a court could grant a divorce on a case-by-case basis even if the marriage's failure did not fulfill narrow grounds specified by statute. His argument was based in part on love: if love vanishes, the marriage should be able to be dissolved.[23] His proposal failed. The same proposal was included in a 1925 draft revision, but the draft was never implemented.[24]

Thirty years later, Allied Occupation authorities sought a revision of the family law system of the patriarchal Civil Code.[25] A committee of Japanese experts drafted new provisions. The committee was familiar with Hozumi's ideas—and even if they had not been, his son Shigeto Hozumi, a law professor and future Supreme Court justice, argued to the committee for the inclusion of his father's "grave reason" concept.[26] The subcommittee included it in its draft, which they translated into English for Occupation officials. The officials approved it with little input.[27]

The draft proceeded to the legislature. In 1947 parliamentary debates, member (and first female Vice-Minister of Justice) Chiyo Sakakibara specifically asked if the "grave reason" provision applied when "for instance, if one person falls out of love [*aijō*] but the other still wants to continue in the marriage." To which member (and future Supreme Court justice) Ken'ichi Okuno responded:

> That depends on the circumstances. For instance, even in a continuing marriage that lacks love, one can imagine a situation in which love might return, so the decision should really be made on a case-by-case basis. It can't be said that lack of love should always be grounds for divorce.[28]

The provision, which passed in 1947, thus gives judges significant discretion.

The Japanese "grave reason," then, originates in Hozumi's concept of love in marriage, and love was an integral part of the legislative history. And yet courts interpret "grave reason" strictly, with little attention to love. The Supreme Court describes "grave reason" as "when the marital relationship is so completely destroyed that the efforts required for a spouse to continue it would be too severe, as viewed by [alternatively, 'in the sense of'] society."[29] The standard has three components. The first—"when the marital relationship is so completely destroyed [or broken down]"—would seem to simplify judicial decision making. Theoretically, a judge need not examine the factors that led to the breakdown; he needs to examine only *whether* a breakdown has occurred.

But the second part of the standard, "that the efforts required for a spouse to continue it would be too severe," complicates matters. The standard is not "when the marital relationship has broken down so completely that it will never recover." Nor is it "when the marital relationship has broken down so completely that a reasonable person would not want to continue." Rather, the standard requires a spouse to stick it out unless making such an effort would be "too severe," a factor that turns a judge's focus away from a mere examination of *whether* a breakdown has occurred toward an examination of *how* it happened and ultimately in most cases to an assessment of fault.

The third element of the standard tells how a judge is to make such a determination: through the eyes of society. This seems to be a particularly difficult place to bring in social views. Is the eyes of society the median view, with the extremes eliminated? Is it the least controversial view? Is it that of an average man? An average woman? An average woman who has internalized some male views, whatever those might be? There are deep and wide disagreements in Japan about fundamental issues of marriage and divorce, and yet court opinions leave those questions unasked.

Writing in 2003, retired judge Chikahiro Tada described the difficulty of discretionary decision making in a memorable grave reason case:

Sometime around 1972 or 1973, in a Tokyo District Court suit, a wife raised the following claims as grounds for divorce:

1. He smokes cigarettes all over the house even though he knows the plaintiff dislikes it.
2. He takes control of the television and never backs down.
3. He walks through the place where the plaintiff sleeps.
4. He farts in front of the plaintiff's face.
5. He tells the plaintiff not to eat dinner until he comes home.
6. He orders the plaintiff around by calling her "hey you" [*oi omae*].
7. He prohibits the plaintiff from taking a bath before him.

She listed more than ten such points, then said, "As the above list shows, because the plaintiff can no longer stand to live with the defendant, the requirement of Article 770(5) of the Civil Code that a grave reason that makes continuing the marriage difficult exist has been met."

When this case came to me, a male clerk looked at the complaint and said, "There's no way this list of daily events meets the 'grave reason that makes continuing the marriage difficult' standard, right?" At the time, there were only two or three female judges on the Tokyo District Court and almost no female clerks.

I have to admit it: my opinion was the same as the clerk's. But when I think about it now, I realize my thinking was mistaken. If the plaintiff and the defendant had been reversed; in other words, if at the time it was the wife who did the things listed in points 1 through 7 every day, the husband would have been unable to bear it. If the husband had claimed that these things constituted a grave reason that makes continuing the marriage difficult, I think the claim would have been upheld.[30]

The "grave reason" provision seems to be difficult to apply, changes over time, and is subject to such judicial scrutiny that it loses its no-fault character. In the midst of this amorphousness, a few standard grave reason fact patterns have emerged. Domestic violence is one: Japanese courts have routinely granted divorces (and awarded damages) in such cases.[31] The Tokyo High Court, for instance, in a 1983 opinion, allowed a man to divorce his wife after she locked him out of the house on the veranda one night while he had nothing but a towel, cut up his neckties, forced him to sleep in bunk beds with their children, cut his arms and face while he slept, and poured water, milk, and *miso* soup on him.[32] Courts look at nonphysical abuse as well; a 2009 Osaka High Court panel granted a divorce to an ill 82-year-old husband whose 59-year-old wife berated him, removed the memorial tablet of his deceased first wife from the family altar, and destroyed his photo albums and other possessions that had sentimental value.[33] Exceptions exist, but domestic abuse is now established as a standard "grave reason" fact pattern.[34]

Two other grave reason patterns exemplify relatively recent trends in Japanese marriages: religion and late-life divorce. The facts of the former, in which the plaintiff is usually the husband, show how courts invoke emotion in cases in which Japanese wives turn to religion, apparently to cope with empty marriages. The latter, in which the plaintiff is usually the wife, evidences court opposition to a growing trend of ending long-term marriages in Japan. In these two types of cases, judges are completely in control as arbiters of both law and emotions, and cases of painful love, emotions matter little here.

Religion

Most Japanese people practice some combination of Buddhism and Shinto. Neither requires regular attendance of any sort, and neither has strong prohibitions. Religion-based divorce cases are usually about other, smaller religions, especially those that require attendance or other objective forms of devotion, as these practices clash with majority norms. Most of the cases concern Jehovah's Witnesses, but a few cases concern other Christian groups, a few nonmainstream Buddhist groups, and cults like Aum Supreme Truth. Stated broadly, the judge's task is to measure the severity, from the view of Japanese society, of living with a nonmainstream spouse. The touchy element of attendance-based religion in Japan seems to make the cases more difficult than other divorce patterns.

The cases can be divided into those in which the suing spouse wins and those in which he—almost always he—loses. In a typical case in which the suing spouse won, Jun and Hiroe were married in 1970 and had three children. Their youngest child was killed in an automobile accident at the age of three. The accident was Hiroe's fault, and she turned to Jehovah's Witnesses for "spiritual answers." Initially a friend came by her house for worship, but by 1978 Hiroe was attending church every Tuesday, Wednesday, and Sunday. When Jun came home from work on those days, the court explained, his dinner was cold.

Hiroe refused to observe holidays like New Year's Day and Girls' Day. She refused to give her children permission to participate in school activities on Sports Day. Jun became an alcoholic. In 1985, Hiroe became an "all-the-time worshiper," logging 1,000 hours per year in services. She read the Bible to the children as often as she could. Jun filed for divorce, citing her religious activity as a grave reason. Hiroe claimed that she was not solely to blame: Jun, fueled by his alcoholism and his anger against the church, had destroyed her belongings and written antireligious statements on them.

The court stated that freedom of religion must be respected (it is constitutionally guaranteed against state intrusion) but that couples also must respect each other's positions, cooperate, and preserve familial stability. If by one spouse's actions the other spouse's "lifestyle [*seikatsu*] and feelings [*kimochi*] are completely ignored, damaging the marital relationship," the divorce can be granted. By not celebrating Japanese customs and attending church services regularly, Hiroe had ignored Jun's lifestyle and feelings. The court awarded Jun a divorce, but because of his antichurch actions, the court found both parties to be at fault for purposes of damages.[35]

This outcome would not be unusual in the United States. Although most contemporary family-law Jehovah's Witnesses cases in the United States are about child custody, a handful of cases from decades before the no-fault divorce revolution show that church activity can constitute "extreme cruelty" or "cruel treatment" grounds for divorce. As in Japan, religious belief is not a ground for divorce.[36] But actions *based on* religious beliefs may be sufficient for divorce. In a 1969 Jehovah's Witnesses case, for instance, a Kansas court granted a divorce where "Hazel had become so obsessed with her religious beliefs and activities that she completely neglected her duties as a wife and mother, and as a result, she and her husband could no longer live together."[37] In a 1944 case, an Arizona court noted that the Jehovah's Witnesses were "a sect of religious fanatics whose methods of propagating their beliefs are so aggressive, obnoxious and obtrusive as to arouse resentment and physical violence," and then held that "if one carries such beliefs to the extent of disrupting and destroying the family life, it seems this conduct becomes cruel treatment."[38]

Despite the differences in the role of religion in society, the U.S. and Japanese rulings sound surprisingly similar. If there is a difference in approach, perhaps it is that the U.S. courts emphasize duty slightly *more* than the Japanese. The Japanese court speaks of wifely tasks, but it also highlights respect, cooperation, and feelings. It is unclear exactly what those feelings are or should have been. The language is mild; perhaps a spouse must simply respect autonomy and independence. Whatever the degree of emotional energy required, the Japanese court seems to acknowledge that nonmainstream religion creates murky issues that are difficult to solve with the language of duty alone.

The discourse of emotion arises more strongly in Japanese cases in which suing spouses lose (they rarely lost in the United States) and are forced to remain with their religious spouse. In one case, the wife had been a Jehovah's Witness for seven years, and the couple had been separated for two years when the husband filed for divorce. The husband explicitly stated in his brief that he had lost his love (*aijō*) for his wife. The court noted that the wife still loved *him* and their three children, and was ready to return to married life. The husband, the court said, should "take her feelings into consideration" (*shinjō wo kumitoru*). Even though she went to services three nights a week, the court said, her absence would not be problematic if she were going out for English or tennis lessons instead of church. The court denied the divorce.[39]

In another case, Yoshitaka and Miki married in 1983, moved in with Yoshitaka's parents, and had two children. In 1988, Miki began attending Jehovah's Witnesses Bible study, and she began attending services two years later. After a fight over her church attendance, she moved to an apartment owned by her father-in-law a few hundred meters away from the house.

Yoshitaka painted a stark description of the results of Miki's church attendance. Miki went to church at least twice a week. She cooked neither breakfast nor lunch on Sundays. She made Yoshitaka put the children to bed at night. She cleaned the veranda so infrequently that giant ants invaded their house. She would not light incense or say prayers to ancestors. She would not allow the children to celebrate holidays. She took the children to services even when they were sick.

The court made a point of saying that Miki was still in love with Yoshitaka and had "strong" love for their children. Yoshitaka, on the other hand, had "absolutely lost his love and trust" (*aijō, shinrai wo mattaku ushinai*) for Miki. But Yoshitaka, the court said, should nevertheless look at her "faith with feelings of generosity and continue to talk to [her] calmly" (*shinkō ni taishi kan'yō no kimochi wo motte reseini hikoku to no hanashiai*). Because the couple had been apart for only two years, their "love for the children"— not for one another—should bring them back together. The court denied the divorce.[40]

The results of these three cases are not easily reconciled. Many other cases serve as further evidence that courts simply have no systematic way of determining whether the burden of living with a religious spouse is too severe in the sense of society.[41] But even without a synthesis, two intriguing patterns emerge.

First, in almost every case, the facts follow a standard pattern in which the religious spouse is the wife. In almost every case, the wife becomes confused, lonely, or alienated and turns to religious activity as an answer.

In almost every case, the religion she turns to is Jehovah's Witnesses, for whom church attendance is vital, or some similar attendance-mandatory organization. Despite the fact that 70 percent of mediated divorces are initiated by women, 100 percent of the published Jehovah's Witnesses divorce cases are initiated by men.

Why is it the wife in particular? In her study of middle-class Japanese women in troubled marriages, anthropologist Amy Borovoy found that marriage was based not on love, romance, or sexual compatibility but on the ability to maintain separate spheres. These spheres, she notes, "offered women a window for establishing distance from their husbands without creating great upheaval."[42] If the husband's sphere is work (or perhaps hostesses), the wife's sphere is the home. For women who want more, an attendance-based religion might hold answers.[43]

Second, Japanese courts explicitly recognize love and other feelings in religion-based cases. But in the battle of emotions, love *loses:* courts instruct a spouse to show "generosity" and remain in a marriage even while acknowledging that he has "absolutely lost his love." To stretch the descriptions of chapter 2 a bit, love in the religion cases seems to be characterized as a resignation to suffering—or, if not suffering, at least to tolerance and endurance.[44] If a spouse can tolerate the other to show a modicum of court-ordered generosity and consideration of feelings, the marriage should continue.

Late-Life Divorce

Bookstores sell guidebooks for spouses considering late-life divorce (*jukunen rikon*). Books aimed at wives focus on legal and financial questions. Books aimed at husbands discuss practical methods for mitigating a wife's desire to divorce ("Prohibited acts: not complimenting your wife on a delicious meal, not responding to your wife's conversation, not thanking your wife when she does something for you." "Don't leave your clothes on the floor or leave the toilet seat up.").[45] For those men who need more than books, the National Chauvinistic Husbands Association (Zenkoku Teishu Kanpaku Kyōkai), with 4,300 members, helps its members learn how to avoid divorce by teaching them how to reconnect, or perhaps connect for the first time, with their wives.[46]

The "Love Letters at Sixty" book series discussed in chapter 2 provides role models for late-life marriage while at the same time hinting at possible reasons for marital discord. A seventy-one-year-old Tokyo man, for instance, wrote to his wife:

> You've gotten pretty good at the computer, haven't you? I'd like to take back the words that I've said over the past forty years: "You're stupid," "How am I supposed to eat this garbage," "Do whatever you please," and "Get out." Can you drag those words to the trash? It's time for us to reboot.[47]

The computer language might be endearing, but the underlying sins for which the man is attempting to atone are less so.

A sixty-one-year-old Saitama man seems to have found himself on less sure footing:

> Thank you for consenting to my retirement at age sixty. There are many cases in which wives swear to divorce their husbands when the husbands announce their retirement, and I'm relieved that, at least for now, we are not one of those cases. When we watched the television drama series "Late-Life Divorce," I suddenly asked you, "Will that happen to us?" and you said, "I've never thought of such a thing." It made me very happy.[48]

The husband was relieved to have avoided a specific Japanese social phenomenon. In a typical late-life divorce, a husband retires from decades of hard work and long hours at a company. The husband begins keeping regular hours at home, a place that once was his wife's exclusive domain. The husband has difficulty filling his days and is unhelpful with housework; the wife realizes she knows nothing of her husband as a person and does not want to do all the housework. She—and it is usually she in late-life divorces as in all divorces—seeks a divorce.[49] Sometimes, as in television drama, women are lauded for their initiative. Sometimes their actions are frowned upon: the Supreme Court ruled in 2004 that statements broadcast on the NHK television network to the effect that a woman "suddenly" requested a divorce after twenty-one years of marriage injured her reputation because they could "give the impression that she was a woman who was unkind to her husband, selfish, and lacking in humanity."[50]

In courtroom examples of late-life divorce, the desire to divorce, along with happiness, love, and kindness, are irrelevant. What matters is that couples that have been together a long time stay together, for, as the Tokyo District Court noted in 2000, "it is extremely unfortunate for an older couple to want divorce."[51] The following two cases exemplify both the fact patterns and the courts' role in blessing the unions.

In the first case, the Kobayashis married in 1960, when they were both twenty-five. Mr. Kobayashi was a company man; Ms. Kobayashi, a home-maker. They had two children. Their roles in the marriage sound like cari-catures of 1960s Japanese marital relations:

> At about the same time that the couple married, [Mr. Kobayashi] began to pour all of his energy into the company he had just joined. He set off to work every morning at 6 a.m., worked until past 9 p.m., and some days worked past 11 p.m. He continued his work after he came home on weekdays as well as on his days off. In accordance with this lifestyle, [Ms. Kobayashi] brought breakfast to [Mr. Kobayashi] in bed each morning, prepared his toothbrush, and put on his jacket and socks for him.

Mr. Kobayashi does not evoke much sympathy. Ms. Kobayashi argued that he did not allow her to have a hobby. Before marriage, she played the *koto* and the *shamisen,* traditional Japanese instruments, but she stopped because Mr. Kobayashi liked Western classical music. Although he "never hit her," he showed little kindness. He expected her to prepare his dinner and his bath every night. He was unsympathetic to her health problems, which were numerous: she was hospitalized for surgeries on an ovarian tumor (1962, age twenty-seven), a herniated lumbar disk (1966, age thirty-one), stomach cancer (1986, age fifty-one), and arthritis (1996, age sixty-one).

After Mr. Kobayashi retired in 1995, Ms. Kobayashi began to think seri-ously about divorce. She seems to have communicated with him mostly in writing. One note she left in 1997 for him said, "I can't take any more of this, both psychologically and physically. From now on, I won't cook for you." Five months later, she left a note saying, "I'm leaving you and want a divorce." At the time, they were both sixty-two years old. Mr. Kobayashi opposed the divorce. When mediation failed, the case went to court.

The Yokohama District Court saw no hope for recovery in the mar-riage. Citing the above facts, it said that Mr. Kobayashi had shown little concern for his wife. The spouses were living separately, their children were adults, and retirement, it noted, "is not temporary." Mr. Kobayashi did not appear to be taking actions to improve the marriage. The court granted the divorce.[52]

Mr. Kobayashi appealed to the Tokyo High Court. Now sixty-five years old, he argued in his brief that he "did not gamble or commit adultery. He was never violent to his wife. He was a serious, hard-working person." And as for the divorce imposed against him by the lower court, Mr. Kobayashi argued:

> For a court to declare that a marriage is destroyed beyond repair simply because one spouse strongly wants a divorce makes the listed grounds for divorce in the Civil Code meaningless. Is it really acceptable, after long years of ups and downs in a marriage, for a divorce to be granted so easily? I turned over all financial matters to my wife, worked hard every day, was promoted to manager of the Technology Section in 1981, to manager of the Information Systems Section in 1986, and to director in 1990....Immediately after I reached retirement age and left the company, I was stabbed out of the blue with "divorce" as if it were a weapon.

Mr. Kobayashi was not a gambler or a cheat, he did not beat his wife, and he worked hard for a company. He was arguing in effect that he had performed his role as a dutiful husband, perhaps even an ideal husband, and it was unjust that his (selfish, ungrateful) wife would now punish him simply because she "strongly wants" a divorce.

Writing in 2001, the high court worked its way through the facts the same way the lower court did but focused on two different issues. First, when Ms. Kobayashi was hospitalized for stomach cancer in 1986, she had left her husband a note in which she thanked him for all he had done for her over the years and expressed her desire to continue life with him. The lower court had glossed over the note, calling it a "will" prepared in case Ms. Kobayashi died in the operation. But to the Tokyo High Court, the letter was evidence that "at least until 1986...the marriage can be said to have been amicable."

Second, the high court focused on feelings—not of the couple but of their son, whose testimony it reproduced:

> He testified, "Inside the house, my father doesn't get involved with minor issues, and my mother is the one who counseled and listened to the children. In matters relating to school or work, my mother would always seek my father's opinion and do as he wished. My mother is the kind of person who pays attention to small things and is helpful. Sometimes she even goes too

far to be helpful. My father is a lord-of-the-manor type who doesn't do anything around the house. It's as if not doing anything is just the natural order of things to him. He's not the kind of person who would say thank you." "Even though my father doesn't say much, when my mother was hospitalized and had surgery for stomach cancer in 1986, he seemed very worried, he wouldn't say a word to us, and he didn't go see her by himself. It's from this point in time that their relations worsened, and our family became the kind of family that you wouldn't brag about to other people."

He opposes his parents' divorce because "I think it's only natural that running a family together over the course of forty years will have its bad moments. It's essential in daily life for a couple to talk to each other and solve their problems, to allow the other person to correct your behavior. I think my parents have reached a point at which they can't do that. They need to discuss things with each other and let each other know how they think, and to strive to satisfy the other person if possible. That might be difficult, but I think that that is the responsibility of people who have lived together for many years." "I have some misgivings about my parents living separate lives in their old age. I'm worried about what kind of lifestyles they would lead if they divorce and have to split income and expenses." "I want my parents to be a regular married couple, even if they can't be one that is said to get along well."

This is not a case that uses a "best interest of the child" standard as seen in U.S. cases; the "child" in question was thirty-three years old. Nor did the thirty-three-year-old reveal anything particularly new and decisive about the marriage. The court's use of the son's testimony suggests that it views marriage as an institution that extends beyond the two parties, even to other adults. As in the engagement cases in which parental desires affected the decision to marry, here a child's desire affects a parent's ability to divorce—a consideration that is not unusual in the Japanese case law.[53]

The court continued:

Examining all the facts of the many years of marriage between [the couple], although it cannot be denied that from the position of [Ms. Kobayashi], the marriage lacked sympathy and kindness [*omoiyaru to iu kozukai*], there was no specific act that could destroy the marital relationship. The relationship of [Mr. and Ms. Kobayashi] does not differ significantly from that of an ordinary [*tsūjō*] married couple.

The court's candor here is surprising: an "ordinary" marriage lacks "sympathy and kindness" and is predicated upon the fulfillment of duties and the absence of gambling or cheating? Even if as a matter of practice that is the norm, it is striking for a court to say so.

The court concluded:

> Mr. Kobayashi has experience in the world and is the kind of person who can be expected to live by societal standards of good sense. The parties should accept the results of this case, reconsider the marriage that has been constructed over the course of many years, change the things they need to change, and, with the help of their oldest son, strive to create a harmonious relationship.

Citing the son's testimony and Mr. Kobayashi's "strong desire" to stay married, the court refused to grant Ms. Kobayashi a divorce. And why should it, if the marriage is ordinary?[54]

Ms. Kobayashi had no choice but to remain married—and recall that legally, she must cohabit as well. As we will see in the at-fault divorce cases, a court might refuse a judicial divorce in order to make the parties bargain over a negotiated divorce. But in this case, the court is not encouraging private negotiation. It is ordering Ms. Kobayashi, who seems to have few financial resources with which to bribe her husband into a consensual divorce, to stay against her will.

A second case makes an even stronger judicial statement against late life-divorce. Mr. and Ms. Tanaka had been married for twenty-eight years, and their two children were adults. Mr. Tanaka ran an automobile repair business, and Ms. Tanaka was a housewife. According to Ms. Tanaka, her husband was violent. In addition to verbal abuse, he had pushed, hit, and poured water on her. He bit his son's finger until it bled, "not for talking back but merely for stating his opinion." Ms. Tanaka's shame, she said, prevented her from going to the doctor with her bruises. She tried unsuccessfully to kill herself. Finally, she left their home, and they lived apart for four years. She filed for divorce.

Ms. Tanaka cited Mr. Tanaka's violence as a "grave reason." She also explicitly acknowledged that she was influenced in part by the late-life divorce phenomenon. Like Mr. Kobayashi, Mr. Tanaka argued that because he worked hard at his business and neither gambled on horses nor cheated with women, there was no "grave reason."

The Nagoya District Court praised Mr. Tanaka with faint damns, acknowledging his violence but noting that it was sporadic. It also repeated Mr. Tanaka's claim that he did not gamble or cheat, a phrase that seems to symbolize a healthy marriage, or at least a dutiful husband, to courts. It then went beyond the facts of the case to mourn the demise of the family in Japan:

> The housework done by housewives used to be quite difficult. But from the end of the 1950s to the 1960s, washing machines, vacuum cleaners, and electric rice cookers, the three so-called "sacred instruments," proliferated, and it is said that the housewife's job became easier. This free time gives women time to contemplate. A woman looks back on her history with her husband and their children, has regrets, and dreams of a world in which she is free [*shōrai no jiyū na sekai wo yumemiru*]. Late-life divorce can be seen as one aspect of this modern trend.

It is not entirely clear what the court is getting at here. It might simply be giving a lesson in social history, or it might be imputing blame to Ms. Tanaka for choosing to end the marriage simply because technological advances made her life more carefree. In any event, the court recognized "late-life divorce" as a social concept (it has no legal significance), suggesting that it differs somehow from other, non-late-life, divorces.

When the court turned to analyze the Tanakas' marriage in particular, it viewed it through the lens of late-life divorce. It noted that during the trial, Mr. Tanaka "looked quite serious" in the corner of the courtroom. "With a compassion-invoking presence, he listened and watched the progression of the trial, looking sad and forlorn." The court concluded:

> It might be difficult for Mr. and Ms. Tanaka to continue their married life. But Mr. Tanaka opposes the divorce and he earnestly wants Ms. Tanaka to return to him. Now that their children have become independent and the couple should be preparing for a period of great change in their lives as they prepare for old age, if Mr. Tanaka can sufficiently reflect on the things written above which deserve reflection, there is a real possibility that this marriage to Ms. Tanaka can continue. If they can give each other, and especially Mr. Tanaka, one final chance, they should search together for the blue bird they were unable to find before no matter how they searched, and they should slowly settle down and leisurely talk with one another. Considering

all the circumstances, the marriage can continue, and accordingly the request to divorce in this case is denied.[55]

The effect of the ruling, like that in the Kobayashis' case, is that Ms. Tanaka must remain married to Mr. Tanaka until he, if ever, consents to a negotiated divorce. Ms. Tanaka, who left Mr. Tanaka for four years after she attempted suicide and endured years of verbal and physical abuse, should now search for the "blue bird." That flash of outsight, apparently a reference to Maurice Maeterlinck's 1908 play (which became a 1980 animated television series in Japan) in which the bird symbolizes happiness, is as jarring in a case about domestic abuse in Japanese as it would be in English. It does not bode well for Ms. Tanaka's future.

With this strange choice of words, the judge has expressed his hope for the future, certainly for the Tanakas, and given the sermon on vacuum cleaners and the family for many other married couples as well. As in the Kobayashis' case, the judge might be attempting to preserve some social order by keeping together families, the fundamental social unit. Given its history, the expectation that this particular social unit will find a bluebird on its shoulder after years of separation and abuse seems a bit optimistic.

At-Fault Divorce

The story of the judicial prohibition of at-fault divorce in Japan begins with a landmark 1952 Supreme Court decision in which the Inoues, husband and wife, were litigants. Mr. Inoue had a mistress, and they had a child together. He wished to live with her. Mr. Inoue claimed that Ms. Inoue dumped water on him and hit him with a broom. He filed for divorce.

Based on these facts, under the 1947 Civil Code revisions, adultery seems to have been established, and there might be a "grave reason" that made the marriage difficult to continue. But perhaps because those provisions had been in effect for such a short time, the Supreme Court raised another issue instead, an issue the Civil Code did not address. The only reason Ms. Inoue was violent, the Court said, was that Mr. Inoue angered her by getting his mistress pregnant. The Court ruled that Mr. Inoue could not divorce, for "if the petition is approved, the wife will be in dire straits [*fundari kettari,* literally, 'stepped on and kicked']. The law cannot tolerate immoral action. The most important role of law is to uphold virtue and not to indulge immorality. Law must always be interpreted in light of this principle."[56]

The immorality of which the court spoke was about not merely spousal equality but sexual activity. It noted that "the unprincipled nature of male-female relations after the end of the war is deplorable." Mr. Inoue, then, was punished not only for leaving his wife but for taking a mistress at a time in which doing so had become socially unacceptable.

But the case had ramifications beyond Mr. Inoue. The case established a Supreme Court precedent that a so-called "responsible" or "culpable" party (*yūseki haigūsha*), the at-fault party responsible for the decline of the marriage (in practice, almost always because of adultery), cannot receive a judicial divorce without the consent of the other spouse. *Ever.* The state guaranteed a faultless spouse lifetime marriage: the couple must remain married until the nonculpable spouse consents to a negotiated divorce.

In addition to the moral lesson, the no-at-fault-divorce rule might have been intended to protect women from financial abandonment. But it did nothing to protect women if the at-fault husband does *not* seek a divorce, as the ability to remain in a paper marriage helps wives little.[57] If the law offered women any protection, it did so only if the husband was the at-fault spouse; if a wife was at fault and wished to divorce, it was she who needed to pay a bribe to leave.

Another explanation for the rule seems likely: judges were distributing money between spouses so that spouses could bargain for divorce privately rather than sue in court.[58] By enforcing the 1952 at-fault rule, Japanese courts set a price at which a simple, negotiated divorce could be reached without further aid of the government. If an at-fault spouse wanted out badly, the bribe would be high; if not, the bribe would be low.

Over the decades that followed after the 1952 rule was announced, the environment for marriage and divorce in Japan changed. Women began to receive and seek university education in greater numbers. Women's employment opportunities increased. Women had fewer children and began to seek hobbies outside the home. Three important figures rose: the divorce rate, the percentage of marriages that were "love" marriages, and the average age at the time of marriage. The crown prince married a commoner to great fanfare as newspapers reported on their "love" (*aijō*).[59] Japan's sexual revolution separated (for some) sex and marriage. Even speech patterns changed; the gender differences in languages diminished as women's words became "rougher" and more masculine.[60] New terms like "feminism," "late-life divorce," and "domestic violence" entered the national vocabulary.

The legislature remained silent on the divorce issue, but the legal academy began to change the legal environment. Scholars like Masayuki Takanashi had long argued against the at-fault rule based on ethical grounds and the view of marriage as a voluntary arrangement.[61] Pressure to change the at-fault rule grew stronger in the 1980s, as academics noted that various countries around the world had begun to eliminate the fault requirement. As one scholar, for instance, noted in a 1985 comparative law journal symposium on changes in divorce law around the world, in the United States:

> [I]f one falls out of love with one's partner, one should divorce, and one should marry [remarry] a new partner with whom one falls in love. If one looks at things this way, adultery and so on mean nothing. A person should not stay married to a spouse he does not love; rather, he should quickly divorce and marry his adultery partner.[62]

In a handful of cases beginning in the 1980s, lower courts, conscious of these trends in society and legal scholarship, pushed the law by carving out exceptions to the 1952 rule. In a 1985 Sendai High Court case, for instance, a sexually unfaithful husband sued his wife for divorce. The court found that the wife's financial situation would not be affected by a divorce and that the couple's separation of thirty-five years was "more than twice as long as the longest statute of limitations, fifteen years." Despite the fact that the husband was at fault, and in seeming direct conflict with the 1952 Supreme Court case, the court granted the divorce.[63]

The Supreme Court of course knew of the lower court decisions, and was aware that its longstanding ruling was becoming out of sync. In the official commentary to the following 1987 Supreme Court case (released after the case was decided), the Court noted that lower courts had begun to diverge, that scholarship had begun to favor liberal divorce, and that several systems had significantly liberalized their divorce regimes (the Court examined in depth England, California, Germany, France, and Sweden). The Court also cited surveys that found that the public favored more liberal divorce rules. It then stated that those surveys were insufficient evidence of changing attitudes but finally noted that "one can feel some change" nonetheless on the issues.[64]

The facts of the monumental 1987 case were as follows. Mr. and Ms. Hiyama were married in 1937. The marriage was peaceful until 1949, when Ms. Hiyama discovered her husband's infidelity. Mr. Hiyama moved out to live with his lover. He filed for divorce in 1951, but the Tokyo District Court dismissed his claim on the ground that his adultery made him the at-fault party. He refiled for divorce after a 1984 attempt at mediation failed.

At the time the case reached the Supreme Court, the couple had lived separately for thirty-eight years after having lived together for only twelve. Mr. Hiyama was seventy-four and Ms. Hiyama was seventy. Their children were adults, Mr. Hiyama had financially supported his wife for years, and he lived a "quite stable economic life." The result under the law in effect at the time was clear: the couple simply would not have been allowed to divorce, no matter how badly Mr. Hiyama wanted out. But the 1987 Supreme Court, noting that divorce must not "go against the concepts of justice, equity, and social ethics," overturned its 1952 precedent. It allowed Mr. Hiyama to divorce despite his adultery, because of factors similar to those already raised by the lower courts: the couple's age (and lack of minor children), the lengthy separation, and the availability of financial support.[65]

The subsequent history of Japanese divorce law is largely about defining and applying the boundaries of this 1987 Supreme Court exception. Table 6.2 summarizes the responsible party cases published in law reporters and online since 1987.

The column headings represent the factors designated by the Supreme Court as important: the ratio of years married to years apart, age of spouses, children at home, and the "situation." The first three factors are self-explanatory and seem designed to measure the seriousness of the parties and to protect children. "Situation" means a "mental, social, or economically harsh situation that is remarkably in opposition to social morals." As the standard is applied in the courtroom, the divorcing spouse is entitled to a divorce upon proof of the first three objective elements—unless the spouse who opposes the divorce can prove a harsh situation.[66]

The list of factors suggests how important the situation of the parties in the 1987 case was. If anyone should be allowed to divorce, surely it is a stable seventy-four-year-old who has been estranged from his spouse for

TABLE 6.2. *Court Rulings on Divorce Requests by an At-Fault Spouse*

Date/Court	Citation	Years together/ Years apart	Ages	Situation	Children home?	Divorce granted?
2/19/1987, Supreme Court	1243 *Hanrei Jihō* 3	12/36	Both over 70	Husband, former corporate director, previously gave wife living expenses; in 1963, gave her $10,000 and an oil painting. Wife had $110,000 pension. Wife never asked for money during separation.	No	Yes
11/24/1987, Supreme Court	1256 *Hanrei Jihō* 28	4/30		Husband previously gave wife $30,000/ year of his $160,000 salary, paid loans, etc. Husband now with another woman, but she was not cause of separation.	No	Yes
2/12/1988, Supreme Court	1268 *Hanrei Jihō* 33	17/22		Husband is tax accountant; gave wife land during marriage.	No	Yes
4/7/1988, Supreme Court	1293 *Hanrei Jihō* 94	21/16		Wife supported by and living with daughter.	No	Yes
12/8/1988, Supreme Court	41(3) *Kasai Geppō* 145	10 months/ 10 years	Husband 37, Wife 39	Husband is cook on foreign ship, salary of $40,000. Wife helps out in family shop. No support from husband.	No	Yes
2/27/1990, Tokyo High Court	714 *Hanrei Times* 217	8/22	Husband 60, Wife 58	Husband is doctor; spent $500,000 for wife's failed business. Sends $200/month in expenses. Wife also owns property.	No	Yes
3/25/1990, Tokyo High Court	42(6) *Kasai Geppō* 40	10/10	Both 47	Husband has money; wife works part time.	Yes	No
3/28/1989, Supreme Court	699 *Hanrei Times* 178	22/8	Husband 60, Wife 57	Husband is local bureaucrat who "overspends."	No	No

Date, Court	Citation		Family	Description		
9/7/1990, Supreme Court	956 *Jurisato Hanrei Card* 99, 1988 (o) 316	5/15	Husband 61, Wife 53	Husband runs publishing business. Wife unemployed but lives in husband's condo. Husband raised daughter from age 4.	No	Yes
11/8/1990, Supreme Court	1370 *Hanrei Jihō* 55	23/8	Husband 52, Wife 55	Wife earns $600/month as dressmaker. Husband regularly sends support payments.	No	Yes
5/26/1992, Osaka High Court	797 *Hanrei Times* 253	24/26	Husband 84, Wife 78	Husband returns once or twice a month to take care of things at home. Wife receives $3,000/month from husband's former employer.	No	Yes
11/2/1993, Supreme Court	46(9) *Kasai Geppō* 40	17/9	Husband 53, Wife 52	Husband unemployed. Wife committed adultery, but husband's violence (grabbing her neck, throwing buckets of water on her when she comes home late) makes him responsible party as well.	No	Yes
2/8/1994, Supreme Court	1505 *Hanrei Jihō* 59	15/12	Husband 56, Wife 54	Husband pays $1,500/month. Youngest of 4 children is 18.	Yes	Yes
2/20/1997, Tokyo High Court	1602 *Hanrei Jihō* 95	27/20	Husband 77, Wife 74	Husband was newspaper company president; returns to take care of wife from time to time. Husband pays $3,000/month.	No	No
11/19/1997, Tokyo High Court	999 *Hanrei Times* 280	6/14	Husband 36, Wife 32	Husband earns $8,000/month, gives $2,500/month to wife.	Yes	No
1/30/1998, Tokyo District Court	1015 *Hanrei Times* 232	3/3		Husband pays $1,500/month.	Yes	No
6/26/2002, Tokyo High Court	1801 *Hanrei Jihō* 80	22/6	Husband 51, Wife 50	Husband works for company; wife teaches Japanese.	No	Yes

(Continued)

TABLE 6.2. (*Continued*)

Date/Court	Citation	Years together/ Years apart	Ages	Situation	Children home?	Divorce granted?
2/21/2003, Nagoya High Court	2001 (ne) 1108	27/7	Husband 62, Wife 60	Both doctors. Separated for 16 years, but 9 of those years were for work-related reasons.	No	No
5/8/2003, Nagoya High Court	2002 (ta) 78	13/17	Husband 57, Wife 56	Husband is retired from Special Defense Forces.	No	No
7/31/2003, Fukuoka High Court	1162 *Hanrei Times* 245	4/9	Husband 42, Wife 35	Husband is doctor, pays $9,000/month.	Yes	Yes
8/26/2004, Fukuoka High Court	58(1) *Kasai Geppō* 91	21/9	Husband 55, Wife 55	Wife works part-time. Husband pays son's tuition and plans to give wife $80,000 upon divorce.	No	No
11/18/2004, Supreme Court	1881 *Hanrei Jihō* 90	7/2	Husband 34, Wife 33	Husband is tax officer, wife unemployed; husband gives wife $800 of his $3,000/ month salary.	Yes	No
3/15/2007, Osaka High Court	1251 *Hanrei Times* 312	8/13	Husband 46, Wife 46	Husband pays $15,000 in consolation and $14,000 for children's education.	Yes	Yes
5/14/2008, Tokyo High Court	61(5) *Kasai Geppō* 44	15/15	Husband 57, wife 50	Husband pays $1,400/month. Family has little money and adult son is handicapped and husband does not appear to want to offer care.	No	No

more than half of his life. The court standard seems to have been tailored to the facts of that case.

The test says nothing about the desires of the parties; it says nothing whatsoever about emotions or feelings. The test looks at the ratio of years married to years apart but makes no attempt to measure the quality of those years. Of course, we might question whether we want judges to determine quality and desires. But as we have seen throughout the book, judges routinely make such determinations. They simply choose not to do so in at-fault divorce cases, relying instead on a mechanical test.

The result is that many marriages in which spouses are unable to reach a negotiated agreement continue over the objections of a spouse, as in the following case. The Nakatas married in 1965 and had four children. Sometime between 1985 and 1991, they began living separately under the same roof; Mr. Nakata lived downstairs and Ms. Nakata lived upstairs. In 2004, Mr. Nakata filed for divorce.

Mr. Nakata argued that "for eighteen years, [Ms. Nakata and I] have had no conversation and have never had a meal together. I'm not even invited to our children's weddings. We live separate lives and our married life is completely destroyed." Ms. Nakata saw things differently: "Although we live separately on the first and second floors of the house, we see each other almost every day, and I inform [Mr. Nakata] about family weddings, funerals, births, and other ceremonial events. Our lifestyle can be thought of as a form of living together, and our married life is not completely destroyed." Ms. Nakata's motivation seems much like that of Ms. Tsunoda's client from earlier in this chapter: to maintain her economic lifestyle, she had to stretch the truth.

Writing in 2005, the Tokyo District Court examined the history of the marriage. In 1986, the court said, the Nakatas began to fight over money. Ms. Nakata wanted pain management therapy for her back and arthritis, but Mr. Nakata refused to pay the required $60 per doctor's office visit. In order to pay for these expenses:

> In 1988, Ms. Nakata began working part-time at a nearby kindergarten, from seven o'clock to nine o'clock in the morning and from four o'clock to six o'clock in the evenings. Because she thought Mr. Nakata would oppose the job, she did not mention it to him beforehand. But after she took the job, Mr. Nakata learned of it when the kindergarten called their house. He told

her that a man's place is to work outside the house to support the family, and the woman's place is to stay in the house to protect it. She responded, "I'm doing it because I want the money," and did not quit the job. This worsened the relationship between the two.

In 1991, the couple fought over how to care for Mr. Nakata's aging mother. Mr. Nakata told Ms. Nakata, "If you're not going to take care of my parents, get the hell out." After that argument:

> Mr. Nakata began to ignore Ms. Nakata and the rest of the family. For a while, Mr. Nakata threw outside any of Ms. Nakata's personal belongings that he found on the first floor. After that, they did not eat together and lived separately on the first floor and the second floor. Because the bathroom was located in the first floor, Ms. Nakata initially went there to bathe. But on November 21, 1991, the defendant put up signs that said "No Bathing Without Permission" and "A Charge of 500 Yen Will Be Assessed for Each Bath Taken Outside of Regular Hours." Ms. Nakata began bathing at a local public bath. Except for chance meetings at the mailbox or to take out the trash, they lived completely separate lives and continue to do so now.

Ms. Nakata financed her meager lifestyle by cashing in life insurance policies, taking out loans, and saving her kindergarten earnings. After more than a decade of this lifestyle, Mr. Nakata filed for divorce.

The court found that Mr. Nakata was at fault, a somewhat rare finding for a nonadultery case but one the facts support. It then applied the standard. The parties lived separately for at least thirteen of their thirty-nine years of marriage, a period the court found sufficiently lengthy. They were both in their sixties. Their children were adults. But, the court said, given that Ms. Nakata was sixty-six years old and her only income was the $1,000 per month that she received from her part-time kindergarten job, a divorce would leave her in an economically harsh situation that was "remarkably in opposition to social morals." The court refused to grant the divorce. If Ms. Nakata continued to refuse to consent to divorce, the couple would remain in their troubled marriage.[67]

Occasionally a court strays from the standard and examines more emotional factors. The Fukazawas were married in 1994 and had a child in 1996. Ms. Fukazawa obsessed about cleanliness. She demanded that her husband remove his socks at the front door and change into his "inside socks." She made him place his briefcase on newspapers. If he played in the sandbox with their child, she required him to bathe before entering the living room. She made him place his head on newspaper ads if he lay on the floor so as not to soil the tatami or carpet.

In 2000, Mr. Fukazawa began an affair. Two months later, he asked his wife for a divorce. Because his mother, in the words of the court, "would not allow him to remarry" if he divorced, the couple began living together again. A year later Mr. Fukazawa opposed his mother and filed for divorce.

The lower court acknowledged the husband's adultery but said that the couple "have completely lost any love and affection for each other as husband and wife, and taking into account the fact that a period of two years and four months has passed since they began living separately, that there has been no interaction as a family between the couple during this period, that there is no chance of conducting a communal life as a normal husband and wife in the future, and that [Ms. Fukazawa's] parents are alive and are relatively well off financially." The lower court granted the divorce. In doing so, it seems to have completely ignored the 1987 test in favor of more emotional criteria of loss of love, affection, interaction, and community.

On appeal, the 2004 Supreme Court paraphrased the decision of the lower court: "Although [Ms. Fukazawa] refuses to divorce [Mr. Fuka-zawa], it is because she can sustain economic stability through the continuation of a legal marital relationship and not because of love and affection [*jōai*]." The Court, then, explicitly *acknowledged* the marriage's lack of love, a factor that mattered to the lower court. It then ignored that lack of love and turned to the established standard: time apart, time together, minor children, and finances. In this case, the time apart was too short, the time together relatively too long, a seven-year-old child was present, and Ms. Fukazawa's financial situation was dire. The Court denied the divorce, dismissing the sentimental lower court's emphasis on love and affection, and leaving the loveless parties to negotiate privately.[68]

In some areas of Japanese law and society, it is difficult to determine whether the perceived problems are societal and enforced by, or perhaps merely described by, courts, or if courts are causing the social problems. In the at-fault divorce context, however, it seems that it is courts that are problematic, as two surveys show that public opinion is far more nuanced and lenient than the law.

First, in 2006, the Cabinet Office conducted on behalf of the Ministry of Justice a nationwide survey on family law and legal institutions.[69] Two questions from that survey are directly on point. First, respondents were asked their opinion on granting divorce to an at-fault spouse after a period of separation. Fifty-eight percent of respondents agreed that an at-fault spouse should be allowed to divorce after the passage of a certain period of time. Sixteen percent disagreed, and 22 percent were undecided.

The next question asked that majority of respondents how long the minimum period of separation should be. The three largest groups of respondents said less than two years (22.1%), two to four years (27.2%), and "decisions must be made on a case-by-case basis" (26.8%). Only 2.8 percent picked the longest term of ten years or more.

A second survey that focused specifically on the at-fault spouse issue was conducted in 2007 by Shozo Ota and his graduate students at the University of Tokyo Law School.[70] In that study, respondents favored a required separation period averaging 3.31 years for a responsible party to divorce.[71] But those average data mask three larger phenomena. First, one-third of respondents said that "zero years"—no time at all—should be required for a responsible party to divorce (those same respondents might nonetheless support the doctrine if, for instance, young children were at home). Second, "respondents had sympathy for wives who were cheated on, but not for husbands who were cheated on": people were more likely to allow at-fault wives to divorce than at-fault husbands and more likely to allow an at-fault husband than an at-fault wife to divorce if the divorce were conditioned on the at-fault spouse providing sufficient economic support.[72] Third, the study also found differences in responses by sex. To a statistically significant degree, male respondents were more likely to allow divorce and to require a longer separation period before divorce than female respondents.[73]

Courts, then, are at odds with the public: their standard is higher and more rigid. The high standard for at-fault divorce set by the courts might force parties into private negotiations that benefit the spouse who wants to stay in the marriage (often the wife), but they do so at what seems to be a high cost.[74]

"The American story about marriage," one U.S. legal scholar writes, "goes something like this: marriage is a relationship that exists primarily for the fulfillment of the individual spouses. If it ceases to perform this function, no one is to blame and either spouse may terminate it at will. After divorce, each spouse is expected to be self-sufficient. If this is not possible with the aid of property division, some rehabilitative maintenance may be in order for a temporary period. Children hardly ever appear in the story; at most they are rather shadowy characters in the background."[75]

What a different story emerges from the Japanese cases. Marriage is not for the fulfillment of individual spouses. It is a publicly recognized contract in which the desire of one spouse is sufficient to maintain it. If a marriage ends, a spouse can terminate only if the other spouse consents. If he or she does not, the government determines whether it can be terminated based in part on its assessment of blame. Children are central to divorce decisions, so central that their existence alone—not simply their best interests, but their existence—can render divorce impossible. Their opinions matter even as adults, as courts take seriously their views that Mom and Dad should stay together, even if Mom or Dad would rather not.

The result is that courts in Japanese divorce cases exercise more control over troubled relationships than cases from other legal contexts. Instead of merely approving of or commenting on the lack of emotion, courts effectively *mandate* that some bad marriages continue if bribes aren't paid. When love is used as a decision-making criterion by a lower court, the appeals court overrules. Courts subjugate the intent of (at least one of) the parties to their own views on appropriateness.

Divorce cases are difficult, and a court's ability to refuse to grant a divorce even if grounds are shown does not make decision making any easier. The judicially mandated use of the sense of society as a yardstick here, as elsewhere, does not sound terribly controversial. But in many divorce cases that use the standard, the judges' opinions seem not to reflect the times, and in some cases we have evidence that they simply are getting the norms wrong. Some in Japan would argue that this result is a product of an insular judiciary; judges would counter that they are simply doing their best to interpret the law.

In the case law that results, love loses. That result is expected; indeed, it is that very expectation that led me to investigate the issues that led to this book. But given the ease with which judges raise love in this context and discuss emotions in others, it now comes as a bit of a surprise. Given the judge's expectation in the Child Predator case that "sex in particular performs the role of cultivating the bond between husband and wife that creates and supports love"; given the highly volatile and potentially violent context for love;, given the judicial expectation that certain relationships will be real, nonmonetary, or earnest; and given the ways judges reach deeply into the emotional aspects of relationships, does it not seem the slightest bit odd that similar factors rarely are important when judges decide the fate of marriages?

CONCLUSION

Mitsutaka, a doctor, had a series of affairs with nurses. His wife, Yuriko, a nurse's assistant and part-time hostess, became angry. They fought, and he killed her and their children. Guilty.

But there's much more. The Yokohama District Court tells the story, picking up after the couple began living together in 1990, as follows:

In January 1991, Mitsutaka learned that Yuriko was pregnant. Because he had no desire to marry her, he had her have an abortion. However, soon thereafter Yuriko became pregnant again. This time, she strongly desired to have the baby. Mitsutaka told Yuriko that he would not marry her even if she gave birth to the child. Yuriko said that she would give birth even if Mitsutaka would not marry her. Mitsutaka then promised that he would acknowledge paternity. A girl was born on November 18, 1991. After the child was born, Mitsutaka adored her, and he thought that a child naturally [*yahari*] should have a father. He thought Yuriko would approach him about marriage after the child's birth, but she did not, and, seeing her gentle manner, he decided to marry her. On November 30 of the same year, he submitted the couple's marriage notification form together with the birth registration for the child, whom they named Matsue.[1]

Within 24 hours of submitting the paperwork for the birth and the marriage to City Hall, Mitsutaka was gone:

> Mitsutaka went to work at a hospital in Hitachi City, where he lived alone, apart from his family, because of his job [*tanshin funin*]. As soon as he began single life, he thought he should not have submitted the marriage notification form, he regretted that he had been in such a rush to submit it, and soon he began to think that Yuriko must somehow have tricked him into it. His fond feelings for Yuriko began to turn cold.
>
> Mitsutaka could not get rid of the feeling that he had wanted to play freely with women until he turned thirty years old. In January 1992, he propositioned nurses at the hospital where he worked, and he began to have affairs. The more affairs he had with nurses, the more emotionally detached from Yuriko he became. As his affairs became more frequent, he began to come home on weekends less frequently. Yuriko figured out that Mitsutaka was having an affair. When she pressed him for answers, he was evasive. She called the other women on the phone and chastised them. After that, she harbored suspicions toward him and began to monitor his behavior. Mitsutaka hated Yuriko for this, he became even further detached from her, and he did not end the affairs, choosing instead to scrape and claw his way out of each situation in one way or another.

In April 1992, Mitsutaka moved home to work in a university hospital, and his relationship with Yuriko and their daughter Matsue improved. Yuriko wanted to move to a house, and they did so. Yuriko became pregnant again, and the couple had a son in February 1993—eleven months after Mitsutaka's return home.

Two months later, Mitsutaka left his job at the university hospital and began to practice medicine at a smaller hospital, which provided him with the considerable salary of $10,000 a month. He paid off credit card debt, "became comfortable in his new job, felt free and rich, and his womanizing habits reemerged; beginning in June, he began to have one affair after another [*tsugitsugito*] with nurses at the hospital where he worked." As for Yuriko:

> As Mitsutaka began coming home late, she realized he was having an affair, and she once again pressed him for answers. Mitsutaka repeatedly avoided

her questions, and gradually they began to lose their effect; instead, Mitsutaka began to pressure Yuriko. From the beginning, Mitsutaka had thought Yuriko was a flawed wife; she was selfish, she had wrong ideas about money, and she did not properly do the housework or childrearing. When the couple fought, Mitsutaka would attack Yuriko with these thoughts, and Yuriko would respond even more strongly. The couple's fights would intensify, with each yelling at the other harshly. At times there was violence.

During these fights, Mitsutaka argued that because Yuriko did not earn a living, she had no right to voice her opinion. Yuriko reacted by taking part-time jobs, first as a hostess and karaoke companion, and then as a night-shift assistant at a medical lab, further neglecting her housework and childrearing. Mitsutaka and Yuriko continued to grow colder, they fought and said that they had no love for each other, and they became meaner and more entrenched in their positions.

As Mitsutaka's relationship with Yuriko worsened, he continued to turn to other women, especially to a nurse at his hospital with whom he began an affair in late August 1994. The court said that he "sweet-talked" the nurse by telling her that he wanted to divorce his wife and marry her. The relationship further impacted the marriage:

> In the beginning of September, as Mitsutaka began to stay out all night, Yuriko pressed him to tell her the name of the other woman, and when she learned the name of the nurse, she met her face-to-face. She was surprised to hear from the nurse that Mitsutaka wanted to marry her, and she vowed never to divorce him. She called the nurse's mother and demanded compensation. She called Mitsutaka's father and told him of the affair. His father expressed his strong opposition to his son. Yuriko told Mitsutaka that she would not permit him to work in the same hospital as the other woman. She began to pressure him to quit his job. Mitsutaka told her that he would not be able to find such good employment easily, and he coaxed her into giving him some time to break off his relationship with the nurse. But all the while, he did not end the relationship with the nurse, and in fact he told her he would leave his wife to be with her.

Faced with this pressure—from his inability to divorce Yuriko, from Yuriko's insistence on compensation from the nurse and her family, from the demand that either Mitsutaka or the nurse quit his or her job, and from a threat that Yuriko would talk directly to the head of the hospital—

Mitsutaka caved. For the month of September, he focused on his family, and even took a vacation with them. But just as it seemed that Yuriko's suspicions had abated:

> On October 18, Yuriko became suspicious that Mitsutaka's [upcoming] company trip was really a trip with the other woman. She also inquired flatly as to what had happened to the decision to quit the hospital, saying it in such a way as to show that she had not forgotten about the incident. Mitsutaka felt the obstinacy of her remarks and realized that Yuriko was always going to insist that he leave the hospital and that she had not appreciated his month of diligence at maintaining his family. He was astonished, and his hatred for Yuriko grew even deeper than in the past. He became angrier, thought that he could no longer continue to stay married and live together with Yuriko, and began to embrace the thought that if he could not divorce her, it would be acceptable for her to die.

The two continued to argue for the next few days, until Mitsutaka went on his company trip. When he returned, Yuriko complained that "even if you bring me souvenirs, I still can't feel your love." Yuriko asked him if he loved her, and his response left little room for interpretation:

> "Of course I don't love you. But I can't divorce you, so we don't have any choice but to keep living together." When Yuriko heard him blurt out the words so bluntly, she became furious, and, while wielding a knife, yelled that she would stab him and kill herself. She chased him, even outside the house, and as the night wore on, their hatred and anger led to intense fighting, at which point, as if there were no other options, she yelled, "You're thinking that it would be good if I weren't around, right? That it would be good if I died. Kill me!" She put the knife to her neck and fell toward Mitsutaka. To hear Yuriko say such things and behave this way made Mitsutaka think she was simply trying to get a rise out of him, and his hatred increased.
>
> After this intense fighting, as if Yuriko had lost all strength, she stopped making dinner and cleaning the house. When Mitsutaka came home at night he would eat a box lunch [*bentō*], and the family would not even eat together.

The inevitable climax occurred four nights later. But let's put that off for one more paragraph for a question: Why does the story not start *here*?

Why did the court begin this narrative four years earlier, when the couple met, when he "had her have" an abortion? Why not begin tonight? Why not three years ago, with Mitsutaka's first affair or the birth of his daughter? With the birth of the son? I assume here, as I have throughout the book, that the court includes facts because they matter to the story. Yuriko's confrontations with the nurse and her mother matter, the lack of souvenirs matters, and the conversation about love matters. These premonitory facts are intended to resonate with readers, to tell us what to expect both in the story and in the judicial outcome.

And now for the conclusion. On Mitsutaka's way home from work, he stopped at a discount shop and bought plastic rope, duct tape, scissors, plastic bags, and gloves—all, the court stated unquestioningly, to fix the doghouse as Yuriko had requested. He fell asleep that night on the sofa. At four in the morning, Yuriko woke him up, saying, "So you hate sleeping with me, huh?" The court continued:

Because Yuriko spoke so coldly in an effort to draw him into a fight, Mitsutaka became enraged. He criticized her for making the house a complete mess, for not cooking and looking after the children as she should have, and for working part-time in the middle of the night. Under pressure, Yuriko responded, "I work because we have loans. I can't quit my job because you might divorce me and I don't know when you'll do it." She became more excited and began to wail about Mitsutaka's affairs. She grabbed his arm with her fingernails. When that happened, Mitsutaka told her that he was living with her even though he didn't like [*suki*] her, and so on. She became hysterical; she said, "I'm going to talk directly to the head of the hospital and make you and that nurse quit," to which he replied, "If I quit now, I won't have a place to work, and we won't be able to survive." As the fight escalated, Mitsutaka at last yelled, "If you go to the hospital, I swear I'll kill [*bukkorosu*] you."

Things were quiet for a while after that, but at 5:30 in the morning, Yuriko suddenly went to the kitchen. She made some noise there, and she soon returned to the living room with a knife and the rope that Mitsutaka purchased the night before. She said, "If you hate me so much, you should kill me [*koroshite moratta hō ga ii*]." When Mitsutaka told her to put down the knife, she told him that he should just strangle her with the rope. When he told her that she should go ahead and die [*jibun de shine*], she wound the rope around her neck and gave it to Mitsutaka, saying, "I want you to kill me. Hold the rope so I can hang myself." Mitsutaka stood on the sofa and held in his hands the rope that was wound around Yuriko's neck. Yuriko joined him on the sofa, saying, "Hold the rope tightly. I'll die for you [if that's what you want] [*shinde ageru wa*]."

She jumped off the sofa, but Mitsutaka's hands slipped, and the rope slipped from her neck. At this point, Yuriko yelled at him, "If you don't kill me I'm going to the hospital tomorrow. Because you messed up my life, it's only natural that I mess up yours. Why don't you just kill me [*nande ko-roshite kurenainoyo*]?" When Mitsutaka heard this, he realized that Yuriko was intent on destroying herself. He remembered all the hatred he felt, and he formed the intent to kill, thinking that Yuriko could not remain alive. He pulled tightly with both hands on the rope that was wound around her neck as Yuriko grasped for his hands. He continued to pull on the rope with all his strength. As Yuriko's hands, with which she had been scratching Mitsutaka, began to fall away, he let go of the rope. Yuriko fell on the floor, gasping for air. Mitsutaka jumped on top of her and put his hands on her nose and mouth. Yuriko (age thirty-one) died of homicide by asphyxiation.

Mitsutaka—whose testimony, reliable or otherwise, must be the source of most of the court's facts—realized that as a murderer, his life "was over." He began to "think of the future of his children, who had a dead mother and a murderer father. He pitied them and thought they would be better off [*shiawase*] dead than alive." He also felt, the court said, "in a corner of his heart" that they would be a "nuisance" (*jama*) to him if left alive. He went up the stairs to their rooms and, using the same rope that he used on Yuriko, he strangled his one-year-old son and two-year-old daughter.

Mitsutaka considered suicide, but before he could reach a decision, he realized that it was past 9 a.m. and he should be at work. He dragged Yuriko's body upstairs, went to work, and came home early. On his way home, he decided not to commit suicide but to dispose of the bodies instead. He wrapped the bodies in plastic and rope and tied weights to them. He took care of an errand in the evening, and when he returned home, he decided to wait until nightfall to move the bodies.

To pass the time, the doctor went to the red-light district of Tokyo's Shinjuku ward. He saw a strip show and went to a soapland. This raises a question: Who cares? The court has already told us of Mitsutaka's deeds, and the outcome does not look good for him. We still might want to know what happens to the bodies, or how the police catch him, but surely the fact that he went to a strip show and a soapland is not directly relevant to his guilt; it could have been left out of the narrative just as easily as the court left out the clothes he wore that day or what he had to eat.

The court is setting us up, of course. Mitsutaka, this despicable human being, has brutally killed his family, and now what does he do? Instead of panicking (good), mourning (better), or turning himself in (best), he casually and selfishly goes in search of sex (bad), and his partner was not his girlfriend but a prostitute (worse?). By adding those facts, the court signals not only the outcome of the case but its understanding of how sex will be coded by readers.

Back to the story. After his sexual escapades, Mitsutaka returned home, loaded the bodies into the trunk of his car around midnight, drove to the bay, and dumped them in the ocean. He then filed a missing person report with the police, met with Yuriko's mother and lied about the events, and attempted to get his girlfriend to formulate an alibi with him. Police found the bodies a few days later and arrested him. He confessed.

The district court, the court from which I have taken the facts, found that Yuriko was in part to blame because the continuous fighting was the result of both spouses' stubbornness. After noting that Mitsutaka showed serious, deep regret for his actions, the court sentenced him to life in prison.

Prosecutors sought the death penalty and appealed the sentence to the Tokyo High Court. Prosecutors protested the district court's characterization of Yuriko's conduct as blameworthy. The cause of the marital strife, they argued, was Mitsutaka's infidelity, and Yuriko should not be blamed for it. Any "hysteria" she experienced was his fault, not hers. Moreover, they argued, Mitsutaka "behaved egotistically," "never fostered love [*jōai*] or tried to raise his level of humanity," was "self-centered" in his "multiple relationships with women," and "clearly had problematic views on women and ethics, considering his multiple affairs."

The high court rejected these arguments. Although it was true, the court said, that Mitsutaka's adultery was a major cause of the fighting, the collapse of his marriage was not entirely his fault, and that fact must be considered in sentencing. It found further that "although it is only natural [*atarimae*] that Yuriko would refuse to grant a divorce and would pressure him about his affair," Mitsutaka's motivations were more complex than simply wanting out. He wanted, for instance, to avoid losing his job, and in the case of his children, he killed them out of pity, thinking they would join their mother "in heaven." The court affirmed the life sentence, saving Mitsutaka from the gallows.

The facts of the case are extreme. Murders of this sort are not everyday occurrences in Japan just as they are not in the United States. But the words of the judges even in a case based on exceptional events tell us much about their vision of love, sex, and marriage. Consider first some of the subjective factors that appear in the court's judgment. The court found Yuriko partly to blame for the situation that led to her murder because of the couple's lack of "mutual respect" and "common understanding," suggesting that she was somehow asking for it. It found it "only natural" that Yuriko would *refuse* to divorce her husband, a serial philanderer in a loveless marriage. It found Mitsutaka's views on women to be "problematic" but raised no eyebrows about Mitsutaka's soapland trip or Yuriko's harassing of the other woman's *parents* for compensation. The court was silent about Yuriko's hostessing except to note that it resulted in Yuriko neglecting her household duties, suggesting that the problem wasn't the hostessing but the lack of maid service. The court expressed no shock at the idea that a parent might prefer death for motherless children. It recited the prosecutorial argument that Mitsutaka never fostered "love" and yet did not mention that love in its sentencing discussion.

The "objective" facts, mined by the judges and uncolored by them except for their lack of commentary, would be such unnatural overkill in a novel as to make it unbelievable. In a single case we have an abortion at the request of the man, a doomed commuter marriage, multiple affairs, compensation demanded of the other woman for an affair, refusals to grant divorce, hostessing, explicit expressions of lack of love in marriage, soaplands, and strip clubs—most presented drolly as if they are ordinary parts of life. Truth might be stranger than fiction, but this is both: a version of the truth shaped by judges into a readable short story laden with the elements of cultural goo that pervade the cases in this book.

The picture that emerges from this story and from others in this book is that of a particular kind of lovesickness in Japan. Love glooms eternal. To judges, at least, love is characterized not by caring, romance, or sentimental warmth but by pain. If people fall in love, they suffer, in the most extreme cases to the point of death, experiencing overwhelming, unavoidable, and disruptive emotions.

Japanese judges also have a particular vision of sex. When sex is consensual, multiple abortions at the request of the man are common, "normal" sex is either violent or shameful, and underage girls are appropriate partners if the man is "earnest"—but not in the throes of passion. When sex is purchased, it comes from a state-sanctioned prostitution industry or from a huge adult video industry that caters to rape fetishes (among others), despite what appears to be a common judicial sentiment that the videos lead to violence and perversion. When sex occurs at a pseudo-brothel, the sex industry charges for it; when it occurs outside of a marriage, it is courts that put a price on it—but as in underage sex, some "real" component short of love often is required.

To Japanese judges, love is central to marriage in the abstract, but it is so unachievable in real-life marriages that its absence is expected. Marriage, then, becomes a partnership, or a contract governed by courts. If spouses stay married until late in life, or if a court simply thinks they should stay together, they may not divorce unless they both consent. If one spouse is responsible for the breakdown of the marriage, that spouse can divorce only under very narrow conditions strictly enforced by courts. Perhaps it's just as well that love remains an unreachable ideal in marriage, as the turbulent love seen in other cases seems unlikely to last over time.

That is a rough cut of the judicial vision, but the discourse on love, sex, and marriage that we have seen in this book is far more complex. Judicial opinions are part of a complicated legal system that attempts to govern an extraordinary range of activity. Within that system, courts reach far more deeply into hearts and psyches than statutes require. Courts view the marital relationship not simply as a contract between two people but as a family bond the dissolution of which can be affected by statements of adult children. Courts have much to say about sex (with the exception of homosexuality), voicing opinions as to which activities are normal and which are decidedly not. And love, which seems unlikely to have legal importance, is often an explicit or implicit factor in decision making.

This lack of separation of love from law is striking. It seems natural that the index to the book *Law in Japan*[2] contains no entry for love, while *Love in Modern Japan*[3] contains no entry for law. We tend to think of human love and state law as distant concepts. Law is rigid, constructed, and precise; love is fuzzy, natural, and undeniably imprecise. And yet in the regulations of the state we have found a Japan complicated by painful love, serial abortions, tortuous Valentine's Days, and late-life divorces; a Japan afflicted with romantic stalkers, compensated dating, and commodified relationships—the details of which we are privy to only because courts delve deeply into the lives of litigants to discover them.

The love-and-law stories are not a faithful representation of the totality of Japanese culture; rather, they are one part of a developing Japanese social environment that judges must navigate. The parties that appear in front of judges carry loads of social, cultural, and personal baggage through which judges sift to determine The Facts. Using the "sense of society" as a guide, judges apply to those facts laws that are the product of lengthy negotiations among competing interest groups. The resulting judicial opinions affect the social environment and the ways in which people carry on their daily affairs (innocent or otherwise) by encouraging change and by shaping incentives for proper behavior.

This embeddedness of judicial opinions in the Japanese social environment suggests linkages and commonalities with other areas of that environment on the issues of love, sex, and marriage. Of course, the judicial vision of Japanese lovesickness cannot be ascribed to all of Japan. People experience lovesickness in different ways and to different degrees, and many people are perfectly satisfied with their lives. But perhaps we can begin to link some of the ideas of judges with those of nonjudges by looking at the people who are closest to the judges' opinions: the litigants. Judges tell the stories, but the factual elements do not appear out of thin air. Mitsutaka's soapland-and-strip-club outing and Yuriko's part-time hostessing, for instance, might have been irrelevant to the ruling, but the facts remain. Litigants and prosecutors bring cases the elements of which suggest an at least partially shared set of conceptions, experiences, and intuitions.

Many of the concepts that arise in the cases also correlate with evidence from outside the courtroom. In the love arena, we have seen that half of unmarried Japanese young adults have no friends of the opposite sex and that the leading male conception of love is that it "is complex and sometimes leads to pain"—the same vision of the judiciary (and in the case of stalking, the legislature as well). As for sex, four out of ten couples leave their pajamas on to do it, a third of abortions are performed for the man, more than half of men have visited a prostitute, and girls want to try to be hostesses far more than lawyers—data that fit well with the judiciary's views of conservatively patterned private and readily available public sex. In marriage, surveys show that sex is a duty and that "keeping romance alive" and "being in love" are far less important than "financial security"—an emotionally detached vision enforced by the courts.

The social and judicial spheres correlate in more amorphous ways as well. Japanese has no easy expression for "soulmate" but has concepts of late-life divorce, compensated dating, vomit pornography, delivery health, and sexlessness. Marriage vows rarely mention love. Private investigators frequently are hired to investigate straying spouses and potential mates. And Japan's much-discussed social problems of a low birthrate, social shut-ins, a rising divorce rate, and high rates of abortion, sexual dissatisfaction, and suicide appear almost as frequently in the cases as they do in the press.

Within these constructs of law and society, Japanese judges translate incidents into legal dramas, morality plays, and cautionary tales. Along the way, subtly or otherwise, intentional or not, they put forth a particular image of love, sex, and marriage in Japan. Their Japan is a place of "sexual hedonism, the collapse of the family system, and adultery," a place where an "ordinary" marriage "lacks sympathy and kindness," a place where Mitsu-taka's retort to his soon-to-be-deceased wife, "Of course I don't love you. But I can't divorce you," is firmly grounded in the law.

Ah, love.

NOTES

Introduction

1. He was charged with violations of the Penal Code (art. 176): "a person who by violence or threat commits an indecent act with a male or female person...shall be punished."

2. See Atsushi Koyano, *Sei to Ai no Nihongo Kōza* [A Course in the Japanese of Sex and Love] 173 (2003); Hikaru Saitō, Hentai—H, in Shōichi Inoue, ed., *Sei no Yōgoshū* [Sex Vocabulary] 45, 53 (2004).

3. Nara District Court, 1257 *Hanrei Times* 336 (Sept. 26, 2006) ("*occhan, ecchi*"); Niigata District Court, 1299 *Hanrei Jihō* 152 (Aug. 26, 1988) ("ano ojisan ecchi na ojisan").

4. See Amy Adler, The Perverse Law of Child Pornography, 101 *Colum. L. Rev.* 209 (2001) (on the "pedophilic gaze").

5. Shizuoka District Court, 1041 *Hanrei Times* 293 (Dec. 1, 1999).

6. Although the note is anonymous, it reveals things that only the judge would know, such as reasons for the denial of bail. The tone also matches that of the opinion.

7. 1041 *Hanrei Times* 293 (Dec. 1, 1999). The shut-in problem is *hikikomori,* a term applied to people, mostly young men, who sequester themselves in their rooms and have no social life. Population estimates vary widely, from eighty thousand to one million. See, e.g., Amy Borovoy, Japan's Hidden Youths: Mainstreaming the Emotionally Distressed in Japan, 32 *Cult. Med. Psychiatry* 552 (2008); Tamaki Saitō, *Hikikomori Kyūshutsu Manyuaru* [Rescue Manual for Hikikomori] 28–29 (2002); Michael Zielenziger, *Shutting out the Sun: How Japan Created Its Lost Generation* (2007).

8. A partial list would include Anne Allison, *Nightwork: Sexuality, Pleasure, and Corporate Masculinity in a Tokyo Hostess Club* (1994); Nicholas Bornoff, *Pink Samurai: Love, Marriage and*

Sex in Contemporary Japan (1991); Catherine Burns, *Sexual Violence and the Law in Japan* (2005) (analyzing twenty rape cases); Sabine Frühstück, *Colonizing Sex: Sexology and Social Control in Modern Japan* (2003); Sheldon Garon, *Molding Japanese Minds: The State in Everyday Life* (1997); Matthews Masayuki Hamabata, *Crested Kimono: Power and Love in the Japanese Business Family* (1990); Sumie Kawakami, *Goodbye Madame Butterfly: Sex, Marriage and the Modern Japanese Woman* (2007); David Leheny, *Think Global, Fear Local: Sex, Violence, and Anxiety in Contemporary Japan* (2006); James E. Roberson and Nobue Suzuki, eds., *Men and Masculinities in Contemporary Japan: Dislocating the Salaryman Doxa* (2003); Sonia Ryang, *Love in Modern Japan: Its Estrangement From Self, Sex and Society* 2 (2006); Christine R. Yano, *Tears of Longing: Nostalgia and the Nation in Japanese Popular Song* (2002); Tamie L. Bryant, Marital Dissolution in Japan: Legal Obstacles and Their Impact, 17 *Law in Japan* 73 (1984).

9. A partial list would include Amy Borovoy, *The Too-Good Wife: Alcohol, Codependency, and the Politics of Nurturance in Postwar Japan* (2005); Harald Fuess, *Divorce in Japan: Family, Gender, and the State 1600–2000* (2004); Yuko Kawanishi, *Mental Health Challenges Facing Contemporary Japanese Society: The Lonely People* (2009); Karen Kelsky, *Women on the Verge: Japanese Women, Western Dreams* (2001); Tiana Norgren, *Abortion before Birth Control* (2001); Tarō Ōhata and Sumie Kawakami, *Tsuma no Koi: Tatoe Furin to Yobaretemo* [The Love of Wives: Even If It's Called Adultery] (2004); Frances Rosenbluth, ed., *The Politics of Japan's Low Fertility* (2007); Leonard J. Schoppa, *Race for the Exits: The Unraveling of Japan's System of Social Protection* (2006); Patrick Smith, *Japan: A Reinterpretation* 135–36, 155–56 (1997) (discussing a "pervasive lovelessness" and an "absence of intimacy" in "every fiber of society"); Merry Isaacs White, *Perfectly Japanese: Marking Families in an Era of Upheaval* (2002); Zielenziger, *Shutting out the Sun;* Borovoy, Japan's Hidden Youths.

10. Mark D. West, *Law in Everyday Japan: Sex, Sumo, Suicide, and Statutes* (2005).

11. See, e.g., *Lawrence v. Texas,* 539 U.S. 558 (2003); *Bowers v. Hardwick,* 478 U.S. 186 (1986). Only one Japanese case centrally concerns same-sex sex acts, a 1999 case in which a "new half" (*nyu-ha-fu*), or transgender, plaintiff fell down a flight of stairs while manually stimulating the defendant's penis. The court found a duty of care of sexual partners to "avoid using force that might cause harm to the other person's body." It awarded the plaintiff damages but offered no commentary about the act itself. *Kōno v. Otsukawa,* Tokyo District Court, 1018 *Hanrei Times* 288 (Apr. 28, 1999).

12. *Japan Association for the Lesbian and Gay Movement v. Tokyo,* Tokyo District Court, 1509 *Hanrei Jihō* 80 (Mar. 30, 1994); *aff'd,* Tokyo High Court, 986 *Hanrei Times* 206 (Sept. 16, 1997). Courts have found the same lack of consensus or thought on other difficult social issues; see, e.g., *Kakunaga v. Sekiguchi,* Supreme Court, 31 *Minshū* 533 (1977) (noting that the average person has little "interest in and consciousness of religion").

13. See, e.g., Robert A. Ferguson, The Judicial Opinion as Literary Genre, 2 *Yale J. L. & Human.* 201, 211, 213 (1990) ("rhetoric of inevitability"); Mark Kelman, Interpretive Construction in the Substantive Criminal Law, 33 *Stan. L. Rev.* 591, 592 (1980–81) (interpretive construction as "processes by which concrete situations are reduced to substantive legal controversies").

1. Judging

1. See William Glaberson, In Tiny Courts of N.Y., Abuses of Law and Power, *N.Y. Times,* Sept. 25, 2006, A1.

2. See Mark D. West, Making Lawyers (and Gangsters) in Japan, 60 *Vand. L. Rev.* 439 (2007).

3. Kamisaka v. Japan, Osaka District Court, 1736 *Hanrei Jihō* 77 (May 26, 2000), *aff'd,* Osaka High Court, 1159 *Hanrei Times* 158 (Oct. 10, 2003).

4. Takao Tanase, *Gendai Hōshakaigaku Nyūmon* [An Introduction to Contemporary Law and Society] 168 (1994).

5. See Hiroshi Takahashi, Career Judiciary, Judicial Reform, and Practicing Attorneys, 27 *J. Japan. Law* 39, 45 (2009).

6. Until 2009, the judiciary had a higher percentage of women than either the procuracy or the bar. See Gender Equality Bureau, Josei Saibankan Kazu to Josei Hiritsu, available at www. gender.go.jp/teppai/sabetsu/5th_report/toukei/63.pdf. The bar topped 16 percent in 2009. See Nichibenren, Bengoshikai Betsukaiin Kazu [Number of Bar Members by Branch], available at http://www.nichibenren.or.jp/ja/jfba_info/membership/data/100101.pdf. Women seem to climb the pay scale and receive promotions at the same rate as men. See J. Mark Ramseyer, Sex Bias in the Japanese Courts, in Kuo-Chang Huang, ed., *Empirical Studies of Judicial Systems* 197 (2008).

7. See Saibankan no Hōshū nado ni Kansuru Hōritsu [Law Concerning Judge Compensation], law no. 75 of 1948, art. 2 and attached chart.

8. A quasi-jury system was introduced in 2009 for serious criminal charges.

9. See, e.g., Hiroshi Segi, Gōgi no Jissai to Sono Kentō [An Investigation and Report on the Conference System], 189 *Hanrei Times* 58, 61 (Dec. 1, 2005).

10. See, e.g., Shihō Kenshūjo, ed., *Minji Hanketsu Kian no Tebiki* [Handbook for Drafting Opinions in Civil Cases] (10th ed. 1998).

11. Code of Civil Procedure art. 253; Tōkyōkō/Chisai Minji Hanketsusho Kaizen Iinkai and Ōsakakō/Chisai Minji Hanketsusho Kaizen Iinkai, Minji Hanketsusho no Atarashii Yōshiki ni Tsuite [Regarding the New Form of Civil Opinions] 715 *Hanrei Times* 4 (1990).

12. Code of Criminal Procedure art. 355; Tōkyō Chisai, Ōsaka Chisai Keiji Hanketsusho Kentō Guru-pu, Keiji Hanketsusho no Minaoshi ni Tsuite [Regarding the Revision of Criminal Opinions], 755 *Hanrei Times* 10 (1991).

13. Etsutarō Iwabuchi, *Akubun* [Terrible Writing] 75 (3d ed. 1979, 16th prtg. 2003).

14. Shihō Kenshūjo, ed., *Minji Hanketsu Kian no Tebiki* [Handbook for Drafting Opinions in Civil Cases] 89 (10th ed. 1998); Jirō Nomura, *Nihon no Saibankan* [Japanese Judges] 78 (1992).

15. Kenji Endō, Minsohō Oyobi Minso Jitsumu ga Hanketsusho ni Kitai Suru Mono ha Nanika [What is Expected of Judicial Opinions from Civil Procedure Law and Practice?], 724 *Hanrei Times* 4, 8 (1990).

16. The standard for criminal elements is beyond a reasonable doubt; see, e.g., Supreme Court, 1253 *Hanrei Times* 118 (Oct. 16, 2007)); the standard is lower in civil cases; e.g., Supreme Court, 29 *Minshū* 1417 (Oct. 24, 1975); see also Kevin M. Clermont, Standards of Proof in Japan and the United States, 37 *Cornell Int'l L.J.* 263 (2004)).

17. See, e.g., Hiroshi Segi, Gōgi no Jissai to Sono Kentō [An Investigation and Report on the Conference System], 189 *Hanrei Times* 58 (Dec. 1, 2005).

18. Minji Soshō Kisoku [Rules of Civil Procedure], Supreme Court Proclamation no. 5 of 1996, art. 155; Keiji Soshō Kisoku [Rules of Criminal Procedure], Supreme Court Rule no. 32 of 1948, art. 35(2). The Code of Criminal Procedure (art. 342) requires that the sentence be read aloud.

19. Shin'ichi Yoshikawa, Minji Soshō ni okeru Saibankan no Yakuwari [The Role of the Judge in a Civil Case], in Shintarō Katō, ed., *Zemināru Saibankanron* [Seminar: Theory of Judges] 147, 191 (2004).

20. Kaoru Inoue, *Kurutta Saibankan* [Crazy Judges] 57 (2007).

21. See J. Mark Ramseyer and Eric B. Rasmusen, Measuring Judicial Independence: The Political Economy of Judging in Japan (2003).

22. Daniel H. Foote, Restrictions on Political Activity by Judges in Japan and the United States: The Cases of Judge Teranishi and Justice Sanders, 8 *Wash. U. Global Stud. L. Rev* 285, 296 (2009).

23. Nihon Minshū Hōritsu Kyōkai, *Zen Saibankan Keireki Sōran* [Overview of Careers of All Judges] (4th ed. 2004).

24. Takao Kokubo and Hiroyuki Nakagawa, Saibankan toshite no Ikigai to Seikatsu [Judges' Passions and Daily Lives], in Katō, ed., Zemina-ru Saibankanron 121, 140.

25. Id.

26. Hanjiho no Shokken no Tokurei nado ni Kansuru Hōritsu [Law Concerning the Special Authority of Assistant Judges], law no. 146 of 1948.

27. Yasuhiro Igaki, Sugao no Saibankan [The Exposed Judge], in Yasuhiro Igaki et al., eds., *Saibansho no Mado Kara* [From the Courthouse Window] 7, 61–62 (2000).

28. The path to becoming a Supreme Court justice is slightly different. Justices are appointed by the cabinet and are often former prosecutors, judges, lawyers, and academics. Five of the fifteen justices need not have legal experience.

29. Shihō Seido Kaikaku Shingikai, Chūkan Hōkoku [Interim Report], Nov. 20, 2000, available at http://www.kantei.go.jp/jp/sihouseido/report/pdfs/naka_honbun.pdf at 27; see also Osaka High Court, 1159 *Hanrei Times* 158 (Oct. 10, 2003) (acknowledging the importance of the factors listed in the report).

30. Etsuo Shimozawa, Kasai no Hito [Family Court People], in Nihon Saibankan Nettowa-ku, ed., Saibankan ha Uttaeru! Watakushitachi no Daigimon [Judges Complain! Our Big Issues] 54, 54–55 (1999).

31. Tokyo District Court, 2003 (*ta*) 956 (Mar. 29, 2005).

32. Jirō Nomura, *Nihon no Saibankan* [Japanese Judges] 65 (1992); see also, e.g., Ryūshō Kadota, *Saibankan ga Nihon wo Horobosu* [Judges Are Destroying Japan] (2005). Survey data show that many citizens agree. Along with his student Hideaki Irie, University of Tokyo law professor Dan Foote polled 400 random citizens about their views on dispute resolution. The survey asked respondents whether they agreed with the statement "Judges understand the sense of ordinary citizens." Nearly 40% disagreed with the statement, either strongly or mildly, 11% agreed with it, and 49% were unsure. When asked their agreement with the statement "Judges have contact with ordinary citizens outside the courtroom," 5% agreed, nearly 50% disagreed, and 47% were unsure. Daniel H. Foote and Hideaki Irie, *Funsō Kaiketsu ni tsuite no Anke-to Chōsa* [Survey Regarding Dispute Resolution] (March 2007) (survey administered by Yoron Kakaku Kyōkai). See also Daniel H. Foote, *Namonai Kaomonai Shihō* [Nameless, Faceless Justice] 192–93 (2007) (citing summary survey data).

33. J. Mark Ramseyer and Eric B. Rasmusen, The Case For Managed Judges: Learning from Japan after the Political Upheaval of 1993, 154 *U. Penn. L. Rev.* 1879, 1879 (2006).

34. Tokyo District Court, 967 *Hanrei Jihō* 17 (Mar. 14, 1980).

35. Masami Itō, *Saibankan to Gakusha no Aida* [Between Judge and Scholar] 45 (1993).

36. Supreme Court 6(2) *Minshū* 110 (Feb. 19, 1952); *Japan v. Shigeto,* Supreme Court, 39(6) *Keishū* 413 (Oct. 23, 1985); *Kōno v. Heikawa,* Tokyo High Court, 1107 *Hanrei Times* 232 (Nov. 30, 2000); Tokyo District Court, 1155 *Hanrei Times* 57 (Apr. 22, 2003).

37. Only *kōjo ryōzoku,* sometimes translated as "public policy and good morals," appears in the Civil Code (art. 90).

38. See, e.g., *Anzai v. Shiraishi,* Supreme Court, 940 *Hanrei Times* 98 (Apr. 2, 1997); *Kakunaga v. Sekiguchi,* Supreme Court, 31 *Minshū* 533 (July 13, 1977).

39. See, e.g., *Shinagawa v. Korobe Railway Co.,* Great Court of Cassation, 14 *Minshū* 1965 (Oct. 5, 1935); John Owen Haley, *The Spirit of Japanese Law* 156–57 (1998).

40. See, e.g., Shioda v. Kōchi Broadcasting Co., Supreme Court, 268 *Rōdō Hanrei* 17 (Jan. 31, 1977).

41. Haley, *The Spirit of Japanese Law* 157.

42. Courts had previously held that a common-law spouse could receive benefits even if her spouse was in another legal marriage, provided that the legal marriage was destroyed and the common-law marriage was socially recognized. See, e.g., Tokyo District Court, 670 *Hanrei Times* 77 (Mar. 28, 1988). A common-law spouse may also be entitled to private pension benefits in the same situation. See Supreme Court, 1180 *Hanrei Times* 171 (Apr. 21, 2005). The Supreme Court had held in an earlier case that a woman in a common-law marriage with the son

(from another marriage) of her deceased husband was ineligible for benefits from the stepson's/ husband's death because the relationship was contrary to social mores. Supreme Court, 1984 (*tsu*) 335 (Feb. 14, 1985).

43. Kōno v. Shakai Hokenchō Chōkan, Supreme Court, 1238 Hanrei Times 177 (Mar. 8, 2007).

44. Of course, U.S. judges are not immune to such biases. See Dan M. Kahan, David A. Hoffman, and Donald Braman, Whose Eyes Are You Going To Believe? *Scott v. Harris* and the Perils of Cognitive Illiberalism, 122 *Harvard L. Rev.* 837 (2009).

45. John O. Haley, The Japanese Judiciary: Maintaining Integrity, Autonomy, and the Public Trust, in Daniel H. Foote, ed., *Law in Japan: A Turning Point* 99, 127 (2007).

2. Love

1. See Dana Goodyear, I ♥ Novels, *New Yorker,* Dec. 22, 2008, 62.

2. See Laura Kipnis, *Against Love: A Polemic* 3 (2003) ("Love is, as everyone knows, a mysterious and all-controlling force, with vast power over our thoughts and life decisions. Love is boss, and a demanding one too: it demands our loyalty. We, in turn, freely comply—or as freely as the average subject in thrall to an all-powerful master, as freely as indendured servants.")

3. Carolyn H. Simmons, Alexander Vom Kolke, and Hideko Shimizu, Attitudes Toward Romantic Love Among American, German, and Japanese Students, 126(3) *J. Soc. Psychology* 327, 332 (1986).

4. National Institute of Population and Social Security Research, Dai13kai Shusshō Dōkō Kihon Chōsa: Kekkon to Shussan ni Kansuru Zenkoku Chōsa, Dokushinsha Chōsa no Kekka Gaiyō 8–9 [13th Survey on Demographic Trends: National Survey on Marriage and Birth, An Outline of the Results of the Survey of Single Persons] (2006), available at http://www.ipss.go.jp/ps-doukou/j/doukou13_s/Nfs13doukou_s.pdf.

5. Susan Sprecher et al., Love: American Style, Russian Style, and Japanese Style, 1 *Personal Relationships* 349 (1994). See also Stella Ting-Toomey, Intimacy Expressions in Three Cultures: France, Japan, and the United States, 15 *Int'l J. Intercultural Relations* 29 (1991) (finding more "love commitment in France and the U.S. than in Japan").

6. Christine R. Yano, *Tears of Longing: Nostalgia and the Nation in Japanese Popular Song* 148–56 (2002).

7. Naho Tanimoto, *Ren'ai no Shakaigaku* [The Sociology of Love] 147–50 (2008).

8. Osaka District Court, 2006 (*wa*) 4737 (Oct. 1, 2007); Kofu District Court, 2005 (*wa*) 270 (Mar. 25, 2006); Intellectual Property High Court, 2005 (*ne*) 10060 (Jan. 25, 2006).

9. Osaka District Court, 2007 (*wa*) 3024 (Feb. 7, 2008); Kofu District Court, 2004 (*wa*) 282 (Apr. 26, 2007).

10. Mito Family Court, 1999 (*ka*) 23 (July 22, 1999).

11. Tokyo District Court, 2002 (*yo*) 21038 (June 20, 2002).

12. Osaka District Court, 2001 (*u*) 605 (Oct. 16, 2001).

13. Okayama District Court, 1593 *Hanrei Jihō* 146 (Aug. 4, 1995).

14. Kyoto District Court, 2000 (*wa*) 1480 (Feb. 26, 2002); Nagoya District Court, 1542 *Hanrei Jihō* 26 (Feb. 9, 1995).

15. Tokyo District Court, 842 *Hanrei Times* 160 (Dec. 16, 1993).

16. Osaka District Court, 1978 (*wa*) 6006 (July 15, 1980).

17. Tokyo District Court, 1796 (*wa*) 818 (Dec. 19, 1986),

18. Tokyo District Court, 1070 *Hanrei Jihō* 106 (Dec. 22, 1982).

19. Fukuoka District Court, 2002 (*wa*) 502 (Feb. 27. 2003).

20. Osaka District Court, 2004 (*u*) 68 (Jan. 18, 2006).

21. Osaka District Court, 1217 *Hanrei Times* 310 (June 14, 2005); Shizuoka District Court, 915 *Hanrei Times* 194 (Feb. 19, 1996); Chiba District Court, 781 *Hanrei Times* 133 (Feb. 21, 1992); Tokyo District Court, 1614 *Hanrei Jihō* 153 (Feb. 19, 1997).

22. Akihiro Nakatani, *Ura Ren'ai Ron* [The Underground Theory of Love] 2 (2001).

23. See Chieko Irie Mulhern, Japanese Harlequin Romances as Transcultural Women's Fiction, 48(1) *J. Asian Stud.* 50 (1989).

24. Masahiro Yamada and Tōko Shirakawa, *Konkatsu Jidai* [The Marriage-Hunting Age] 154 (2008).

25. Mitsuba, *30sai no Hoken Taiiku* (2008).

26. Takayuki Yokota-Murakami, *Don Juan East/West: On the Problematics of Comparative Literature* 41 (1998).

27. Susumu Itō, *Nihonjin no Ai* [Japanese Love] 95 (1996).

28. Junko Saeki, *Ren'ai no Kigen: Meiji no Ai wo Yomitoku* [The Origins of Love: Reading Love in the Meiji Period] 16 (2000).

29. Id. at 223–24; Junko Saeki, *"Iro" to "Ai" no Hikaku Bunkgakushi* [A Comparative Literary History of Love] 10 (1998); Yūko Tanaka, *Edo no Koi* [Love in the Edo Period] (2002).

30. Akira Yanabu, *Hon'yakugo Seiritsu Jijō* [The Establishment of Standard Language] 93 (1982).

31. The orthodox account holds that translators invented *ren'ai* not only because Japan lacked the word but also because it lacked the concept. The novelist Yukio Mishima noted the foreignness of "Western" love:

> *Koi* in Japan began to take shape in the Heian period. From then until now, there is no philosophical background for *ren'ai*. Like the Greek concept, *ren'ai* in Japan is an instinctual desire that grows naturally, but that is the only commonality with the Greek. In Greece, unlike Japan, there was a philosophy of love that became clarified into a comprehensive worldview. For the Japanese, *ren'ai* is simply instinct plus emotion. In Japan, emotions developed significantly, but those emotions have no connection whatsoever to philosophy, and the world that developed was based on emotion. Therefore, in Japan, to speak bluntly, *koi* between a man and a woman is just a desire to sleep together.

Yukio Mishima, Shin Ren'ai Kōza [Lecture on New Love] (1955) in 29 *Ketteiban Mishima Yukio Zenshū* [The Complete Yukio Mishima] 15, 22 (2003). Some commentators argue that the lack of a word does not necessarily indicate the lack of a concept and that Japanese had been "loving" for centuries before Western literature appeared in Japan. See, e.g., Atsushi Koyano, *Ren'ai no Shōwashi* [A History of Love in the Shōwa Era] 8–10 (2005); Atsushi Koyano, Romantikku Rabu to ha Nanika [What Is Romantic Love?], in Tamoki Aotsu et al., eds., *Ai to Kunan* [Love and Suffering] 65, 68–69 (1999).

32. *Natural Plants K.K. v. Club Cosmetics K.K.*, Intellectual Property High Court, 2075 *Hanrei Jihō* 110 (Apr. 27, 2009); see also *Natural Plants K.K. v. Koezuka*, Intellectual Property High Court, 2008 (*gyōke*) 10042 (June 25, 2008) (turning to dictionary to find *rabu* equivalent to *ai, aijō, koi, ren'ai*). Other words that courts use to convey emotions that resemble love include, with rough and overlapping English equivalents, *miren* (lingering affection or attachment), *itoshii* (dear or beloved), *renbo* (longing), *bojō* (longing), *koishii* (yearning), and *horeru* (fall in love).

33. When a landlord sued neighbors whose dog had barked so incessantly that the tenant broke the lease early, the Tokyo District Court found that the neighbors did not have the proper "love" (*aijō*) for the dogs that was necessary to fulfill their duty to care for them by feeding and walking them. *Inoue v. Kōno*, Tokyo District Court, 1536 *Hanrei Jihō* 66 (Feb. 1, 1995). When an American Shorthair show cat died due to a botched surgery, the Utsunomiya District Court calculated damages for the owners based not only the cat's worth as a show cat but specifically noted that

Myuzu "was not just a show cat; she was loved [*aijō*] as a member of the family." Utsunomiya District Court, 1997 (*wa*) 529 (Mar. 28, 2002). When a man's elderly mother died in the hospital as the result of negligence, the Tokyo District Court noted not only the plaintiff's requests to the hospital to take safety measures but also the fact that the son "lived alone with Hana, and his love [*aijō*] for her was deep." *Kōno v. Tōkyō,* Tokyo District Court, 1588 *Hanrei Jihō* 117 (Apr. 15, 1996).

34. *Koibito* (boyfriend and girlfriend) and *ren'ai kankei* (love affair) are used to describe romantic relationships. *Aijin* (lover) carries a more illicit nuance.

35. Kushiro District Court, 2006 (*wa*) 34 (Aug. 21, 2006); Tokyo District Court, 1229 (*wa*) 275 (Aug. 30, 2002); *Kōno v. Otsuyama,* Tokyo District Court, 915 *Hanrei Times* 171 (June 7, 1996).

36. Tanimoto, *Ren'ai no Shakaigaku* 170; see also Yoshimasa Kuribayashi, Ren'ai ni Okeru Kokuhaku no Seihi no Kiteiin ni Kansuru Kenkyū [Research on the Factors that Lead to Success or Failure of Love Confessions], 41 *Hokusei Gakuen Daigaku Shakai Fukushigakubu Hokusei Ronshū* 73 (2004), available at http://db1.wdc-jp.com/cgi-bin/jssp/wbpnew/master/download.php?submission_id=2003-E-0192&type=1 (noting success of expressing fondness).

37. Kyoko Seki, David Matsumoto, and T. Todd Imahori, The Conceptualization and Expression of Intimacy in Japan and the United States, 33 *J. Cross-Cultural. Psych.* 303, 317 (2002); Susan L. Kline, Brian Hortin, and Shuangyue Zhang, Communicating Love: Comparisons Between American and East Asian University Students, 32 *Int'l J. Intercultural Relations* 32 (2008).

38. Kensuke Sugawara et al., *Tsuma he no Aijō Hyōgen ni Shitagau Shūchi no Mekanizumi ni Tsuite* [Regarding the Mechanism Behind the Embarrassment of Expressions of Love to One's Wife], Nihon Shakai Shinrigakkai Dai 40kai Taikai Happyō Ronbunshū [Collection of Papers From the 40th Meeting of the Japanese Social Psychology Association] (1999), available at http://www5b.biglobe.ne.jp/~sken/hp/articles/papers/ken.1999a.pdf.

39. Amy Borovoy, *The Too-Good Wife: Alcohol, Codependency, and the Politics of Nurturance in Postwar Japan* 94 (2005).

40. Dai 8kai "60sai no Rabu Reta-" Taishō Jushō Rabu Reta- [Grand Prize Winner, Eighth "Love Letters at 60"] (2008), available at http://www.sumitomotrust.co.jp/about-us/love/grand-prize.html.

41. Nihon Hōsō Kyōkai, ed., 7 *Otto kara Tsumahe, Tsuma kara Otto he: 60sai no Rabu Reta-* [From Husband to Wife, from Wife to Husband: Love Letters at 60] 177 (2007).

42. Nihon Hōsō Kyōkai, ed., 6 *Otto kara Tsumahe, Tsuma kara Otto he: 60sai no Rabu Reta-* [From Husband to Wife, from Wife to Husband: Love Letters at 60] 29 (2006).

43. Nihon Hōsō Kyōkai, ed., 5 *Otto kara Tsumahe, Tsuma kara Otto he: 60sai no Rabu Reta-* [From Husband to Wife, from Wife to Husband: Love Letters at 60] 51 (2005).

44. Nihon Hōsō Kyōkai, ed., 6 *Otto kara Tsumahe, Tsuma kara Otto he* 62.

45. Nihon Hōsō Kyōkai, ed., 8 *Otto kara Tsumahe, Tsuma kara Otto he: 60sai no Rabu Reta-* [From Husband to Wife, from Wife to Husband: Love Letters at 60] 69 (2008).

46. Jun'ichi Watanabe, *A Lost Paradise* 346 (Juliet Winters Carpenter trans. 2000) (original Japanese, *Shitsurakuen,* published 1997).

47. See Junko Saeki, Shinjū no Kindai [Love Suicides and Modernity], in Tamoki Aotsu et al., eds., *Ai to Kunan* [Love and Suffering] 25, 29–42 (1999).

48. Shunsuke Serizawa, Gendai Shinjūron [Modern Shinjū Theory], in Chizuko Ueno et al., eds., *Sekushuaritei to Kazoku* [Sexuality and the Family] 195 (1991). Psychiatrist Yoshitomo Takahashi calculates that the murder-suicide rate as a percentage of suicides in Japan is the same in the United States but also notes that the concept of love suicide differs significantly. Yoshitomo Takahashi, *Chūkōnen Jisatsu* [Middle-Aged Suicide] 80–81 (2003).

49. See Mark D. West, *Law in Everyday Japan: Sex, Sumo, Suicides, and Statutes* 145–89 (2005).

50. Jisatsu Sōgō Taisaku Kaigi, Jisatsu Sōgō Taisaku Taikō [Fundamental Principles of the Comprehensive Antisuicide Plan], available at http://www8.cao.go.jp/jisatsutaisaku/sougou/taisaku/kaigi_2/data/s2.pdf 19.

51. Osaka District Court, 2006 (*wa*) 1261 (Aug. 15, 2006).

52. *U.S. v. Bright,* 517 F.2d 584, 585 (2d Cir. 1974).

53. Supreme Court, 62(5) *Keishū* 1559 (Apr. 25, 2008).

54. See, e.g., A. Van Gastel, C. Schotte, and M. Maes, The Prediction of Suicidal Intent in Depressed Patients, 96(4) *Acta Psychiatrica Scandinavica* 254 (1997).

55. Japanese police are required to categorize and record the causes of each suicide for which a note is left. In 2009, police determined—somehow—the cause of suicide in 24,434 of 32,854 cases, or nearly three-fourths. 393 people killed themselves over "lost love," and 194 did so over "adultery." In total, 1,121 people killed themselves over "male-female problems" such as these. 4,117 people committed suicide over "family problems," the largest category of which, with 1,087 deaths, was "marital discord." Another 653 people killed themselves over "loneliness." Combined, these problems are the number two cause of suicide for women (after health problems) and number three for men (after economics and health). Keisatsuchō Seikatsu Anzenkyoku Chiikika, Heisei 21nenchū ni okeru Jisatsu no Gaiyō Shiryō [2009 Outline of Suicide Records] (May 2010), available at http://www.npa.go.jp/safetylife/seianki/220513_H21jisatsunogaiyou.pdf. A study at one Japanese hospital of patients who had attempted or completed suicide found the most common precipitants to be loss of love, divorce, loneliness from living alone, and family conflicts. Takao Hattori, Kazuo Taketani, and Yumi Ogasawara, Suicide and Suicide Attempts in General Hospital Psychiatry: Clinical and Statistical Study, 49 *Psychiatry and Clinical Neurosciences* 43 (1995).

56. See Amy Borovoy, Japan's Hidden Youths: Mainstreaming the Emotionally Distressed in Japan, 32 *Cult. Med. Psychiatry* 552, 555–57 (2008).

57. Yoshio Mino, Hideyasu Aoyama, and Jack Froom, Depressive Disorders in Japanese Primary Care Patients, 11(4) *Family Practice* 363 (1994).

58. Yoshibumi Nakane et al., Public Beliefs About Causes and Risk Factors for Mental Disorders: A Comparison of Japan and Australia, 5(33) *BMC Psychiatry* (2005), available at http://www.biomedcentral.com/1471–244X/5/33.

59. Anthony F. Jorm et al., Public Beliefs About Treatment and Outcome of Mental Disorders: A Comparison of Australia and Japan, 3(12) BMC Medicine (2005), available at http://www.biomedcentral.com/1741–7015/3/12.

60. See, e.g., Kathryn Schulz, Did Antidepressants Depress Japan, *N.Y. Times,* Aug. 22, 2004, Section 6, 39. The stigma that attaches to the label for schizophrenia (*seishin bunretsubyō*) is worse; see Tomoko Sugiura et al., Labeling Effect of *Seishin-Bunretsu-Byou,* the Japanese Translation for Schizophrenia: An Argument for Relabeling, 47(2) *Int'l J. Social Psychiatry* 43 (2001).

61. Nagoya High Court, 61(2) *Kasai Geppō* 240 (Apr. 8, 2008). Family Court opinion dated Mar. 3, 2007 appended at page 251.

62. Sapporo District Court, 1089 *Hanrei Times* 298 (May 10, 2001). Article 43 of the Penal Code provides that a penalty may be reduced "if the perpetration of the crime has been voluntarily stopped."

63. Tokyo District Court, 2001 (*wa*) 2983 (Feb. 26, 2002).

64. Maebashi District Court, 1(7) *Kakeishū* 1707 (July 27, 1959).

65. Kyoto District Court, 135 *Hanrei Jihō* 5 (Nov. 8, 1957).

66. Sapporo District Court, 2007 (*wa*) 137 (Dec. 21, 2007). In another 2007 case, the defendant attempted to use the motif of parent-child suicide to cover up a murder. He strangled with a belt his thirty-six-year-old adultery partner, then took her body to the bathroom, tied the belt into a noose, and hung her from the shower head with it. To complete the standard parent-child suicide pattern, he brought their three-month-old son from his crib and placed him in the bathroom near his mother, where he suffocated him with a blanket. The court used forensic evidence to determine that the deaths were murders and sentenced the defendant to life imprisonment. Sendai District Court, 2007 (*wa*) 59 (Sept. 21, 2007). See also Kushiro District Court, 2006 (*wa*) 86, Nov. 27,

2006 (father kills three-year-old after killing his wife); Tokyo District Court, 668 *Hanrei Times* 226 (Mar. 10, 1988) (mother kills three-year-old when convinced she herself has mental illness); Tokyo District Court, 683 *Hanrei Times* 213 (July 28, 1988) (mother kills two children when convinced *that* she has infected her family with AIDS); Tokyo District Court, 462 *Hanrei Times* 130 (Nov. 30, 1981) (father kills fifteen-year-old problem child) see also Oita District Court, 2007 (*wa*) 1 (May 24, 2007) (sixty-eight-year-old husband kills sixty-four-year-old wife at her request and then kills eighty-six-year-old mother-in-law because wife had said that leaving her alive would be "pitiful"). See generally Taimie L. Bryant, Oya-Ko Shinju: Death at the Center of the Heart, 8(1) *Pacific Basin L.J.* 1 (1990).

67. Kushiro District Court, 2006 (*wa*) 34 (Aug. 21, 2006).

68. William Johnston, *Geisha, Harlot, Strangler, Star: A Woman, Sex, and Morality in Modern Japan* 101 (2005).

69. Id.

70. Tokyo District Court, 1229 (*wa*) 275 (Aug. 30, 2002). See also Sapporo District Court, 1005 (*wa*) 1664 (Nov. 2, 2007), *aff'd*, Sapporo High Court, 2007 (*u*) 332 (Mar. 13, 2008) (defendant attempted to murder two women because he felt lonely after his girlfriend of four years left him, he felt worse when he saw his friends "with their boyfriends and girlfriends" having fun, and he "wanted to make his victims, their families, and their lovers feel pain").

71. Simmons, Vom Kolke, and Shimizu, Attitudes Toward Romantic Love 332.

72. *Japan v. Miura,* Tokyo District Court, 849 *Hanrei Times* 165 (Mar. 31, 1994).

73. *Japan v. Hara,* Tokyo District Court, 2002 (*wa*) 620 (June 11, 2003). Names are from published press accounts.

74. Wakayama District Court, 2(506) *Kakeishū* 894 (June 13, 1960).

75. The percentage is similar to that of Texas. Japan sentences roughly ten persons per year to execution. See David T. Johnson, Where the State Kills in Secret: Capital Punishment in Japan, 8(3) *Punishment and Society* 251, 267 (2006).

76. *Japan v. Shonen N,* Supreme Court, 37(6) *Minshū* 609 (July 8, 1983).

77. Tokyo High Court,1422 *Hanrei Jihō* 142 (Oct. 22, 1991).

78. Yūji Kanemasa, Jun'ichi Taniguchi, and Masanori Ishimori, Ren'ai no Ime-ji to Kōi Riyū ni Oyobosu Isei Kankei to Seibetsu no Eikyō [Effects of Opposite Sex Relationships and Sex on Images of Romantic Love and Reasons for Attraction], 1 *Tainin Shakai Shinrigaku Kenkyū* 147 (2001).

79. See generally Chizuko Ueno, *Suka-to no Shita no Gekijō* [The Stage under the Skirt] 59 (1992) (discussing nineteenth-century taboo of female genitalia touching an object).

80. See Shōichi Inoue, Aijin, in Shōichi Inoue, Hikaru Saitō, Tomomi Shibuya, and Junko Mitsuhashi, eds., *Seiteki na Kotoba* [Sexual Words] 18 (2010) (noting also that until the twentieth century, the word did not have the connotation of infidelity).

81. Tokyo District Court, 2004 (*wa*) 17193 (Sept. 30, 2005).

82. Fukuoka District Court, 1581 *Hanrei Jihō* 143 (July 12, 1996).

83. Supreme Court, 4(9) *Keishū* 1806 (Sept. 27, 1950).

84. Fukuoka High Court, 1633 *Hanrei Jihō* 147 (Dec. 4, 1997).

85. *Japan v. Ōyama,* Hiroshima High Court, 2005 (*u*) 115 (Oct. 16, 2007). See also Kobe District Court, 2009 (*wa*) 106 (June 15, 2009) (defendant claims that he murdered his girlfriend, whom he loved [*ai*], eleven days before she was to give birth to his child, because he wanted to make her his own and not because he feared that his wife and boss would learn of her existence); cf. Saitama District Court, 2008 (*wa*) 1139 (June 8, 2009) (court finds that accomplice has no reason to frame his wife because he proclaimed his love for her in open court).

86. See also Tokyo District Court, 1602 *Hanrei Times* 145 (Feb. 12, 1997) (mother kills daughter whom she "loved above all others").

87. *Japan v. Yamauchi,* Nagoya High Court, 144 *Hanrei Times* 175 (Dec. 22, 1962).

88. Kochi District Court, 742 *Hanrei Times* 224 (Sept. 17, 1990).

89. See Osaka District Court, 879 *Hanrei Jihō* 158 (Nov. 30, 1977) (one-year sentence for husband who killed sick wife whom he "loved deeply"); Kagoshima District Court, 333 *Hanrei Times* 352 (Oct. 1, 1975) (no liability for husband who killed sick wife whom he "loved"); Takamatsu High Court, 2001 (*u*) 231 (Jan. 17, 2002) (seven-year sentence for man who killed adulterous wife whom he "loved"). The same pattern occurs in cases of parental love; see Osaka District Court, 2006 (*wa*) 1078 (May 23, 2006) (fifteen-year sentence for man who killed twenty-one-year-old son who he "in fact, loved").

90. Suto-ka- Kōi no Kisei nado ni Kansuru Hōritsu [Antistalking Law], Law No. 81 of 2000.

91. See Transcript at Sangiin, Naikaku Iinkai Kaigiroku [Minutes of House of Councillors, Cabinet Committee], No. 3, Mar. 22, 2001, available at http://kokkai.ndl.go.jp/SENTAKU/sangiin/151/0058/main.html (statement of Reiko Ōmori on difficulty of prosecution in the absence of love); Transcript at Kokka Kihon Seisaku Iinkai Gōdō Shinsakai Kaigiroku [Minutes of Joint Committee on the Fundamental Issues of Government], No. 5, April 19, 2000, available at http://kokkai.ndl.go.jp/SENTAKU/ryoin/147/9001/main.html (statement of Yoshirō Mori on drafting difficulties).

92. Based on a search at the Japanese government's comprehensive e-gov site, http://law.e-gov.go.jp/cgi-bin/idxsearch.cgi. The word *aijō* (love) appears in one statute, Shintai Shōgaisha Hojokenhō [Law Concerning Service Dogs for Physically Disabled Persons], Law no. 49 of 2002, and in one ministry provision, Shōnen Kanbetsusho Shogū Kisoku [Rules Pertaining to Treatment of Juvenile Detention Facilities], Ministry of Justice Order no. 58 of 1949. The word *ai* (love) appears in forty-five statutes, including thirteen in which the character appears merely as part of the names of prefectures (Aichi or Ehime).

93. Ark. Code Ann. § 9–15-103(4)(A) (2005), Colo. Rev. Stat. § 13–14-101(2) (2006), Fla. Stat. ch. 784.046 (2005), Iowa Code § 236.2(e) (2006), Minn. Stat. § 518B.2 (2005), N.H. Code Admin. R. Ann. 173-B:1 (2004); see Commission on Domestic Violence Report, American Bar Association Recommendation 110, Adopted Aug. 7–8, 2006, available at www.abanet.org/leadership/2006/annual/dailyjournal/hundredten.doc.

94. *Fuller v. State,* 259 S.W.3d 486 (Ct. App. Ark. 2007).

95. *Andrews v. Rutherford,* 832 A.2d 379 (Sup. Ct. N.J. 2003). California defines a "dating relationship" as "frequent, intimate associations primarily characterized by the expectation of affection or sexual involvement independent of financial considerations." Cal. Fam. Code § 6210 (2008). Before the statutory definition was codified, California courts defined a dating relationship as "a serious courtship. It is a social relationship between two individuals who have or have had a reciprocally amorous and increasingly exclusive interest in one another, and shared expectation of the growth of that mutual interest, that has endured for such a length of time and stimulated such frequent interactions that the relationship cannot be deemed to have been casual." *Oriola v. Thaler,* 84 Cal. App. 4th 397, 412 (Ct. App. Cal. 2000). See *People v. Rucker,* 126 Cal. App. 4th 1107 (Ct. App. Cal. 2005); *People v. Atchison,* 2007 Cal. App. Unpub. LEXIS 2645 (Ct. App. Cal. 2007).

96. Haigūsha Kara no Bōryoku Oyobi Higaisha no Hogo ni Kansuru Hōritsu [Law for the Prevention of Spousal Violence and the Protection of Victims], Law no. 31 of 2001. "Spouse" includes common-law spouses. Art. 1.

97. Transcript at Sangiin, Chihō Gyōsei Keisatsu Iinkai Kaigiroku [Minutes of House of Councillors, Local Administration and Police Committee], No. 10, May 16, 2000, available at http://kokkai.ndl.go.jp/SENTAKU/sangiin/147/0004/main.html.

98. Kumiko Okada, Suto-ka- Kōi Nado Kiseihō [The Antistalking Law], Hōgaku Semina-Oct. 2000, 61, 62.

99. Transcript at Sangiin, Chihō Gyōsei Keisatsu Iinkai Kaigiroku [Minutes of House of Councillors, Local Administration and Police Committee], No. 10, May 16, 2000, available at http://kokkai.ndl.go.jp/SENTAKU/sangiin/147/0004/main.html.

100. The Supreme Court has held that the law is not overbroad and does not violate a person's right to have feelings of love, a right implied by articles 13 (right to life, liberty, and pursuit of happiness) and 21 (freedom of expression) of the constitution. *Japan v. Shigeno,* Supreme Court, 1141 *Hanrei Times* 132 (Dec. 11, 2003).

101. Tokyo High Court, 1860 *Hanrei Jihō* 154 (Mar. 5, 2003).

102. Tokyo High Court, 1172 *Hanrei Times* 308 (Oct. 20, 2004).

103. Kobe District Court, 1997 (*wa*) 125 (July 3, 2007).

104. As a convicted stalker, he received a suspended sentence and subsequently became the sixth judge in Japanese history to be impeached (and the first since 2001, when a Tokyo High Court judge was impeached after violating child prostitution laws). See, e.g., Hanji Shimoyama, Sotsui Jijitsu Mitomeru, Suto-ka- de Dangai Hatsukōhan [First Public Hearing in Stalker Impeachment Trial of Judge Shimoyama], *Nihon Keizai Shinbun,* Dec. 3, 2008, available at http://www.nikkei.co.jp/news/main/20081203AT1G0301K03122008.html (accessed Dec. 8, 2008).

105. 1 Corinthians 13:4–8.

3. Coupling

1. See Kalman D. Applbaum, Marriage with the Proper Stranger: Arranged Marriage in Metropolitan Japan, 34 (1) *Ethnology* 37 (1995).

2. The theory has deep roots—see Kaoru Matsuda, *"Ketsuekigata to Seikaku" no Shakaishi* [A Social History of "Blood Type and Personality"] (1994)—and was most popularly set forth in Hiroshi Nomi, *Ketsuekigata de Wakaru Aishō* [What Blood Types Reveal about Compatibility] (1971).

3. Erika Kudō, Tainin Ninchi Katei ni Okeru Ketsuekigata Sutereotaipu no Eikyō [The Effect of Blood Stereotypes on Interpersonal Perception], 43(1) *Jikkei Shakai Shinrigaku Kenkyū* 1 (2003).

4. Matthews Masayuki Hamabata, *Crested Kimono: Power and Love in the Japanese Business Family* 125 (1990).

5. Nanae Ogino, Isamu Saitō, and Masatoshi Kojima, Ren'ai no Gen'in Kizoku to Kotoba ni yoru Kikō Teiki no Jisshōteki Kenkyū: Seikaku, Gaiken, Taiō, Un e no Kizoku Keikō [Self-Presentation and Causal Attribution of Romantic Love: Attribution to Character, Looks, Reaction, and Luck], 42 *Shiraume Gakuen Daigaku/Tanki Daigaku Kiyō* 29 (2006).

6. Nexco Higashi Nihon Kantō Shisha, Ren'ai "Kōsoku" do Chōsa [Survey of High-Speed Love], May 19, 2007, available at http://www.e-nexco.co.jp/pressroom/press_release/kanto/h19/0615/pdfs/data.pdf.

7. Automobile Liability Security Law, Jidōsha Songai Baishō Hoshōhō Shikōrei, Ordinance no. 286 of 1955, art. 2.

8. Parties rely on one of two books for charts published by the Federation of Bar Associations Accident Consultation Center: the so-called "Blue Book" (*Aohon*), published biennially and used throughout Japan with the exception of Tokyo, Osaka, and Nagoya (see Nichibenren Kōtsū Jiko Sōsan Senta- Kōtsū Jiko Songaigaku Santei Kijun [Standard Damage Amounts for Traffic Accident Liability]), and the so-called "Red Book" (*Akahon*), published annually by the Tokyo branch of the Federation of Bar Associations for use in Tokyo (see Nichibenren Kōtsū Jiko Sōsan Senta- Tōkyō Shibu, Minji Kōtsū Jiko Soshō Songai Baishōgaku Santei Kijun [Standard Damage Amounts for Traffic Accident Liability in Civil Suits]).

9. *Kōno v. Kawaguchi,* Kobe District Court, 935 *Hanrei Times* 193 (July 11, 1996).

10. Fukuoka District Court, 1509 *Hanrei Jihō* 123 (Oct. 7, 1993). See also Tokyo District Court, 986 *Hanrei Times* 271 (Nov. 11, 1997) (eyelid); Osaka District Court, 710 *Hanrei Jihō* 80 (Apr. 18, 1973) (eyelid); Osaka District Court, 1784 *Hanrei Jihō* 108 (Apr. 5, 2001) (breasts).

11. Naha District Court, 2004 (*wa*) 396 (Feb. 28, 2008).

12. *Kōno v. Otsukawa,* Tokyo District Court, 1018 *Hanrei Times* 288 (Apr. 28, 1999).

13. Kyoto District Court, 1998 (*u*) 39 (May 27, 2010).

14. See Shōichi Inoue, *Bijinron* [Theory of Beauty] 64–92 (1991); Shōichi Inoue, ed., Ansoroji- "Bijinron" no Hensen [Anthology: The Transformation of the Theory of Beauty], 23 Kindai Nihon no Sekushuaritii [Sexuality in Modern Japan] (2007).

15. Nancy F. Cott, *Public Vows: A History of Marriage and the Nation* 150 (2000); see also Michiko Suzuki, Progress and Love Marriage: Rereading Tanizaki Jun'ichirō's *Chijin no ai,* 31(2) *J. Japan. Stud.* 357, 367–68 (2005);

16. Naoki Sugita, Fūfu Ren'ai no Shinriteki Seiteki Kōsatsu [A Spritual and Sexual Examination of Marital Love], in Hisashi Satō, ed., *Sei to Ren'ai no Kenkyū* [Studies in Sex and Love] 415 (1922), reprinted as 17 *Kindai Nihon no Sekushuaritii* [Sexuality in Modern Japan] (2007).

17. See Junko Saeki, *Ren'ai no Kigen: Meiji no Ai wo Yomitoku* [The Origins of Love: Reading Love in the Meiji Period] 41–42 (2000); Ken K. Ito, The Family and the Nation in Tokutomi Roka's *Hototogisu,* 60(2) *Harv. J. Asiatic Stud.* 489 (2000).

18. At least as late as 1959, some villages practiced "marriage by capture," marriage forced by rape. Kagoshima District Court, 1959 (*wa*) 104 (June 19, 1959).

19. See, e.g., Tokyo District Court, 2004 (*wa*) 17193 (Sept. 30, 2005).

20. *Itō v. Itō,* Tokyo High Court, 13(2) *Kaminshū* 288 (Feb. 26, 1962).

21. In rural areas, arranged marriage continues. A 1990 survey found arranged marriages in 16.7% of twenty-somethings, 47.3% of thirty-somethings, 67.4% of forty-somethings, and 81.6% of fifty-somethings. Takayoshi Naitō, *Nōson no Kekkon to Kekkonnan* [Marriage and Marriage Difficulties in Farming Villages] 107 (2004).

22. National Institute of Population and Social Security Research, Dai13kai Shusshō Dōkō Kihon Chōsa 18. See also Masahiro Yamada, *Shoshi Shakai Nihon* [The Japan with the Declining Birth Rate] 172 (2007).

23. Aya Kitamura and Masahiro Abe, *Gōkon no Shakaigaku* [The Sociology of Gōkon] 8–9 (2007).

24. Nagoya High Court, 1057 *Hanrei Times* 199 (Jan. 26, 2000).

25. Kitamura and Abe, *Gōkon no Shakaigaku* 42–3.

26. Id. 108.

27. Takashi Kadokura, *Sekkusu Kakusa Shakai* [Sexual Gap Society] 129 (2008). International services that arrange matches beween Japanese women and foreign (white) men are apparently especially prosperous. See Karen Kelsky, *Women on the Verge: Japanese Women, Western Dreams* 178–80 (2001).

28. Ministry of Economy, Trade, and Industry, Shōshika Jidai no Kekkon Kanren Sangyō no Arikata ni Kansuru Chōsa Kenkyū [Investigative Study of Marriage-Related Industries in the Age of the Declining Birth Rate], May 2006, available at http://www.meti.go.jp/press/20060502001/houkokusho-set.pdf.

29. Ministry of Economy, Trade, and Industry, Kekkon Sōdangyō, Kekkon Jōhō Sa-bisuguō ni okeru Kujō, Sōdan Naiyō ni Kansuru Chōsa Hōkokusho [Investigative Report on Complaints and Consultations Related to the Marriage Introduction Industry], Sept. 2007, available at http://www.meti.go.jp/press/20070921006/03_chousa.pdf.

30. *Kōno v. Otsuyama,* Tokyo District Court, 915 *Hanrei Times* 171 (June 7, 1996).

31. In Japan, to win a breach of engagement case, a spurned fiancé must show two elements: (a) an engagement existed and (b) the defendant spouse-to-be ended it without appropriate reason. Evidence of the existence of an engagement, according to courts, includes telling parents, telling friends, setting a wedding date, reserving a wedding hall, and setting a time to submit the marriage registration form to city hall. See Tokushima District Court, 478 *Hanrei Times* 112 (June 21, 1982) (engagement found when parties told parents and friends, reserved hall for wedding); Tokyo District Court, 2005 (*wa*) 10186 (Sept. 13, 2005) (engagement found; defendant said he did not tell his parents of engagement, but his e-mail suggested otherwise; court considered factor heavily); Tokyo District Court, 2004 (*wa*) 22296 (Sept. 5, 2005) (no engagement found when defendant did

not tell his parents, no time was set for a wedding or applying for marriage, and questions as to whether defendant presented himself as engaged). Breach of engagement is an action that has died in the United States, where, as a general rule, a spurned fiance may sue his bride-to-be only for the return of the engagement ring; see Margaret F. Brinig, Rings and Promises, 6 *J. Law, Econ. & Org.* 203, 206 (1990); Rebecca Tushnet, Rules of Engagement, 107 *Yale L.J.* 2583 (1998).

The question in most breach of engagement cases is element (b), whether the defendant had appropriate reason to end the engagement. Some reasons are categorically appropriate: another lover, homosexuality, pre-existing marriage or pregnancy, violence, insult, verbal abuse, rape, abandonment, mental illness such as schizophrenia, incurable sexual disease, and inability to have sexual relations. Other reasons can be appropriate if properly specified: "We agreed that we would live separately from his parents, but now he's pressuring me to live with them," "He promised that I would continue to work after marriage, but now he wants me to be a full-time housewife," or "He made the wedding and honeymoon plans without even talking to me." Still other reasons have been held to be insufficient: hypoplastic (small) uterus, tuberculosis, lack of virginity, and astrological incompatibility. See, e.g., Aiichi Munabe et al., *Gendai Kaji Chōtei* Manyuaru [Manual on Modern Family Mediation] 204 (2002); Mizuho Fukushima, *Bengoshi ga Mitsumeta Yureru Onnatachi: Otoko to Onna, Kekkon, Kazoku, Shigoto* [Wavering Woman as Gazed upon by a Lawyer: Men and Women, Marriage, Family, and Work] 79 (1997). The factors are similar to the reasons used by Japanese judges in prewar cases. See J. Mark Ramseyer, *Odd Markets in Japanese History: Law and Economic Growth* 95–103 (1996).

32. Kofu District Court, 2004 (*u*) 405 (Feb. 5, 2008).

33. Aomori District Court, 1003 *Hanrei Times* 307 (Nov. 11, 1998).

34. The National Police Agency reported 790 *deaikei*-site-related crimes against women, 720 of whom were under 18, in 2008. Keisatsuchō, Abunai! Deaikei Saito [The Dangers of *Deaikei* Sites], 2009, available at http://www.npa.go.jp/cyber/deai/data/index.html.

35. See, e.g., Tokyo District Court, 2004 (*wa*) 25263 (July 22, 2005).

36. The advertising company's website is http://pure-i.net/awbr. The ubiquitous ad was reproduced (with commentary similar to mine) by Arudou Debito on his website at http://www.debito.org/wp-content/uploads/2008/04/sankeisports040208.jpg.

37. Tokyo District Court, 2004 (*wa*) 24911 (Oct. 19, 2005).

38. See e.g., Osaka District Court, 2008 (*wa*) 3179 (Aug. 8, 2008) (man lured to hotel by woman where he is robbed by a waiting man).

39. Miyazaki District Court, 2007 (*wa*) 192 (Apr. 16, 2009).

40. *Kōno v. Heikawa,* Tokyo High Court, 1107 *Hanrei Times* 232 (Nov. 30, 2000).

41. Michio Matsuda, *Ren'ai Nanka Yameteoke* [Don't Fall in Love!] 10 (1970).

42. Id. 221.

43. Ichirō Yasuda, *Nihonjin no Seikōdō* [Japanese Sexual Activity] (1966).

44. Robert O. Blood, *Love Match and Arranged Marriage: A Tokyo-Detroit Comparison* 80–84 (1967).

45. Id. 86–88.

46. *Imai v. Imai,* Osaka High Court, 500 *Hanrei Jihō* 32, 23(10) *Minshū* 1916 (June 26, 1967).

47. Masayuki Tanamura, *Kekkon no Hōritsugaku* [The Law of Marriage] 149 (2d ed. 2006). See also Luigi M. Civisca, *The Validity of Naien* 18, 30–31 (1957) (citing statistics on couples who fail to file or file late). On historical acceptance of common-law marriage in courts, see, e.g., *Yanaka v. Nozawa,* Daishin'in [Supreme Court], 21 *Minroku* 49 (Jan. 26, 1915).

48. Kyōko Yoshizumi, *Kindai Kazoku wo Koeru—Hihōritsukon Kappuru no Koe* [Getting beyond the Modern Family: The Voices of Legally Unmarried Couples] 43 (1997). See Gifu District Court, 41(9) *Kasai Geppō* 116 (June 23, 1989); see also Tokyo District Court, 835 *Hanrei Times* 58 (Nov. 19, 1993) (constitutional for national university to require professor to use married name, not maiden name).

49. *X v. Y,* Supreme Court, 1240 *Hanrei Times* 118 (Apr. 24, 2007). See also *Terao v. Hoshino,* Supreme Court, 147 *Hanrei Jihō* 4 (Apr. 11, 1958) ("a so-called common-law marriage [*naien*] exists when a man and a woman fail to file a marriage notice, which would make the marriage a 'legal marriage,' but live together as jointly cooperating husband and wife"). Unlike a legal spouse, a common-law spouse does not receive a mandatory spousal share (*iryūbun*) upon a spouse's death. See Civil Code art. 1028. A common-law spouse would still be entitled to the deceased spouse's property through a will (subject to any mandatory claims from other successors), if there is no successor, through an application to the family court as a person with a "special relationship" (*tokubetsu na enko*) to the deceased. See Civil Code art. 958(3). Only 913 actions were filed in 2008. Saikōsai Jimusōkyoku, *Shihō Tōkei Nenpō, Kaji Hen* [Annual Report of Judicial Statistics, Family Cases] 7 (2009).

50. Id.

51. Article 24: "Marriage shall be based only on the mutual consent of both sexes." The provision remained virtually unchanged since Beate Sirota Gordon's initial draft. See Beate Sirota Gordon, *The Only Woman in the Room: A Memoir* 209 (1997).

52. *Snetsinger v. Montana University System,* 104 P.3d 445 (Mont. 2004). Rhode Island requires that the parties intended to enter a "husband-wife relationship" and that "the parties' conduct is of such a character as to lead to a belief in the community that they were married," *De Melo v. Zompa,* 844 A.2d 177 (R.I. 2004). Utah recognizes common-law marriage for a couple who are of age, are legally capable of marriage, have cohabitated, mutually assume rights, duties, and obligations, and "who hold themselves out as and have acquired a uniform and general reputation as husband and wife," Utah Code Ann. 30–1-4.5 (2004). See also Henry Baskin, Family Law: The Abolition of Common Law Marriage, 79 *Mich. Bar. J.* 176 (2000).

53. See Ariela R. Dubler, Wifely Behavior: A Legal History of Acting Married, 100 *Colum. L. Rev.* 957 (2000). Only eleven states and the District of Columbia recognize common-law marriage; the concept died in the early decades of the twentieth century.

54. Japanese contracts require no consideration. The court did not address Toshihide's claim that his signature on the oath was coerced.

55. Toshihide claimed that Mie forged his signature and seal and that he did not learn of his marriage to her until he tried to register his marriage with Chizuko on the twenty-ninth. Mie claimed that Toshihide had given power of attorney to submit the papers. The court found that at a minimum Toshihide was aware that the papers were being submitted.

56. A marriage can be annulled only by a court and not by mutual consent. Such actions initially proceed in family court mediation. Kosekihō [Family Registry Law], Law no. 224 of 1947, art. 114. If the spouses agree as to the lack of intent to marry, the family court may simply enter a judgment based on the statement of the mediator as to the agreement. Kaji Saiban Hō [Family Court Law], Law no. 152 of 1947, art. 152. If the parties disagree, the case proceeds to trial in family court. Jinji Soshō Hō [Social Status Proceedings Law], Law no. 109 of 2003, art 2(1). Before 2003, such cases were heard in district court.

57. *Imai v. Imai,* Supreme Court, 577 *Hanrei Jihō* 67, 23(10) *Minshū* 1894 (Oct. 31, 1969). See also *Kubota v. Kubota,* Kagoshima District Court, 2(12) *Kaminshū* 1491 (Dec. 21, 1951) (marriage annulled when marriage was entered into for purpose of avoiding internment in Manchuria); *Ōta v. Ōta,* Tokyo High Court, 1147 *Hanrei Jihō* 99 (Feb. 27, 1985) (annulled when marriage entered into for purpose of acquiring Japanese citizenship for child); *Imada v. Kane,* Osaka District Court, 550 *Hanrei Times* 248 (Dec. 24, 1984) (annulled when marriage entered into for purpose of receiving visa). But see *Yoshioka v. Tei,* Supreme Court, 235 *Hanrei Times* 105 (Apr. 3, 1969) (finding "intent to marry" when representative of unconscious husband filed marriage notification on husband's behalf after husband dies).

58. *Kōno v. Kōno,* Tokyo District Court, 692 *Hanrei Jihō* 51, 53 (Sept. 21, 1972); *Toda v. Toda,* Osaka High Court, 27(4) *Kasai Geppō* 56 (June 28, 1984).

59. A provision courts did not enforce consistently. See Ramseyer, *Odd Markets in Japanese History* 82–84.

60. Kurt Steiner, The Revision of the Civil Code of Japan: Provisions Affecting the Family, 9(2) *Far. East. Q.* 169, 182 (1950).

61. *Noguchi v. Noguchi,* Okayama Family Court, 20(1) *Kasai Geppō* 89 (June 22, 1967) (holding that husband may not receive a cohabitation order for his third wife because he beat her, drank a lot, and was in fact still married to his second wife).

62. Atsushi Ōmura, Kon'inhō, Rikonhō [Marriage Law and Divorce Law], 1384 *Jurisuto* 6, 11–13 (2009).

63. See, e.g., *Yoda v. Yoda,* Sapporo Family Court, 51(5) *Kasai Geppō* 57 (Nov. 18, 1998); *Nakai v. Nakai,* Tokyo High Court, 54(3) *Kasai Geppō* 66 (Apr. 6, 2001).

64. *Petition of Kichizō Sorano,* Daishin'in [Supreme Court], 9 *Minshū* 926 (Sept. 30, 1930); see also Shūhei Ninomiya, *Kazokuhō* [Family Law] 36 (1999).

65. See *Toda v. Toda,* Osaka High Court, 27(4) *Kasai Geppō* 56 (June 28, 1984). If the strategic use of the order is obvious, it may be void as an abuse of right. See *Kōno v. Kōno,* Supreme Court, 413 *Hanrei Jihō* 3 (June 30, 1965).

66. Saikōsai Jimusōkyoku, *Shihō Tōkei Nenpō, Kaji Hen* 14–15.

67. *Nashimoto v. Nashimoto,* Fukuoka Family Court, 20(9) *Kasai Geppō* 84 (Apr. 13, 1968); *Inoue v. Inoue,* Tokyo High Court, 18(4) *Kasai Geppō* 65 (Oct. 13, 1965); *Higashitani v. Higashitani,* Matsuyama Family Court, 19 (3) *Kasai Geppō* 54 (Aug. 15, 1966).

68. Kōsei Rōdōsho, Heisei 16nen Shūrō Jōken Sōgō Chōsa Kekka no Gaiyō [Outline of Results of 2004 Survey on Working Conditions] (Sept. 2004), available at http://www.mhlw.go.jp/toukei/itiran/roudou/jikan/syurou/04/index.html.

69. Sumiko Iwao, Hiroko Saitō, and Mamoru Fukutomi, *Tanshin Funin* [Job-Induced Family Separation] 116–17 (1991).

70. Rōdō Daijin Kanbō Taisku Chōsa Bu, ed., *Tenkin to Tanshin Funin* [Moving Because of Work and Separating Because of Work] 151 (1991). Some parents fear a disruption in entrance exam preparation, but the largest group by far (49.3%) chooses not to move their childeren because of the psychological pressures of moving to another school. Id. 153.

71. Id. 180. Families rarely come to visit: 30.8% never do, 30.2% come once a year, 22.9% come two or three times a year. Id. *at* 181.

72. Iwao, Saitō, and Fukutomi, *Tanshin Funin* 139.

73. *Kōno v. Kōno,* Tokyo High Court, 1633 *Hanrei Jihō* 90 (Sept. 29, 1997) (lower court opinion, Niigata Family Court, 1996 (ka) 5439 (May 2, 1997), attached at p. 93).

74. Sugu Tsukaeru! Chikai no Kotoba Bunreishū [You Can Use Them Right Away! Sample Marriage Vows], available at http://www.walkerplus.com/wedding/tokushu/joshiki/bunrei/.

75. Sandra Buckley, *Broken Silence: Voices of Japanese Feminism* 274 (1997) (interview with Chizuko Ueno). Field research points to the same conclusions. One study of marriage in Japan from the 1990s found that romantic love in one wife was "real, almost instinctive, but essentially shapeless. It left her feeling disconnected and unfulfilled" because "there were no rules, no obligations, no points of references." Hamabata, *Crested Kimono* 160–61.

76. Roper/Dentsu Survey, presented in Sumiko Iwao, *The Japanese Woman: Traditional Image and Changing Japan* 69–73 (1993); see also Elaine Hatfield and Susan Sprecher, Men's and Women's Preferences in Marital Partmers in the United States, Russia, and Japan, 26 *J. Cross-Cultural Psych.* 728, 756 (1995) (finding Americans "most choosy"; Japanese "least choosy" in mate selection factors).

77. National Institute of Population and Social Security Research, Dai13kai Shusshō Dōkō Kihon Chōsa: Kekkon to Shussan ni Kansuru Zenkoku Chōsa, Dokushinsha Chōsa no Kekka Gaiyō 8–9 [13th Survey on Demographic Trends: National Survey on Marriage and Birth, An Outline of the Results of the Survey of Single Persons] (2006), available at http://www.ipss.go.jp/ps-doukou/j/doukou13_s/Nfs13doukou_s.pdf.

78. Chikahiro Tada, *Rikon Chōtei no Ōgi* [The Heart of Divorce Mediation] 119–20 (2003).

79. *Otsu v. Japan,* Tokyo District Court, 1247 *Hanrei Jihō* 82 (July 29, 1987).

80. Introduction to the Blessing Ceremony, available at http://www.unification.org/intro_blessing.html.

81. *Imai v. Imai,* Supreme Court, 577 *Hanrei Jihō* 67, 23(10) *Minshū* 1894 (Oct. 31, 1969).

82. Ofra Goldstein-Gidoni, *Packaged Japaneseness: Weddings, Business, and Brides* (1997).

83. *Kōno v. Kōno,* Fukuoka District Court, 831 *Hanrei Times* 258 (Oct. 7, 1993). See also Fukuoka District Court, 940 *Hanrei Times* 250 (Mar. 12, 1996) (Unification Church wedding "merely a religious ritual"); *Kōno v. Otsu,* Nagoya District Court, 1562 *Hanrei Jihō* 98 (Feb. 17, 1995) (Unification Church case in which annulment is granted because the couple would not "live a lifestyle of mutual support").

84. *X v. Y,* Supreme Court, 1169 *Hanrei Times* 144 (Nov. 18, 2004).

4. Private Sex

1. Ministry of Health, Labor, and Welfare, Shōshika ni Kansuru Ishiki Chōsa Kenkyū [Survey Research on Consciousness of the Declining Birth Rate], Aug. 13, 2004, available at http://www.mhlw.go.jp/topics/bukyoku/seisaku/syousika/040908/dl/0010.pdf.

2. Merry Isaacs White, *Perfectly Japanese: Making Families in an Era of Upheaval* 95 (2002); see also Matthews Masayuki Hamabata, *Crested Kimono: Power and Love in the Japanese Business Family* 124 (1990) (for one subject, "marriage would be a strategic factor in determining his future life in enterprise").

3. *Kōno v. Otsuyama,* Okayama District Court, 1410 *Hanrei Jihō* 100 (Mar. 29, 1991). Another court has held that "marriage requires an understanding and recognition of, first, [a potential spouse's] physical condition as well as such things as economic conditions, plans for the future, views on family, philosophies of life, hobbies, and tastes." When a spouse bases the decision to marry on false information of this sort, tort liability arises. *Kōno v. Otsuyama,* Tokyo District Court, 1217 *Hanrei Jihō* 83 (Aug. 26, 1986).

4. Durex Global Sex Survey (2005), available at http://www.durex.com/cm/gss2005results.asp (accessed Jan. 15, 2009).

5. Durex Sexual Wellbeing Global Survey (2007/08), available at http://www.durex.com/cm/sexual_wellbeing_globeflash.asp (poll conducted by Harris Interactive) (accessed Jan. 15, 2009).

6. Id.

7. 1984 More Report on Male Sexuality, cited in Yoshiro Hatano and Tsuguo Shimazaki, Japan, in Robert T. Francoeur, ed., *The International Encyclopedia of Sexuality* (1997), online edition, available at http://www2.hu-berlin.de/sexology/IES/index.html; see also Sakurako Ogata, Moa Ripo-to no 20nen: Onnatachi no Sei ni Mitsumete [20 Years of the More Report: Looking at Women's Sexuality] (2001).

8. Kokuritsu Kokusai Iryō Senta-, *Nihonjin no HIV/AIDS Kanren Chishiki, Seikōdō, Seichishiki ni tsuite no Zenkoku Chōsa* [National Survey Japanese Knowledge of HIV and AIDS, Sexual Activity, and Sexual Knowledge] (2005).

9. Kōshū ni Ichijirushiku Meiwaku wo Kakeru Bōryoku Furyō Kōi Nado no Bōshi ni Kansuru Jōrei [Ordinance Pertaining to Public Violence and Other Improper Acts that Create Extreme Nuisance], Hokkaidō Prefectural Ordinance 34, art. 2(2)(1)(4) (Aug. 2, 1965).

10. Supreme Court, 2050 *Hanrei Jihō* 158 (Nov. 10, 2008). The high court opinion noted that the defendant had adorned some of his photos with "heart marks." Sapporo High Court, 2007 (*u*) 73 (Sept. 25, 2007).

11. *Kōno v. Shimizu Construction Co.,* Tokyo High Court, 1673 *Hanrei Jihō* 89 (Nov. 20, 1997).

12. Tokyo District Court, 1172 *Hanrei Times* 216 (Jan. 23, 2004).

13. Supreme Court, 5(6) *Minshū* 1026 (May 10, 1951).

14. *Japan v. Benno,* Supreme Court, 196 *Keishū* 653 (June 19, 1975). See also Tokyo District Court, 1028 *Hanrei Jihō* 145 (Apr. 30, 1981) (finding that unlike a kiss between family members, indecent kisses, like the one in question in which a man kissed a woman on the street whom he had never met or spoken to, create sexual shame of an ordinary person and are contrary to sexual morals).

15. Mark McLelland, "Kissing Is a Symbol of Democracy!" Dating, Democracy and Romance in Occupied Japan 1945–1952, 19(3) *J. History of Sexuality* 508 (2010).

16. See Christopher Gerteis, The Erotic and the Vulgar: Visual Culture and Organized Labor's Critique of U.S. Hegemony in Occupied Japan, 39(1) *Critical Asian Stud.* 3, 13 (1997); see also Ronald P. Dore, *Shinohata: A Portrait of a Japanese Village 109–10* (1978) (from a late 1950s/early 1960s interview on affection in films: "The kissing. To us Japanese it seems just rather unpleasant."). The Osaka High Court divides kisses into three types: customary (*shūkanteki*), love (*aijō*), and sexual (*seiai*). Osaka High Court, 199 *Hanrei Times* 187 (Sept. 7, 1966).

17. Shigemitsu Dandō, *Waga Kokoro no Tabiji* [Journeys of My Heart] 90–93 (1986). Age of other judges from Nihon Minshū Hōritsu Kyōkai, *Zen Saibankan Keireki Sōran* [Overview of Careers of All Judges] (4th ed. 2004).

18. See, e.g., Kyoko Hirano, *Mr. Smith Goes to Tokyo: The Japanese Cinema under the American Occupation, 1945–1952* 154–65 (1992).

19. McLelland, "Kissing Is a Symbol of Democracy!"

20. *Japan v. Matsui,* Supreme Court, 3(6) *Keishū* 711 (May 10, 1949). Still, some courts frame rape cases in language of consent. See Kumamoto District Court, 1638 *Hanrei Jihō* 135 (June 25, 1997); Yokohama District Court, 813 *Hanrei Times* 247 (Mar. 23, 1993).

21. Wakayama District Court, 1240 *Hanrei Times* 345 (June 28, 2006).

22. William Blackstone, 2 *Commentaries on the Laws of England* 209 (1895).

23. See, e.g., *State v. Powell,* 438 So. 2d 1306 (La. App. 1983) (acquitting defendant despite victim's nonconsent because she did not sufficiently resist).

24. See, e.g., *In the Interest of M.T.S.,* 609 A.2d 1266 (N.J. 1992).

25. Osaka District Court, 2007 (*wa*) 4146 (June 27, 2008). But see Osaka High Court, 2004 (*ku*) 442 (Dec. 8, 2004) (examining consent).

26. *Japan v. Tsutsumi,* Yamaguchi District Court, 1(3) *Kakeishū* 611 (Mar. 22, 1959).

27. Hiroshima District Court, 235 *Hanrei Times* 285 (Mar. 26, 1969).

28. Hiroshima High Court, 922 *Hanrei Jihō* 111 (Nov. 20, 1978).

29. See generally Anne M. Coughlin, Sex and Guilt, 84 *Va. L. Rev.* 1 (1998) (arguing that rape law can be understood only when situated in the context of prohibitions against nonmarital sex).

30. Tokyo District Court, 1817 *Hanrei Jihō* 166 (Jan. 16, 2002). Forced oral sex as a substitute for rape is not uncommon. See, e.g., Wakayama District Court, 1240 *Hanrei Times* 345 (June 28, 2006) (sixteen-year-old girl proposed fellatio after defendant was unable to insert his penis); Tokyo District Court, 13 (*wa*) 4008 (June 26, 2003) (sixteen-year-old victim performed oral sex given the option of oral sex or intercourse); Tokyo High Court, 853 *Hanrei Times* 277 (Dec. 13, 1993) (woman avoided rape by performing fellatio). Forced oral sex that occurs after an attempted rape does not affect the punishment for attempted rape. Urawa District Court, 717 *Hanrei Times* 244 (Oct. 3, 1989).

31. See, e.g., Osaka High Court, 802 *Hanrei Times* 233 (Mar. 12, 1992); Tokyo District Court, 1961 *Hanrei Jihō* 72 (May 23, 2006).

32. Maebashi District Court, 1911 *Hanrei Jihō* 167 (Feb. 7, 2003) (eighteen-year-old in attempted rape that was compensated dating); Urawa District Court, 837 *Hanrei Times* 135 (Mar. 31, 1993) (fifteen-year-old in case of attempted rape by teenagers).

33. See Atsushi Koyano, *Sei to Ai no Nihongo Kōza* [A Course in the Japanese of Sex and Love] 62–71 (2003).

34. See, e.g., Chizuko Ueno, *Hatsujō Sochi: Erosu no Shinario* [The Erotic Apparatus] 50–53 (2005).

35. Chizuko Ueno, *Onna Asobi* [Woman's Play] 29–30 (1998); Chizuko Ueno, *Suka-to no Shita no Gekijō* [The Stage Under the Skirt] 173–74 (1992).

36. A panic to which U.S. judges are not immune. Legal scholar Amy Adler brilliantly argues that in nude dancing cases, U.S. Supreme Court justices "were driven by fantasies and anxieties surrounding female sexuality." Amy Adler, Girls! Girls! Girls!: The Supreme Court Confronts the G-String, 80 *N.Y.U. L. Rev.* 1108 (2005).

37. See, e.g., *Takei v. Mizutani,* Supreme Court, 368 *Hanrei Jihō* 54 (Dec. 20, 1963) (sex equals engagement); cf. Tokyo District Court, 2004 (*wa*) 16809 (June 8, 2005)(sex not precondition for engagement).

38. Kōsei Rōdōshō, Heisei 17nen Shusshō ni Kansuru Tōkei no Gaikyō [2005 Outline of Birth-Related Statistics], available at http://www.mhlw.go.jp/toukei/saikin/hw/jinkou/tokusyu/syussyo05/syussyo4.html. The highest rates are in Okinawa (46.8%) and other rural prefectures; the lowest are in Yokohama (Kanagawa Prefecture, 20.3%) and Tokyo (21.0%).

39. More precisely, 58.3% and 81.7%. Naikakufu, *Kokumin Seikatsu Hakusho* [White Paper on Lifestyles] 54 (2005).

40. Mayumi Futamatsu and Shinji Yamasaki, *Rasuto Rabu* [Last Love] 97 (2006); Sanae Kameyama, *Sei wo Ou Onnatachi* [Women Who Pursue Sex] 11 (2006).

41. More precisely, 34.6%. See Sekusuresu Fūfu, Sanbun no Ichi Koeru, Kōrōshō Shirabe [Ministry of Health Survey Finds More than One Third of Married Couples Sexless], *Yomiuri Shinbun,* Apr. 9, 2007, available at http://www.yomiuri.co.jp/iryou/news/kyousei_news/20070409ik05.htm (accessed Apr. 9, 2007).

42. 1146nin Anke-to de Akirakani [Revealing 1146-person Survey], *anan,* May 31, 2006, 69.

43. NHK "Nihonjin no Sei" Purojekuto, ed., *De-tabukku NHK Nihonjin no Seikōdō, Seiishiki* [NHK Databook on Sexual Trends and Attitudes] 18 (2002).

44. Id. 240.

45. Shigemitsu Dandō, 4 *Chūshaku Keihō* [Annotated Penal Code] 298 (1965).

46. When the victim when refused to marry the defendant formally, he became angry. As he strangled her, he told her, "You fucked with me; now I'm going to fuck with you." The court found liability, but questions remained as to whether the two were actually married. *Japan v. Kasai,* Sapporo High Court, 8(6) *Kōtō Saibansho Hanreishū* 179 (Sept. 15, 1955).

47. In 1984, after the wife had once again returned to her parents' home, the husband, along with a friend, forced her into his car. He became increasingly angry and suspicious that she was having an affair, he pulled the car to the side of the road, and they raped her. The district court found him guilty. Tottori District Court, 624 *Hanrei Times* 250 (Dec. 17, 1986). On appeal, the Hiroshima High Court held that in a marriage, each party has the right to demand sex and the responsibility to respond to such demands. In an ordinary marriage, the defendant could not be guilty of marital rape. In this case, because the marriage was destroyed, they were not actually "married." Hiroshima High Court, 1234 *Hanrei Jihō* 154 (June 18, 1987).

48. Utsunomiya District Court, 2003 (*wa*) 366 (Apr. 7, 2004).

49. *Moroi v. Koyama,* Tokyo District Court, 2(2) *Kaminshū* 165 (Feb. 9, 1951). Although lack of sex is grounds for divorce, it is not grounds for annulment if the parties otherwise had the intent to marry. See Asahikawa District Court, 1977 (*ta*) 13 (May 10, 1979).

50. Tokyo District Court, Feb. 14, 1985, unreported case discussed in Kiyoku Kinjō, *Hōjoseigaku* [The Study of Women's Law] 276–77 (2d ed. 1996).

51. *Jacobsen v. Jacobsen,* 130 N.Y.S.2d 762 (1954).

52. *Kunzmann v. Kunzmann,* 508 P.2d 70 (Ct. App. Ariz. 1973).

53. *Youngs v. Youngs,* 33 Ill. App. 223 (Ct. App. Ill. 1889); *Coles v. Coles,* 130 Ky. 349 (Ct. App. Ky. 1908).

54. Michael Fetters, Cultural Clashes: Japanese Patients and U.S. Maternity Care, 4(2) *J. Int'l Inst.* (Winter 1997), available at http://hdl.handle.net/2027/spo.4750978.0004.207 (discussing

surprise among Japanese mothers in the United States when presented routinely with the circumcision option for their infant sons).

55. See Laura Miller, *Beauty Up: Exploring Contemporary Japanese Body Aesthetics* 112–14 (2006); see also *Kōno v. Kōno,* Tokyo High Court, 739 *Hanrei Times* 197 (May 11, 1989) (mother-in-law criticizes daughter-in-law who does not fix her grandson's phimosis); Tokyo District Court, 1155 *Hanrei Times* 57 (Apr. 22, 2003) (lawsuit over failed phimosis correction surgery).

56. Miller, Beauty Up 113.

57. *Kōno v. Kōno,* Yokohama District Court, 1238 *Hanrei Jihō* 116 (Oct. 6, 1986). Shinobu countersued for divorce, claiming that when Seiko returned to her parents' home, she abandoned him maliciously. The court denied his claim. It is not clear why Shinobu and Seiko did not enter into a consensual divorce.

58. *Akasaka v. Akasaka,* Kyoto Family Court, 25(10) *Kasai Geppō* 67 (Jan. 25, 1973).

59. Mitsuba, *30sai no Hoken Taiiku* [Health and Physical Education for Thirty-Year-Olds] 88 (2008).

60. Hiroyoshi Ishikawa, Shigeo Saitō, and Hiroshi Wagatsuma, ed., *Nihonjin no Sei* [Japanese Sex] 129, 190–95 (1984).

61. *Kōno v. Kōno,* Tokyo High Court, 1069 *Hanrei Jihō* 79 (Jan. 27, 1983).

62. *Otsukawa v. Kōno,* Fukuoka High Court, 827 *Hanrei Times* 270 (Mar. 18, 1993). The clearest statement of the law in the United States, such as it is, appears to be *Clough v. Clough,* 84 N.W. 2d 16 (Iowa 1957), in which the plaintiff claimed that "the defendant was guilty of repeated acts of masturbating." "Fortunately," the court said, "we are spared the necessity of analyzing the evidence upon this question" because the plaintiff knew before she married the defendant that he masturbated.

63. *Kōno v. Kōno,* Urawa District Court, 614 *Hanrei Times* 104 (Sept. 10, 1985).

64. A 1982 issue of Japan's leading law journal *Jurisuto* was headlined by a roundtable of academics who discussed "Humans and Sex." One participant remarked: "At least through our generation, there were masturbation contests in the university dorms. This was around 1951 or 1952. I would have been a freshman or a sophomore. You'd hear lots of stories about contests to see who could ejaculate or pee the farthest. I wonder when people stopped doing this?" Zadankai, Ningen to Sei [Humans and Sex], 25 *Jurisuto Zōkan Tokushū* 8, 25 (1982) (statement of Hiroyoshi Ishikawa).

65. Tokyo District Court, 2003 (*ta*) 623 (Mar. 25, 2005).

66. Tokyo District Court, 2003 (*ta*) 591, 2004 (*wa*) 3939 (May 30, 2005). Even if such child pornography were found, depending on what the materials depicted, possession alone might not have been illegal under the Child Pornography Act. See Act on Punishment of Activities Relating to Child Prostitution, Child Pornography, and the Protection of Children (Law no. 52 of 1999), art. 7.

67. Tokyo District Court, 2003 (*ta*) 460 (Aug. 25, 2005).

68. Rōdō Kijun Hō, Law no. 49 of 1947.

69. See Margaret Lock, *Encounters with Aging: Mythologies of Menopause in Japan and North America* (1993).

70. See Yasutaka Teruoka, *Nihonjin no Ai to Sei* [Japanese Love and Sex] 22–25 (1989); Kiyoko Segawa, Menstrual Taboos Imposed upon Women, in Richard M. Dorson, ed., *Studies in Japanese Folklore* 239 (1963).

71. Mitsuba, 30sai no Hoken Taiiku 94.

72. William Johnston, *Geisha, Harlot, Strangler, Star: A Woman, Sex, and Morality in Modern Japan* 134–35 (2005).

73. See, e.g., Osaka District Court, 2006 (*wa*) 2099 (Dec. 8, 2006). Menstrual fears appear less frequently in U.S. nonconsensual sex cases, but see *March v. U.S.,* 362 A.2d 691, 694 (D.C. App. 1976) ("Apparently dissuaded from rape by his discovery that she was menstruating, he forced her to perform fellatio").

74. Tokyo District Court, 890 *Rōdō Hanrei* 42 (Jan. 25, 2005). Most men don't care. One survey finds that 63% of men would have sex with a woman on her period "if she were OK with it." Danshi no Riaru Sex Raifu [Real Men's Sex Life], *anan,* Apr. 21, 2010, 53, 59.

75. *A-ko v. B-o,* Osaka District Court, 237 *Hanrei Jihō* 27 (June 23, 1960).

76. *Stockton v. Stockton,* 203 So. 2d 806 (Miss. 1967).

77. *Houssiere v. Houssiere,* 389 S.W. 2d 533 (Ct. App. Tex. 1965).

78. Tokyo High Court, 1125 *Hanrei Jihō* 166 (Jan. 25, 1984); Tokyo District Court, 1125 *Hanrei Jihō* 169 (Oct. 27, 1980).

79. Ueno, *Suka-to no Shita no Gekijō* 172.

80. Tokyo High Court, 853 *Hanrei Times* 277 (Dec. 13, 1993). Similarly, courts mention the single status of women when their chastity is challenged. See, e.g., Yokohama District Court, 831 *Hanrei Times* 244 (Aug. 4, 1993) (defendant in criminal defamation case sentenced to eighteen months in prison for printing handouts that listed his ex-girlfriend's phone number with the phrase "I like pussy" (*omanko ga daisuki*), making a collage of his ex-girlfriend's face from their company's internal newsletter and genitals from magazines, and distributing them widely; court found her pain to be especially severe because she was a "twenty-three-year-old unmarried woman"); *Sato v. Mens,* 23(9) *Minshū* 1727 (Sept. 26, 1969) (taking of "chastity" entitles woman to damages).

81. Osaka District Court, 283 *Hanrei Times* 332 (Mar. 27, 1972).

82. Urawa District Court, 796 *Hanrei Times* 236 (Mar. 9, 1992).

83. Tokyo District Court, 1562 *Hanrei Jihō* 141 (Dec. 16, 1994).

84. See, e.g., Urawa District Court, 717 *Hanrei Times* 24 (Oct. 3, 1989) (defendant had "had sex with many men"); Tokyo District Court, 1304 *Hanrei Times* 147 (Mary 11, 1989) (defendant "lost her virginity"). See also Catherine Burns, *Sexual Violence and the Law in Japan* 84–130 (2005).

85. Hanne Blank, *Virgin: The Untouched History* 193 (2007).

86. Hiroshima District Court, 2008 (*u*) 22 (Dec. 12, 2009).

87. Shizuoka District Court, 2009 (*wa*) 345 (Jan. 21, 2010).

88. Osaka District Court, 2008 (*wa*) 2245 (Apr. 19, 2010).

89. Shizuoka District Court, 2009 (*wa*) 581 (May 20, 2010).

90. Niigataken Seishōnen Hogo Ikusei Jōrei, Ordinance no. 6 of 1977.

91. Niigata Family Court, 32(10) *Kasai Geppō* 104 (Oct. 1, 1979).

92. Fukuokaken Seishōnen Hogo Ikusei Jorei, Ordinance no. 32 of 1956.

93. In one government survey, 41.8% of respondents said that the age of marriage for women should be raised from sixteen to eighteen to be equal with the age for men, 23.3% said that the age should remain as it is, and 32.1% said that they could not choose between the two options. Naikakufu Daijin Kanbō Seifu Kōhōshitsu, Kazoku no Hōsei ni Kansuru Seron Chōsa [Survey of Law and Legal Institutions of the Family], Dec. 2006, available at http://www8.cao.go.jp/survey/h18/h18-kazoku/index.html.

94. See generally Ariela R. Dubler, Immoral Purposes: Marriage and the Genus of Illicit Sex, 115 *Yale L.J.* 756 (2006) (marriage transformed illicit sex into licit).

95. See, e.g., *Burr v. Clay,* 2010 U.S. Dist. LEXIS 36469 (C.D. Cal. 2010) ("union/meaningful relationship" and "mutual love and commitment 'marriage' before God" insufficient); *Kingery v. Dretke,* 2006 U.S. Dist. LEXIS 33557 (S.D. Tex. 2006) (common-law marriage insufficient); see also Kelly C. Connerton, Comment: The Resurgence of the Marital Rape Exemption: The Victimization of Teens by Their Statutory Rapists, 61 *Alb. L. Rev.* 237 (1997).

96. *Japan v. Shigeto,* Supreme Court, 39(6) *Keishū* 413 (Oct. 23, 1985).

97. Unreported case, Nagoya Summary Court (May 23, 2007); Joshi Kōsei to "Kankei" no Dansei: Ren'ai Mitome Muzai Nagoya Kansai ["Relationship" with High-schooler Confirmed as Love: Not Guilty, Nagoya Summary Court], asahi.com, available at http://www.asahi.com/national/update/0524/NGY200705230023.html (accessed May 24, 2007).

98. Supreme Court, 371 *Hanrei Times* 43 (Oct. 20, 1978).

99. Nagoya District Court, 2007 (*wa*) 3946 (Feb. 5, 2010).

100. *Kōno v. Heikawa,* Tokyo High Court, 1107 *Hanrei Times* 232 (Nov. 30, 2000). In a murder case (in which sex was at issue), the Tokyo High Court found that the defendant went to a hotel room with two female acquaintances and then called one of his employees to the room, where "the four of them together had sexual relations" (it is unclear how the couplings worked out). The court stated that the defendant's "relations with women are a departure from the norm, and the way he views women and the thoughts that form the foundation for that view, are abnormal [*futsū de nai*]." *Japan v. Miura,* Tokyo High Court, 999 *Hanrei Times* 102 (July 1, 1998).

101. Sabine Frühstück, *Colonizing Sex: Sexology and Social Control in Modern Japan* 190 (2003).

102. Tiana Norgren, *Abortion Before Birth Control* 129 (2001).

103. Frühstück, *Colonizing Sex* 186–93.

104. Teruko Inoue and Yumiko Ehara, eds., *Josei no De-tabukku* [Women's Data Book] 35 (4th ed. 2005).

105. Frühstück, *Colonizing Sex* 190.

106. Tomomi Shibuya, Kondo-mu [Condom], in Shōichi Inoue, ed., *Sei no Yōgōshū* [Sex Vocabulary] 135–41 (2004).

107. See White, *Perfectly Japanese* 149.

108. Frühstück, *Colonizing Sex* 190.

109. Yūji Taketani, *Zenkokuteki Jittai Chōsa ni Motozuita Jinkō Ninshin Chūzetsu Genshō ni Muketa Hōkatsu Kenkyū* [Comprehensive Research on Reducing Abortion Based on National Survey Data] (2006).

110. Teruko Inoue and Yumiko Ehara, eds., *Josei no De-tabukku* [Women's Data Book] 36–37 (4th ed. 2005).

111. Hiromi Maruyama, James H. Raphael, and Carl Djerassi, Why Japan Ought to Legalize the Pill, 379 *Nature* 579 (1996).

112. Guttmacher Institute, Facts on Induced Abortion in the United States, January 2008, available at http://www.guttmacher.org/pubs/fb_induced_abortion.html#2.

113. Teruko Inoue and Yumiko Ehara, eds., *Josei no De-tabukku* 36–37.

114. Kenji Hayashi, Nozomanai Ninshin Nado no Bōshi ni Kansuru Kenkyū 10 [Research of Methods to Prevent Unwanted Pregnancy], Ministry of Health Working Paper (1996), available at http://www.niph.go.jp/wadai/mhlw/1995/h070802.pdf.

115. Durex Global Sex Survey(2005), available at http://www.durex.com/cm/gss2005results.asp (accessed Jan. 15, 2009). Japan is calculated as 45 times per year times 35 million women of childbearing age; United States as 113 times per year times 70 million women.

116. Hayashi, Nozomanai Ninshin Nado no Bōshi ni Kansuru Kenkyū 10.

117. See, e.g., *Kō v. Otsu,* Nagoya High Court, 344 *Hanrei Times* 233 (June 29, 1976) (in divorce suit, wife has sex with boyfriend while husband in jail; has three pregnancies and three abortions).

118. Tokyo District Court, 2003 (*wa*) 6244 (Oct. 28, 2005).

119. Tokyo District Court, 530 *Hanrei Times* 178 (Feb. 23, 1984).

5. Commodified Sex

1. Jidō Fukushihō [Child Welfare Act], Law no. 164 of 1947, art. 34(6).

2. Tokyo Family Court, 55(5) *Kasai Geppō* 172 (June 10, 2002).

3. Dansei to Baishun wo Kangaeru Kai, *Baishun ni Taisuru Dansei Ishiki Chōsa* [Survey of Male Awareness of Men and Prostitution] (1998); see also Ryōko Tada, "Ecchi Goko" ni Mukau Otoko Takachi [Men Who "Play Sex"], in Shinji Miyadai, Izumi Tsuji, and Takayuki Okai, eds.,

Otoko Rashisa no Kairaku [The Pleasure of Masculinity] 169, 175 (2009) (45.1% have visited a sex shop, including 9.9% in the previous year).

4. Prostitution Prevention Law [Baishun Bōshihō], Law no. 118 of 1956.

5. See, e.g., Tokyo High Court, 1980 (*u*) 2041 (Mar. 2, 1981) (criminal liability for woman in "makeup and clothes that made her look younger than her age" standing in front of hotel asking men "do you want to go out?"). Posting of bills advertising prostitution service, though widespread, is illegal under the provision, see, e.g., Tokyo High Court, 752 *Hanrei Times* 246 (Dec. 10, 1990) (accessory liability for printer of bills); Osaka High Court, 721 *Hanrei Times* 254 (July 7, 1989) (liability for posting of bills in public telephone boxes).

6. Related actions that violate public morals under the Civil Code, none of which involve the sex act itself, are voidable. See, e.g., Yūgen Gaisha X Shōji v. Otsuyama, Tokyo District Court, 1223 *Hanrei Times* 200 (Nov. 30, 2005) (loan-based indentured servitude of prostitute in soapland made contract unconscionable).

7. Shigemitsu Dandō, *Wa ga Kokoro no Tabiji* [My Inner Journey] 178 (1986).

8. Sheldon Garon, *Molding Japanese Minds: The State in Everyday Life* 202, 204 (1997).

9. Fūzoku Eigyō tō no Kisei oyobi Gyōmu no Tekiseika tō ni Kansuru Hōritsu [Entertainment Law], Law No. 22 of 1948.

10. Id. art. 2(6)(1–3).

11. Id. art. (2)(7)(1).

12. Id. art. (2)(9–10)

13. If there is ambiguity in the law, it is in its enforcement, which may be loose in part because of connections to organized crime. See Tokyo District Court, 1272 *Hanrei Jihō* 149 (Dec. 24, 1987) (soapland may not deduct protection payments to organized crime as business expenses). The law is potentially overbroad. As some critics have noted, the definition of telephone clubs far exceeds limitations on typical prostitution. See Yoshikazu Nagai, *Fūzoku Eigyō Torishimari* [The Regulation of the Entertainment Business] 220–21 (2002).

14. See Ayumi Mitsuishi, Toruko, in Shōichi Inoue, Hikaru Saitō, Tomomi Shibuya, and Junko Mitsuhashi, eds., *Seiteki na Kotoba* [Sexual Words] 225, 234 (2010).

15. Atsushi Koyano, *Nihon Baishunshi* [A History of Prostitution in Japan] 182 (2007).

16. See, e.g., Kobe District Court, 858 *Hanrei Times* 277 (May 12, 1994), *aff'd,* Osaka High Court, 1563 *Hanrei Jihō* 147 (July 7, 1995); see also *People v. Lauria,* 251 Cal. App. 2d 471 (Cal. Ct. App. 1967) (discussing difficulties of proving intent for answering service owner whose services were used by prostitutes).

17. Tokyo High Court, 1992 *Hanrei Jihō* 157 (Aug. 29, 2007).

18. Rōdōsha Hakenhō, Law no. 88 of 1985.   •

19. See Kazuo Sugeno, *Koyō Shakai no Hō* [Employment Society and Law] 206 (1996).

20. Yokohama District Court, 1277 *Hanrei Jihō* 169 (May 25, 1988).

21. Tokyo District Court, 2002 (*wa*) 651 (Mar. 28, 2003).

22. See *City of Erie v. Pap's A.M.,* 529 U.S. 277 (2000); *Barnes v. Glen Theatre, Inc.,* 501 U.S. 560 (1991). See also Amy Adler, Girls! Girls! Girls!: The Supreme Court Confronts the G-String, 80 *N.Y.U. L. Rev* 101 (2005) (arguing that these cases can "be fully understood only when placed within a broader context: the highly charged terrain of female sexuality").

23. Joan Sinclair, *Pink Box: Inside Japan's Sex Clubs* 46 (2006).

24. Nicholas Bornoff, *Pink Samurai: Love, Marriage and Sex in Contemporary Japan* 315 (1991)

25. Ian Buruma, *Behind the Mask* 12–13 (1984).

26. Kokoro no Kyōiku [Heart Education], 745 *Tōdai Shinpō* 4 (June 15, 1998), available at http://www.t-shinpo.com/745/kokoro.html; See generally Andrew Morrison, Teen Prostitution in Japan: Regulation of Telephone Clubs, 31 *Vand. J. Trans. L.* 457 (1998). One court, finding that clubs promote "prostitution and crime," upheld the firing of a public servant who ran such a

business on the ground that the business was "contrary to society." Osaka District Court, 759 *Rōdō Hanrei* 28 (Feb. 3, 1999).

27. See, e.g., Sinclair, Pink Box.

28. Keisatsuchō, *Heisei 19nen Keisatsu Hakusho* [White Paper on Police] 111 (2007). More recent figures are available but differ because of a new licensing procedure.

29. Sanae Kameyama, *Sei wo Ou Onnatachi* [Women Who Pursue Sex] 46 (2006).

30. Josei Sen'yō Seikan Massa-ji Osaka B-Pleasure, available at http://aroma.tnsjpn.com/senden-2.html.

31. See, e.g., Sumie Kawakami, *Goodbye Madame Butterfly: Sex, Marriage and the Modern Japanese Woman* (2007); Tarō Ōhata and Sumie Kawakami, *Tsuma no Koi: Tatoe Furin to Yobaretemo* [The Love of Wives: Even if It's Called Adultery] (2004); Justin Curry, Japan's Virgin Wives Turn to Sex Volunteers: Lustless Matches Put Country on Brink of Demographic Disaster, *The Guardian,* Apr. 4, 2005, 14; Abigail Haworth, Would You Trust This Man with Losing Your Virginity? 13(5) *Marie Claire* 88 (May 1, 2006).

32. Osaka High Court, 1006 *Hanrei Times* 282 (July 16, 1998). See also Tokyo District Court, 730 *Hanrei Times* 246 (Dec. 21, 1989) (man who killed two workers at S&M clubs sentenced to life imprisonment and not death, in part because the court found some fault with the victims); Tokyo High Court, 671 *Hanrei Times* 249 (June 9, 1988) (prostitute received suspended sentence in killing of a man who called her to his hotel room, where he had a vibrator, a screwdriver, rubber gloves, an enema kit, a video camera, and duct tape, and he bound her, called her a men's toilet, and threatened her life with a knife).

33. *United States v. Stevens,* 559 U.S. __ (2010).

34. Nagoya District Court, 2002 (*u*) 46 (June 25, 2003).

35. Fukuoka High Court, 1984 (*u*) 597 (Mar. 12, 1985) ("men's clinic" offering oral and manual sex); Tokyo District Court, 204 *Hanrei Times* 180 (Dec. 16, 1966) (turkish bath offering "special service," defined elsewhere contemporaneously as manual sex, see Yamagata District Court, 661 *Hanrei Jihō* 25 (Feb. 29, 1972) (defining "special" as manual sex and "double special" as manual sex with two hands).

36. Fukuoka High Court, 2006 (*ne*) 806 (Feb. 1, 2007).

37. *Ryūen v. Kōdansha,* Tokyo District Court, 1773 *Hanrei Jihō* 104 (Sept. 5, 2001). In the same suit, the court awarded an additional $20,000 based on swimsuit photos that appeared in another magazine produced by the same publisher without Ryūen's permission. Still, it would not have been completely unthinkable for a successful announcer to have had the job. The 1997 murder of a thirty-nine-year-old woman who worked as an "office lady" for the Tokyo Electric Power Company by day and for an S&M club by night and on weekends brought attention in Japan to the issue of moonlighting prostitution by women with full-time day jobs. See Tokyo District Court, 1029 *Hanrei Times* 120 (Apr. 14, 2000), *rev'd,* Tokyo High Court, 1050 *Hanrei Times* 83 (Dec. 22, 2000); Valerie Reitman, Japan's Case of the Unlikely Streetwalker: An Economist Moonlighting as a Prostitute and the Foreigner Declared Guilty of Her Death Highlight Overlooked Aspects of the Society, *L.A. Times,* Mar. 19, 2001, A1. A 1986 Prime Minister's Office survey on prostitution found that 10% of prostitutes were housewives, 10% were office employees, and 4% were students. March 1986 survey cited in Bornoff, *Pink Samurai* 334.

38. See, e.g., Kōji Maruta, *Dare ga Dare ni Nani wo Urunoka? Enjō Kōsai ni Miru Sei Ai Komunikeshon* [Who Sells What to Whom? Sex, Love, and Communication as Seen in Compensated Dating] 51–55, 107–15 (2001).

39. Kokoro no Kyōiku, 745 *Tōdai Shinpō* 4.

40. Mitsuru Shirakawa, *Shōwa Heisei Nippon Seifūzokushi: Baibaishun no 60nen* [A History of Sexual Entertainment in the Showa and Heisei Eras: 60 Years of Prostitution] 228 (2007). Men who participate in this sort of prostitution with underage (18) girls may be liable under the Act on

Punishment of Activities Relating to Child Prostitution, Child Pornography, and the Protection of Children (Law no. 52 of 1999), which specifically targets child prostitution and child pornography, and under local prefectural regulations.

41. David Leheny, *Think Global, Fear Local: Sex, Violence, and Anxiety in Contemporary Japan* 49–113 (2006).

42. Tokyo Family Court, 57(7) *Kasai Geppō* 51 (Nov. 14, 2003).

43. Wakayama District Court, 2008 (*shoi*) 2 (Feb. 5, 2009). The court similarly framed the case as one of prostitution when it sentenced the girl's mother for her complicity. Wakayama District Court, 2008 (*shoi*) 2 (Dec 25, 2008).

44. Utsunomiya District Court, 2009 (*wa*) 34 (June 4, 2009).

45. Japan v. Fukumoto, Kobe District Court, 1097 *Hanrei Times* 312 (Mar. 25, 2002), *aff'd*, Osaka High Court, 1807 *Hanrei Jihō* 155 (Nov. 26, 2002).

46. Tokyo District Court, 2002 (*wa*) 5926 (June 20, 2003).

47. Jidō Kaishun Jidō Poruno ni kakaru Kōi nado no Shobatsu oyobi Jidō no Hogo nado ni Kansuru Hōritsu, Law no. 52 of 1999.

48. Maebashi District Court, 1911 *Hanrei Jihō* 167 (Feb. 7, 2003); see also Tokyo Family Court, 58(8) *Kasai Geppō* 94 (June 8, 2005) (compensated dating in history of juvenile accused of murder); Tokyo District Court, 1040 *Hanrei Times* 242 (Nov. 26, 1998) (four-year "financially-supported sexual relationship").

49. Rōdōsha Hakenhō, Law no. 88 of 1985.

50. Tokyo District Court, 1530 *Hanrei Jihō* 144 (Mar. 7, 1994). See also Tokyo District Court, 942 *Hanrei Times* 261 (Nov. 26, 1996) (employment law liability for a person who advertised for models for adult movies who were required to have oral sex, simulated sex, and masturbation scenes).

51. *Kuroki v. Shiba Holdings, K.K.*, Tokyo District Court, 1961 *Hanrei Jihō* 72 (May 23, 2006). Japanese courts are highly protective of honor. See Mark D. West, *Secrets, Sex, and Spectacle: The Rules of Scandal in Japan and the United States* 58–113 (2006).

52. *Japan v. Fukumoto*, Kobe District Court, 1097 *Hanrei Times* 312 (Mar. 25, 2002), *aff'd*, Osaka High Court, 1807 *Hanrei Jihō* 155 (Nov. 26, 2002).

53. Aoyama District Court, 2005 (*wa*) 314 (Mar. 16, 2006).

54. Osaka District Court, 2006 (*wa*) 2099 (Dec. 8, 2006). If courts do not make the link from sexual deviance to pornography, the media do it for them. In the case of child murderer Tsutomu Miyazaki, the media focused on his home, which contained a room filled with over 5,000 pornographic videos, many of which focused on rape, pedophilia bondage, and mutilation. See *Japan v. Miyazaki*, Supreme Court, 1205 *Hanrei Times* 129 (Jan. 16, 2006); Mark Schreiber, *The Dark Side: Infamous Japanese Crimes and Criminals* 225–26 (2001).

55. See Aoyama District Court, 17 (*wa*) 314 (Mar. 16, 2006) (serial murderer who chose his victims off of Internet suicide pages suffocated them "to receive a sexual high" and masturbated over their photos "to satisfy his sexual desires"). Even in cases in which rape is not explicitly tied to the unavailability of consensual sex, courts link it to lost love: in one case, the Tokyo District Court acknowledged that the fact that "a woman who had promised to marry [the defendant] broke up with him" was the motivation for rape. Kanazawa District Court, 1974 (*wa*) 258 (Mar. 10, 1975).

Richard Posner similarly argues, contrary to the views of many feminists (see, e.g., Susan Brownmiller, *Against Our Will: Men, Women, and Rape* [1975]), that "rape appears to be a substitute for consensual sex rather than an expression of hostility to women." Richard A. Posner, *Sex and Reason* 370, 384 (1992). He notes that Japan in particular has a low incidence of rape even though "pornography is sold more openly and more widely than in the United States—and most of it is rape or bondage pornography." Id. 369–70. Japanese court opinions concur that rape is about lack of sex, but they see a link between pornography and rape where Posner finds none.

56. Tokyo High Court, 949 *Hanrei Times* 281 (May 12, 1997), *aff'd*, Supreme Court, 1018 *Hanrei Times* 219 (Nov. 29, 1999).

57. Kensuke Sugawara, Shūchi Baben de no Teisai no Toritsukuroi ni Kansuru Jireiteki Kenkyū: Aduruto Bideo no Rentaru Bamen ni Okeru Kyaku to Bideo Mise no Taisho Hōryaku [An Empirical Analysis of Varnishing One's Appearance in an Embarrassing Situation: Coping Strategies for Coping With Clerks and Customers in an Adult Video Rental Situation], 6 *Edogawa Daigaku Kiyō, Jōhō to Shakai* 49 (1996), available at http://www5b.biglobe.ne.jp/~sken/hp/articles/papers/ken.1996.pdf.

58. Shinsuke Shimada and Hitoshi Matsumoto, *Matsushin* 68 (2004).

59. Tokyo District Court, 1209 *Hanrei Times* 60 (Mar. 31, 2006). Identity of plaintiff from Dauntaun Matsumoto, Shōso AVten Eizō "Junindo Koeru" [Downtown's Matsumoto Prevails in Suit against Adult Video Store: "Exceeds Limits of Acceptability"], *Zakzak*, April 1, 2006, available at http://www.zakzak.co.jp/gei/2006_04/g2006040104.html.

60. See Nobuhiro Motohashi, *AV Jidai: Muranishi Tooru to Sono Jidai* [The Age of Adult Videos: Tooru Muranishi and His Times] 221–64 (2005).

61. See, e.g., Osaka District Court, 1034 *Hanrei Times* 283 (Mar. 19, 1999); Okayama District Court, 972 *Hanrei Times* 280 (Dec. 15, 1997)

62. *Kuroki v. Shiba Holdings,* K.K., Tokyo District Court, 1257 *Hanrei Times* 181 (May 23, 2006).

63. Television broadcasters state clearly that "display of total nudity, as a rule, shall be avoided" and agree to monitor especially the 7 p.m. to 9 p.m. time slots, saving the more explicit fare—bare breasts—for after 9 p.m., presumably after children have gone to bed. See Broadcasting Standards Review Board, The National Association of Commercial Broadcasters in Japan (NAB), NAB Take Actions on the Issue of Children's Broadcasting, June 17, 1999, available at http://nab.or.jp/index.php?plugin=attach&refer=Broadcasting%20ETHICS&openfile=actionCB.pdf.

64. The leading Supreme Court case on the topic is The Lady Chatterley's Lover Decision, 11(3) *Keishū* 997 (Mar. 13, 1957). The Tokyo District Court in 1985 banned a film on erotic *shunga* woodblock prints because the prints showed genitals and acts of intercourse (the prints themselves were illegal for sale as well) despite the acknowledged historical and artistic value of the prints. See, e.g., Tokyo District Court, 580 *Hanrei Times* 67 (Oct. 23, 1985); see also see, e.g., Shōichi Inoue, Rekishi no Naka no Waisetsu: Waisetsu ha Geijutsu ni Ippōteki Makasaretekita [The History of Obscenity: Obscenity Lost to Art], in Junji Ishii, ed., *Waisetsu Daikōshin* [The Grand Obscenity Procession] 236, 237 (1993); Yoshihiko Shirakura, *Shunga de Yomu Edo no Seiai* [Erotic Love in the Edo Era as Seen Through Shunga] (2006).

65. *U.S. v. Handley,* S.D. Iowa Criminal No. 1:07–030, Plea Agreement, Attachment A: Stipulation of Facts, Apr. 16, 2009.

66. 18 U.S.C. § 1466A(b).

67. *U.S. v. Handley,* S.D. Iowa Criminal No. 1:07–030, Sentencing Brief, Feb. 10, 2010, at 5–6.

68. As a legal matter, the depiction of sexual conduct matters in Japan only when a real minor (not a cartoon one) is involved, and even then possession is not a crime if there is no intent to distribute or display. Act on Punishment of Activities Relating to Child Prostitution, Child Pornography, and the Protection of Children (Law no. 52 of 1999), art. 7. Japan and the United States have similar conceptions of what it means to exhibit a child. Japan punishes the presentation of a "wholly or partially naked child that arouses a viewer's sexual desire." Act on Punishment of Activities Relating to Child Prostitution, Child Pornography, and the Protection of Children (Law no. 52 of 1999), art. 3(3). In the United States, the "lascivious exhibition of the genitals or pubic area" of a minor is punished. At least one federal court has famously held that "exhibition" does not require nudity. *U.S. v. Knox,* 977 F.2d 815 (1992); *Knox v. U.S.* 32 F.3d 733 (1994).

69. The prosecution did not list full titles of Handley's seven books in the sentencing brief, but it gave enough information to determine that they were (1) Yuki Tamachi, *Mikansei Seifuku Shōjo* [Unfinished School Girl], ISBN 9784812607640 (LE Comics), (2) Makafushigi, *Ai Do-ru* [Idol/I Love Dolls], ISBN 4894652798 (Seraphim Comics), (3) "Kemono for Essential 3" (The Animal

Sex Anthology Vol. 3) (Izumi Comics), (4) Nekogen, *Otonari Kazoku* [Next Door Neighbors], ISBN 9784896136500 (MD Comics), (5) Makafushigi, *Eromon,* ISBN 4894651726 (Seraphim Comics), (6) Makafushigi, *Kono Man○ga* Sugoi! [This Pusxx is Awesome/This Comic is Awesome], ISBN 4894652226 (Seraphim Comics), and (7) Makafushigi, *Hina Meikyū* [Doll Labryinth], ISBN 4894651939 (Seraphim Comics). *U.S. v. Handley,* S.D. Iowa Criminal No. 1:07–030, Sentencing Brief, Feb. 10, 2010, 4. They are available at many online stores and until roughly 2009 at the mainstream www.amazon.co.jp.

70. *U.S. v. Handley,* S.D. Iowa Criminal No. 1:07–030-JEG, Order, Defendant's Motion to Dismiss (July 2, 2008).

71. *Japan v. Kishi,* Tokyo District Court, 1853 *Hanrei Jihō* 151 (Jan. 13, 2004). Had the publisher whited out more of the offending organ (industry whiteout standard is 40%), the book would have been legal, and it would have been legal no matter what the organ was doing.

72. *Asai v. Japan,* Tokyo High Court, 2002 (*ko*) 50 (Mar. 27, 2003).

73. A few publications, including some in the mainstream, received official police warnings when they occasionally ignored the ban. See Shōko Takeda, Waisetsu Nendaiki [Annual Record of Obscenity], in Junji Ishii, ed., *Waisetsu Daikōshin* [The Grand Obscenity Procession] 10 (1993).

74. *Asai v. Japan,* Supreme Court, 2003 (*tsu*) 157 (Feb. 19, 2008). The majority's number of pages is correct.

75. See, e.g., Tokyo District Court, 2004 (*wa*) 17711 (July 14, 2005). The suit must be filed within three years of either an adultery-grounds divorce or knowledge of the affair. Minpō [Civil Code] art. 724. See also *Kōno v. Otsuyama,* Tokyo High Court, 1202 *Hanrei Times* 280 (June 22, 2006). A spouse who forgives her spouse forfeits the right to sue the adultery partner. See *Ōhara v. Honda,* Yamagata District Court, 599 *Hanrei Jihō* 76 (Jan. 29, 1970).

76. Saori Matsuda, Hosutesu [Hostess], in Shōichi Inoue, ed., *Sei no Yōgōshū* [Sex Vocabulary] 101 (2004).

77. Tokyo District Court, 2004 (*u*) 14643 (Nov. 16, 2005) (Mizuno, Yūko, J.).

78. Fukuoka District Court, 1185 *Hanrei Times* 246 (Oct. 27, 2004) (unsuccessful suit by hostess over failure to explain acne scar removal process); Tokyo High Court, 415 *Hanrei Times* 178 (Apr. 24, 1980)(case dismissed because defendant had already paid adequate damages; plaintiff was not entitled to high expected wages as hostess).

79. Anne Allison, *Nightwork: Sexuality, Pleasure, and Corporate Masculinity in a Tokyo Hostess Club* 19 (1994).

80. Itsumi Hino, *Furin no Ri-garu Ressun* [Legal Lessons: Adultery] 70 (2003). See Tokyo District Court, 2003 (*ta*) 600, 2003 (*ta*) 603 (June 24, 2005) (court avoids comment on whether visit to soapland constitutes adultery). Of 126 surveyed sex workers, 79.4% agree that sex with them is not adultery. See *Yukiko Kaname and Nozomi Mizushima,* Fūzokujō Jōshiki Chōsa [Common Sense Survey of Sex Workers] 64–65 (2005). See also *Tanaka v. Tanaka,* Supreme Court, 156 *Hanrei Times* 104 (June 4, 1963) (wife's prostitution constitutes adultery).

81. Tokyo District Court, 2002 (*u*) 26959 (Feb. 19, 2004).

82. Atsushi Miura and Tamao Yanauchi, *Onna ha Naze Kyabakurajō ni Naritainoka?* [Why Do Women Want to Become Cabaret Club Hostesses?] 106–7 (2008).

83. *Ichikawa v. Murai,* Tokyo High Court, 338 *Hanrei Times* 168 (Dec. 22, 1975).

84. *Ichikawa v. Murai,* Supreme Court, 33(2) *Minshū* 303 (Mar. 30, 1979) (Motobayashi, J., dissenting). The Court split on the issue of whether a minor child could sue the third party for alienation of affections. The majority held that there was no causation between a father taking his love (*aijō*) from a child and the actions of the mistress. The rare dissenting opinion held that regardless of whether the mistress's actions are intentional, a causal link exists between living with a mistress and damage to a child.

On the same day, the same Supreme Court panel decided a similar case in which a father and his children sued his wife's lover. *Kimura v. Mori,* Supreme Court, 922 *Hanrei Jihō* 8 (Mar. 30, 1979).

85. See, e.g., Hisao Izumi, Oya no Futei Kōi to Ko no Isharyō Seikyū [Parental Infidelity and Child Support], 694 *Jurisuto* 88 (1979) (no duty of fidelity exists for spouses who are separated but remain legally married); Teruo Nogawa, Haigūsha no Chii Shingai ni yoru Songai Baishō Seikyū: Kantsū ni yoru Baai wo Chūshin Toshite [Suits for Damages Based on Invasion of Spousal Status: The Case of Adultery], in Gendai Kazokuhō Taikei Henshū Iinkai, ed., 2 *Gendai Kazokuhō Taikei: Kon'in Rikon* [Compendium of Modern Family Law: Marriage and Divorce] 371 (1980) (no duty of fidelity after marriage is destroyed); Noriko Mizuno, Otto to Dōyō Shita Josei ni Taishite Tsuma Mata ha Ko kara Isharyō Seikyū Dekiru ka [May a Wife or a Child Bring Suit against a Woman Who Lives with the Husband?], 97(3) *Hōgaku Kyōkai Zasshi* 163 (1980) (no tort liability for third party under any circumstances).

86. *Yamazoe v. Itagaki,* Supreme Court, 908 *Hanrei Times* 284 (Mar. 26, 1996). For a similar U.S. case, see *Pankratz v. Miller,* 401 N.W.2d 543 (S.D. 1987). The 1979 case is still cited. See Tokyo Summary Court, 2002 (*ha*) 15837 (Mar. 25, 2003).

87. See also *Kōno v. Otsuno,* Osaka District Court, 395 *Hanrei Jihō* 38 (June 29, 1964).

88. Tokyo District Court, 1044 *Hanrei Times* 153 (July 31, 1998). If a wife forgives a husband for his adultery, she can no longer sue either the husband or the other woman. Ōhara v. Honda, Yamagata District Court, 599 *Hanrei Jihō* 76 (Jan. 29, 1970) (wife's forgiveness of husband removes liability of other woman); *Kōno v. Kōno,* Tokyo High Court, 1446 *Hanrei Jihō* 65 (Dec. 24, 1992) (husband's forgiveness of wife's adultery removes her liability).

89. *Yatsushiro v. Kitagawa,* Supreme Court, 48(12) *Kasai Geppō* 39 (June 18, 1996). In March, Jōji attacked Mika on the street; her wounds took a week to heal. Jōji paid a $500 criminal fine. Mika sued him for damages based on his adultery. They eventually settled for $20,000. Id.

90. See, e.g., *Doe v. Doe,* 747 A.2d 617 (Md. Ct. App. 2000). Technically, criminal conversation actions require sexual intercourse, and alienation of affections actions require only the alienation of affection of the spouse. Japan does not distinguish between the two, and neither did many U.S. jurisdictions. See Robert C. Brown, The Action for Alienation of Affections, 82 *U. Penn. L. Rev* 472, 473 (1934) ("It is not always easy to determine which of these actions is involved.").

91. See Posner, *Sex and Reason* 81–82; Eric Rasmusen, An Economic Approach to Adultery Law, in Antony W. Dnes and Robert Rowthorn, eds., *The Law and Economics of Marriage and Divorce* 70, 83–84 (2002).

92. "The modern family system of one man and one woman brings psychological peace, feelings of happiness, and the profits of mutual love." Adultery destroys the system and eliminates those "profits." Tokyo District Court, 234 *Hanrei Times* 202 (Feb. 3, 1969).

93. Japanese couples do not have prenuptial agreements even though Japanese law specifically provides for them. The Civil Code (art. 756) allows a husband and a wife to contract around property distribution default rules prior to marriage by registering property separately prior to marriage. The Ministry of Justice recorded only five such registrations in 2006. Hōmushō, 1 *Minji Shōmu Jinken Tōkei Nenpō* [Annual Report of Statistics on Civil Affairs, Litigation, and Civil Liberties] 81 (2007). Contracts between spouses are void. Art. 754. Courts have construed "during the marriage" to mean "not merely the continuation of a formal marriage, but a marriage that in reality is continuing"; therefore, a spouse in a "destroyed" marriage may void a contract with the other spouse even without divorce. *Fukutomi v. Fukutomi,* Supreme Court, 477 *Hanrei Jihō* 11 (Feb. 2, 1967). Yet spouses do contract with each other; courts drolly gloss over contracts in which unfaithful husbands vow never to cheat again. Tokyo District Court, 2004 (*ta*) 37 (June 14, 2005).

94. *Kōno v. Otsuyama,* Tokyo High Court, 1048 *Hanrei Jihō* 109 (Apr. 28, 1982).

95. Courts examine the "realness" of relationships in other areas of the law. In a long line of will contest cases, for instance, courts uphold testamentary gifts by married men to their lovers— often hostesses—as long as the money was given to "secure her future" or "sustain their relationship" and not simply to continue the sex. See, e.g., *Kōno v. Heikawa,* Supreme Court, 1216 *Hanrei*

Jihō 25 (Nov. 20, 1986); *Takeda v. Ishida,* Osaka District Court, 557 *Hanrei Jihō* 257 (Aug. 16, 1968). See also Tokyo High Court, 1692 *Hanrei Jihō* 68 (June 16, 1999) ("lovers contract" voided on public morals grounds).

6. Divorce

1. In 1992, two-thirds of survey respondents stated that divorce based on personality differences was "unacceptable." By 2004, that figure had dropped to roughly half. National Institute of Population and Social Security Research, Dai13kai Shusshō Dōkō Kihon Chōsa: Kekkon to Shussan ni Kansuru Zenkoku Chōsa, Dokushinsha Chōsa no Kekka Gaiyō [Thirteenth Survey on Demographic Trends: National Survey on Marriage and Birth, an Outline of the Results of the Survey of Single Persons] 15 (2006), available at http://www.ipss.go.jp/ps-doukou/j/doukou13_s/Nfs13doukou_s.pdf. Another government survey asked if divorce was acceptable if a mate does not satisfy. In 1972, 21% said yes. In 2004, 52% said yes. Naikakufu, Danjo Kyōdō Sankaku Shakai ni Kansuru Seron Chōsa (2004), available at http://www8.cao.go.jp/survey/h16/h16-danjo/index.html.

2. Ministry of Health, *Rikon ni Kansuru Tōkei* [Statistics Regarding Divorce] (2009); see also Harald Fuess, *Divorce in Japan: Family, Gender, and the State 1600–2000* (2004); James M. Raymo, Miho Iwasawa, and Larry Bumpass, Marital Dissolution in Japan: Recent Trends and Pictures, 11 *Demographic Research* 395 (2004).

3. Data from Saikōsai Jimusōkyoku, *Shihō Tōkei Nenpō, Kaji Hen* [Annual Report of Judicial Statistics, Family Cases] 36–37 (2009). A blank form is provided by the court system as an example at http://www.courts.go.jp/saiban/tetuzuki/syosiki/pdf/01huhukankeityoutei.pdf.

4. The same hypotheses emerge from survey data on why older couples *don't* divorce even though they are thinking of doing so. Among married people in their fifites and sixties, the most common reasons not to divorce were problems for the children and economic reasons. Mayumi Futamatsu and Shinji Yamasaki, *Rasuto Rabu* [Last Love] 67 (2006).

5. Keisatsuchō Seikatsu Anzenkyoku Chiikika, Heisei 21nenchū ni okeru Jisatsu no Gaiyō Shiryō [2009 Outline of Suicide Records] (May 2010), available at http://www.npa.go.jp/safetylife/seianki/220513_H21jisatsunogaiyou.pdf.

6. Haruo Kitamura, ed., *Gyōretsu no Dekiru Hōritsu Sōdanjo* [The Legal Consultation Office That Is So Good That People Form Lines] 103–8 (2003)

7. Ministry of Health, Labor, and Welfare, Heisei 21nen Jinkō Dōtai Tōkei no Nenkan Suikei [2009 Yearly Estimates of Vital Statistics] (2010), available at http://www.mhlw.go.jp/toukei/saikin/hw/jinkou/suikei09/dl/suikei.pdf.

8. Utsunomiya Family Court, 48(4) *Kasai Geppō* 75 (Sept. 22, 1995).

9. See, e.g., Tokyo High Court, 1982 (*u*) 61 (Nov. 22, 1982), *aff'd,* Supreme Court, 500 *Hanrei Times* 138 (May 6, 1983) (mediators encouraged spouses to stay together for the sake of their three children; a month later, the husband attempted to murder his wife by throwing her off a 7.3-meter building).

10. Saikōsai Jimusōkyoku, *Shihō Tōkei Nenpō, Kaji Hen* 34–35. For some people, resorting to mediation for divorce is shameful. According to a former judge, some couples who initially petitioned for mediation request that their divorces be recorded in their family registries not as mediation but as negotiation, for fear that their children will look at the registries and realize their parents could not come to divorce terms on their own. Chikahiro Tada, *Rikon Chōtei no Ōgi* [The Heart of Divorce Mediation] 166 (2003). In 2006, about five percent of mediated divorces either were recorded as negotiated divorces or withdrawn by the parties in order to file for negotiated divorce.

11. Masayuki Tanamura, *Kekkon no Hōritsugaku* [The Jurisprudence of Marriage] 67 (2d ed. 2006) (citing Ministry of Health, Labor, and Welfare data).

12. Civil Code art. 770. For factors not covered in the text, see, e.g., *Ōiwa v. Ōiwa,* Supreme Court, 168 *Hanrei Times* 93 (Sept 17, 1964) (malicious abandonment does not arise when the complaining spouse is partially responsible); *Ōhashi v. Ōhashi,* Supreme Court, 616 *Hanrei Jihō* 67 (Nov. 24, 1970) (mental-illness divorce is not granted in every case of illness, but only upon consideration of the entirety of the facts). By statute, adultery in prewar Japan was grounds for divorce for husbands only, but courts enforced it for wives as well. See J. Mark Ramseyer, *Odd Markets in Japanese History: Law and Economic Growth* 103–7 (1996).

13. Editorial, New York's Antique Divorce Law, *N.Y. Times,* Jan. 17, 2010, at 7.

14. Betsey Stevenson and Justin Wolfers, Bargaining in the Shadow of the Law: Divorce Laws and Family Distress, 121(1) *Q. J. Econ.* 267 (2006). In a series of experiments, Tess Wilkinson-Ryan and Jonathan Baron found no-fault rules to conflict with moral intuitions about punishment for at-fault spouses. See Tess Wilkinson-Ryan and Jonathan Baron, The Effect of Conflicting Moral and Legal Rules on Bargaining Behavior: The Case of No-Fault Divorce, 37 *J. Legal Stud.* 315 (2008).

15. Tokyo District Court, 2004 (*wa*) 24911 (Oct. 19, 2005).

16. Kyoto District Court, 2005 (*wa*) 341 (Jan. 24, 2006).

17. Tokyo District Court, 2004 (*wa*) 17193 (Sept. 30, 2005).

18. http://www.c-splash.com/naiyou/naiyou.html.

19. http://www.gnc.co.jp.

20. http://gulu.go.jp/c-156.html.

21. *Inoue v. Inoue,* 51 *Hanrei Jihō* 12 (May 6, 1955). In a widely circulated 1996 draft revision, legislators proposed an additional hurdle: in the case of adultery or abandonment, a judge may *not* grant a divorce if evidence exists that the marriage can still recover. The provision would have made mandatory what was previously in the judge's discretion. At the same time, the plan would have made some divorces easier through a no-fault system for when "the marriage was destroyed and recovery was impossible, as evidenced by five years' separation that denied the purpose of marriage" (the *tanshin funin* exception). Both proposals failed. Hōmushō Minjikyoku Sanjikan-shitsu, ed., *Kon'in Seido Nado ni Kansuru Minpō Kaisei Yōkōshikian Oyobi Shian no Setsumei* [An Explanation of the Plan to Amend the Marriage Provisions of the Civil Code] 90–92 (1994).

22. See Herbert Jacob, *Silent Revolution: Routine Policy Making and the Transformation of Divorce Law in the United States* 30 (1988).

23. Harald Fuess, *Divorce in Japan* 110–14. As Fuess notes, Hozumi was not prepared to pursue his argument to its logical end and allow unilateral divorce. Hozumi also was not thoroughly Western in his ideas; he was a strong advocate, for instance, of ancestor worship. See Hitoshi Aoki, *Nobushige Hozumi: A Skillful Transplanter of Western Legal Thought into Japanese Soil in Rethinking the Masters of Comparative Law* 129 (Annelise Riles ed. 2001); Byron K. Marshall, Professors and Politics: The Meiji Academic Elite, 3(1) *J. Japan. Stud.* 71 (1977).

24. Kanyū Uramoto, *Hatanshugi Rikonhō no Kenkyū* [A Study of No-Fault Divorce Law] 73–76 (1993).

25. Courts did not necessarily interpret the Civil Code in such a way as to institutionalize patriarchy. See Ramseyer, *Odd Markets in Japanese History* 80–108.

26. Uramoto, *Hatanshugi Rikonhō no Kenkyū* 380–83; Kanyū Uramoto, *Rikonhō no Hendō to Shisō* [Ideas and Change in Divorce Law] 75 (1999); Atsushi Ōmura, *Kazokuhō* [Family Law] 146 (2d ed. 2004).

27. The officials, Thomas Blakemore and Alfred Oppler, made one point about "grave reason": it was broad enough that it made superfluous the ground of "mistreatment of (or by) the ancestors of the other spouse," an artifact from the old Civil Code that the drafters had allowed to remain. That concern had been raised by Japanese academics and committee members as well (most notably by Hanako Muraoka, one of the Women's Club members of the committee, who later would achieve fame as the translator of *Anne of Green Gables*), and the subcommittee dropped ancestor mistreatment from the draft. Uramoto, *Hatanshugi Rikonhō no Kenkyū* 383–91.

28. Saikō Saibansho Jimusōkyoku, 3 *Minpō Kaisei ni Kansuru Kokkai Kankei Shiryō, Katei Saiban Shiryō* [Parliament-Related Documents Pertaining to Civil Code Revisions, Documents Related to Family Courts] 197–98 (1953).

29. Supreme Court, 6(2) *Minshū* 110 (Feb. 19, 1952).

30. Tada, *Rikon Chōtei no Ōgi* 93–94.

31. Aiichi Munabe et al., *Gendai Kaji Chōtei Manyuaru* [Manual on Modern Family Mediation] 155–61 (2002). See Supreme Court, 10(2) *Kasai Geppō* 39 (Feb. 25, 1958) (divorce allowed when husband threw ashtray at wife's face); Tokyo High Court, 350 *Hanrei Times* 309 (Oct. 29, 1976) (divorce allowed in case of violence and alcoholism). In 2001, Japan passed the Law for the Prevention of Spousal Violence and the Protection of Victims. Haigūsha Kara no Bōryoku Oyobi Higaisha no Hogo ni Kansuru Hōritsu, Law no. 31 of 2001. For convictions under the law, see, e.g., Kofu District Court, 2004 (*wa*) 4 (Mar. 2, 2004) (eight-month sentence suspended for three years); Chiba District Court, 2002 (*wa*) 2706 (Feb. 7, 2003) (six-month sentence suspended for three years).

32. Tokyo High Court, 1091 *Hanrei Jihō* 89 (Aug. 4, 1983).

33. Osaka High Court, 62(4) *Kasai Geppō* 85 (May 26, 2009).

34. See, e.g., *Ōse v. Ōse,* Tokyo High Court, 485 *Hanrei Jihō* 44 (Apr. 11, 1967).

35. *Kōno v. Kōno,* Tokyo High Court, 1351 *Hanrei Jihō* 61 (Apr. 25, 1990).

36. See, e.g., *Hoppes v. Hoppes,* 214 N.E.2d 860 (Ohio Ct. Comm. Pleas 1964); *Frantzen v. Frantzen,* 349 S.W.2d 765 (Ct. App. Tex. 1961); *Krauss v. Krauss,* 111 So. 683 (La. 1927).

37. *Sinclair v. Sinclair,* 461 P.2d 750, 752 (Kan. 1969).

38. *Smith v. Smith,* 149 P.2d 683, 684 (Ariz. 1944).

39. *Yamamoto v. Yamamoto,* Nagoya High Court, 789 *Hanrei Times* 29 (Nov. 27, 1991).

40. *Kōno v. Kōno,* Tokyo District Court, 872 *Hanrei Times* 273 (Sept. 17, 1993).

41. See, e.g., Nagoya High Court, 1725 *Hanrei Jihō* 144 (Mar. 11, 1998) (granting divorce because husband lacks love and marriage cannot continue); *Kōno v. Kōno,* Osaka District Court, 1367 *Hanrei Jihō* 78 (May 14, 1990) (denying divorce and stating that husband should look at wife with "forgiving and respectful feelings"), rev'd, Osaka High Court, 1384 *Hanrei Jihō* 55 (Dec. 14, 1990) (granting divorce because wife could not care for children and manage household and husband adamantly wanted out); *Kohara v. Kohara,* Nagoya District Court, 682 *Hanrei Times* 212 (Apr. 18, 1988) (granting divorce because "events and functions like *koinobori* are nothing more than customs to Japanese people, and things like Buddhist funerals, worship at memorial services, and manner of dress are all within the realm of social customs that cannot be said to interfere with freedom of religion"); *Kōno v. Kōno,* Kyoto District Court, 1259 *Hanrei Jihō* 95 (Mar. 27, 1987) (denying divorce despite four-year separation because marriage can still recover); *Kōno v. Kōno,* Oita District Court, 1242 *Hanrei Jihō* 407 (Jan. 29, 1987) (granting divorce despite wife's declaration of love, finding that "[the wife] says she loves her husband because God loves him, but we cannot sweep away the suspicion that this is nothing more than a surface, conceptual idea, and we cannot possibly think that these words will ever become real or be put into practice").

42. Amy Borovoy, *The Too-Good Wife: Alcohol, Codependency, and the Politics of Nurturance in Postwar Japan* 89, 94 (2005).

43. See generally Alan S. Miller, A Rational Choice Model of Religious Behavior in Japan, 34(2) *J. for the Scientific Study of Religion* 234 (1995) (people in Japan without social groups more likely to join New Religion).

44. U.S. courts occasionally use roughly similar language of generosity and feelings. In a 1966 Iowa case, for instance, a court noted, "It seems a little more patience, a restrained tongue, a thanksgiving for the blessings at hand, a willingness to forgive and encourage rather than fault-finding, and a spirit of kindly tolerance of the frailties of each, would bring the peace and contentment they seek here in the courts." Still, the court found that the husband had been subjected to statutorily required "inhuman treatment" and "cruelty" by the wife, who slapped him once,

berated him, yelled at him, called him a son-of-a-bitch, and "would not let him watch T.V., would turn it down or off, preventing him from seeing the Iowa football team play." *Lehmkuhl v. Lehmkuhl,* 145 N.W. 2d 456, 459, 462 (Iowa 1966).

45. Atsuko Okano, *Otto no Tame no Jukunen Rikon Kaihi Manyuaru* [Husband's Guide to Avoiding Divorce] 27, 30 (2006).

46. See Jukunen Rikon wo Fusegu Shin Teishu Kanpakumichi [The New Husbands' Chauvinism: Avoiding Late Life Divorce], *Mainichi Shinbun,* Mar. 25, 2006, 1 (evening edition); Blaine Harden, Learn to Be Nice to Your Wife Or Pay the Price: Japan's Salarymen, With Pensions at Stake, Learn to Work on Their Marriages, *Wash. Post,* Nov. 26, 2007, A1.

47. Nihon Hōsō Kyōkai, ed., 5 *Otta kara Tsuma he, Tsuma kara Otto he: 60sai no Rabu Reta-* [From Husband to Wife, from Wife to Husband: Love Letters at 60] 93 (2005).

48. Nihon Hōsō Kyōkai, ed., 6 *Otta kara Tsuma he, Tsuma kara Otto he: 60sai no Rabu Reta-* [From Husband to Wife, from Wife to Husband: Love Letters at 60] 200 (2006).

49. See Allison Alexy, Deferred Benefits, Romance, and the Specter of Later-Life Divorce, 19 *Japanstudien* 169 (2007).

50. Supreme Court, 1169 *Hanrei Times* 125 (Nov. 25, 2004).

51. *Kōno v. Kōno,* Tokyo District Court, 1053 *Hanrei Times* 215 (Sept. 26, 2000). See also *Kōno v. Kōno,* Tokyo High Court, 1602 *Hanrei Jihō* 95 (Feb. 20, 1997) (in commuter marriage case, court finds that "we cannot say the marital relationship has been in a failed condition for a long time and to such an extent that it is appropriate for the responsible spouse to request a divorce when the relationship, even with its problems, has remained stable for a long period of time").

52. Yokohama District Court, 1708 *Hanrei Jihō* 142 (July 30, 1999).

53. See Tokyo High Court, 532 *Hanrei Times* 249 (May 30, 1984) (divorce granted after court cites daughter's approval).

54. *Kōno v. Kōno,* Tokyo High Court, 1060 *Hanrei Times* 240 (Jan. 18, 2001).

55. *Kōno v. Kōno,* Nagoya District Court, 1409 *Hanrei Jihō* 97 (Sept. 20, 1991). The number of marriages of over twenty years that end in divorce has risen along with marriages of all other lengths. Marriages of more than twenty years accounted for 7.7% of divorces in 1980 but hovered around 15% after 1990.

56. Supreme Court, 6(2) *Minshū* 110 (Feb. 19, 1952). In a few exceptional cases, courts have considered relative fault and granted a divorce if the at-fault plaintiff's fault is less than the defendant's. See, e.g., *Nishigata v. Nishigata,* Supreme Court, 53 *Hanrei Times* 46 (Nov. 24, 1955) (husband's adultery trumps wife's fighting); *Kō v. Otsu,* Nagoya High Court, 344 *Hanrei Times* 233 (June 29, 1976) (husband's incarceration trumps wife's adultery with *yakuza*). The "destroyed marriage" test applies to responsible-party cases: adultery after a marriage has been destroyed does not make the spouse a responsible party. *Naga v. Naga,* Supreme Court, 264 *Hanrei Times* 192 (May 21, 1971).

57. See Yukiko Tsunoda, *Sei no Hōritsugaku* [The Jurisprudence of Sex] 99 (1991).

58. See Gary Becker, *A Treatise on the Family* 331–36 (1991) (showing that rules of divorce change price of divorce, not its incidence).

59. See Ren'ai to Kekkon [Love and Marriage], 1 *Asahi Shinbun 100nen no Kiji ni Miru* [As Seen in 100 Years of the Asahi Shinbun] 284–85 (1979).

60. See Orie Endō, *A Cultural History of Japanese Women's Language* 75–98 (2006).

61. Masayuki Takanashi, *Nihon Kon'inhōron* [Japanese Marriage Law] 250 (1957).

62. Akira Yonekura, Rikon no Hikakuhōteki Kenkyū (Amerika) [A Comparative Legal Analysis of Divorce: America], 47 *Hikakuhō Kenkyū* 48, 55 (1985); see also Aiko Noda, Rikon Gen'inhō to Kaji Jiken [Divorce Cause Law and Family Cases], in Tōichirō Kigawa et al., eds., 8 *Shin Jitsumu Minshōhō Kōza* 167 (1981) (similar analysis by sitting judge).

63. Sendai District Court, 548 *Hanrei Times* 257 (Dec. 14, 1984); see also Tokyo District Court, 624 *Hanrei Times* 97 (Dec. 24, 1986) (allowing divorce after twenty-three-year separation).

64. Hōsōkai, *Saikō Saibansho Hanrei Kaisetsu Minhijen* [Supreme Court Case Law Commentary: Civil Cases] 540, 551 (lower courts), 553–57 (scholarship), 557–66 (other countries), 567–68 (surveys) (1987).

65. Supreme Court, 41 *Minshū* 1423 (Sept. 2, 1987). The Tokyo High Court subsequently established alimony payments, a rarity in Japan, where lump-sum payments are common. Mr. Hiyama split the marital property with Ms. Hiyama, paid her $150,000 in apology money, and agreed to pay $1,000 per month for ten years. Tokyo High Court, 42(3) *Kasai Geppō* 80 (Nov. 22, 1990).

66. See Shigeo Itō, *Yōken Jijitsu no Kihon* [The Foundation of the Ultimate Facts in Civil Litigation] 6 (2000).

67. Tokyo District Court, 2004 (*ta*) 190 (May 16, 2005).

68. *X v. Y,* Supreme Court, 1881 *Hanrei Jihō* 90 (Nov. 18, 2004).

69. Naikakufu Daijin Kanbō Seifu Kōhōshitsu, *Kazoku no Hōsei ni Kansuru Seron Chōsa* [Survey of Law and Legal Institutions of the Family], Dec. 2006, available at http://www8.cao.go.jp/survey/h18/h18-kazoku/index.html.

70. Masako Mizumachi, *Yūseki Haigūsha kara no Rikon Seikyū wo Meguru Kokumin Ishiki* [Survey Regarding Divorce by Responsible Parties], in Shōzō Ōta, ed., *Charenji Suru Tōdai Hōka Daigakuinsei: Shakai Kagaku toshite no Kazoku Hō/Chiteki Zaisan Hō no Tankyū* [Tokyo Law School Students Take Up the Challenge: A Social Science Investigation into Family Law and Intellectual Property Law] 25 (2007).

71. For couples who had been married ten years, respondents wanted an average of 2.51 years apart; for couples who had been married for thirty years, the average time respondents wanted was 4.10 years. Id.

72. Id. at 62–63.

73. Id.

74. In a 1990 case, the Supreme Court allowed a divorce after only an eight-year separation, in part because financial support from the husband was assured. *Kōno v. Kōno,* Supreme Court, 1370 *Hanrei Jihō* 55 (Nov. 8, 1990). Sill, most courts enforce the standard strictly. See, e.g., Tokyo District Court, 2003 (*ta*) 591 (May 30, 2005) (three-year separation insufficient for couple in early thirties despite the absence of children); *Kōno v. Kōno,* Osaka High Court, 1281 *Hanrei Jihō* 99 (Nov. 26, 1987) (divorce not granted when each step was met except financial support). Courts treat non-Japanese spouses under non-Japanese law differently. See, e.g., Tokyo District Court, 1925 *Hanrei Jihō* 121 (Feb. 18, 2005) (Texas no-fault divorce regime not contrary to Japanese public morals despite divorcing spouse's adultery); Tokyo Family Court, 1995 *Hanrei Jihō* 114 (Nov. 11, 2007) (Australian no-fault divorce is not "automatically contrary to public policy").

75. Mary Ann Glendon, *Abortion and Divorce in Western Law* 108 (1987).

Conclusion

1. All long quotes and most of the facts are from Yokohama District Court, 914 *Hanrei Times* 260 (Feb. 22, 1996). A few additional facts are from the appellate opinion, Tokyo High Court, 914 *Hanrei Times* 281 (Jan. 31, 1997).

2. Daniel H. Foote, ed., *Law in Japan: A Turning Point* (2007); see also Arthur Taylor von Mehren, ed. *Law in Japan: The Legal Order in a Changing Society* (1963).

3. Sonia Ryang, *Love in Modern Japan: Its Estrangement from Self, Sex and Society* (2006).

Index